Black Power

Reconfiguring American Political History

Ronald P. Formisano, Paul Bourke, Donald DeBats, and Paula M. Baker, *Series Founders*

Black Power
Radical Politics and
African American Identity

Jeffrey O. G. Ogbar

The Johns Hopkins University Press
Baltimore and London

© 2004 The Johns Hopkins University Press
All rights reserved. Published 2004
Printed in the United States of America on acid-free paper

Johns Hopkins Paperbacks edition, 2005
9 8 7 6 5 4 3 2 1

The Johns Hopkins University Press
2715 North Charles Street
Baltimore, Maryland 21218-4363
www.press.jhu.edu

The Library of Congress has cataloged the hardcover edition of this book as follows:

Ogbar, Jeffrey Ogbonna Green.
  Black power : radical politics and African American identity / Jeffrey O. G. Ogbar.
    p. cm. — (Reconfiguring American political history)
  Includes bibliographical references (p.) and index.
  ISBN 0-8018-7957-4 (hardcover: alk. paper)
  1. African Americans—Politics and government—20th century. 2. African
Americans—Civil rights—History—20th century. 3. Civil rights movements—United
States—History—20th century. 4. African Americans—Race identity. 5. Black
power—United States—20th century. 6. Black nationalism—United States—History—
20th century. 7. Radicalism—United States—History—20th century. 8. Nation of
Islam (Chicago, Ill.)—History. 9. Black Panther Party—History. I. Title. II. Series.
  E185.615.O34 2005
  323.1196'073'009046—dc22   2004000433

    ISBN 0-8018-8275-3 (pbk.: alk. paper)

A catalog record for this book is available from the British Library.

Contents

Illustrations follow page 92

Preface and Acknowledgments

The two most significant organizations in the Black Power movement, the Nation of Islam and the Black Panther Party—though by no means the only important organizations leading to the rise of radicalized black nationalist discourse, symbolism, and activity in the 1960s—were essential in shaping the contours of the Black Power era. This book has built on this thesis and grows around this interpretive framework, while also giving attention to other organizations. The rise of radical politics and African American identity owe a great deal—may have been inextricably tied to—the Nation and the Panthers.

My interest in the topic grows from my personal and intellectual connection to the ways in which people respond to racial oppression. Though my parents were raised in Chicago, I grew up hearing occasional family stories of life in Mississippi before the move north. I was perplexed by the tales of such brutality experienced by black people in Panola County and equally perplexed by the black collective reaction to white supremacy. My grandparents could not vote, hold office, or serve on a jury in the state where they paid taxes and provided for their family. I was led to believe that my maternal grandparents had no particular animus to whites, despite the fact that the overwhelming majority of white people in their home state supported the morally repugnant system of racial subjugation and injustice. In the 1940s my grandparents moved to Illinois during the Great Migration. Their children were raised in the urban, all-black world of Chicago's Southside. By the early 1970s my uncle Carlos Eduardos (who "became" Latino) worked as a Spanish-speaking liaison for the Chicago branch of the Black Panther Party. One aunt briefly considered joining the Nation of Islam, which had a powerful presence in Chicago. My mother attended Operation Push rallies with my father and insisted that she would have become a Panther. When I was born in 1969, my parents argued over naming me either Toussaint L'Ouverture, after the Haitian insurgent, or Bayo, a Nigerian name. (As it turned out, I looked so much like my father that they had to go with "junior".) Ultimately, my parents' generation shifted profoundly from their parents' generation in the ways that they articulated racial politics. They were connected to Africa and its Diaspora in new and important ways. Without doubt, this was their response to living in a racially hostile country.

Most of my family members were similar to most African Americans politically, socially, and culturally. Most were not organized or radical. In many respects my family represents a microcosm of larger historical phenomena. The generational and regional shifts are clear among the group. Born in 1969, I represented a new generation raised in the aftermath of the civil rights and Black Power movements. Reactions to racial oppression are often different, since racism itself has assumed many new forms. The rise of black consciousness in the late 1980s was coterminous with the litany of depressing news about African Americans: unemployment, crime, imprisonment, "endangered" black males, and other maladies fomented a renewed sense of alarm. During my college years this had a profound effect on my intellectual development and interest in how groups negotiate relationships with each other on micro and macro levels. History offered a fascinating medium for the exploration of these relationships and helped provide context to current events. I grew to see the rise and decline of black nationalism in the United States as demonstrative of race relations at any given time. Nat Turner was a proto-nationalist not because race relations were great but because they were horribly inhumane. From this premise I began my work on black nationalism.

Although I will never have the definitive birthing experience, writing this book has been less like giving birth and more like raising a child (though decidedly less costly). It began as a research idea in graduate school and grew through the dissertation stages and subsequent years of manuscript revision, and it now stands on its own. I have arrived at this point with the help, support, and guidance of many people, including family, friends, and colleagues. My parents, Gelinda Green Condos and the late Jeffrey A. Green Sr., always offered inspiration in their pride of my academic progress and other accomplishments. I forever appreciate their love and direction in life. My aunts Rosie, Annie, Maudie, Carrie, Helen, and Dorothy and my uncles Mickey, Bill, and Junior, as well as Artie and Sandy Miller (and the entire Miller clan), have inspired me with their unconditional love and encouragement. I also thank Kristen Plott, William Green Jr., and Diane and Raymond Heller. Many other cousins, aunts, and uncles, too many to name here (really!), also provided important sustenance for me. Indeed, some of my earliest lessons about humanity, America, race, and their troubled nexus were taught by family members. Their personal stories helped provide a rich contextual framework for my academic work and intellectual development. These stories texture this book as well.

I owe considerable gratitude to the Committee on Institutional Cooperation (CIC) Pre-Doctoral Fellowship for facilitating my graduate work at Indiana University. The former CIC director, the late Dr. Ronald E. Smith, was particularly inspirational with his dedication to scholarship and humanity. The assistance of St. Lawrence University and the Jeffrey Campbell Dissertation Fellowship were also important, especially the support of Peter Bailey and David Lloyd. Postdoctoral revisions were partially due to the support of the W. E. B. Du Bois Institute for African and African-American Research at Harvard University and the thoughtful comments of and conversations with fellowship director Richard Newman and others, including Patricia Sullivan, Cornel West, and Waldo E. Martin, during those summer sessions.

Numerous friends helped keep me sane and grounded, including Adisa Iwa, Kondo Kirk Bradley, Alex Torres, and Fanon C. Wilkins, who remain solid brothers of old. Much respect and appreciation to Richard E. Pierce II, Keith Maull, Darroll Lawson, Philip Azim Boyd, Terry-Ann Jones, Reginald Roberts, Fred Roberson, Kupenda Auset, Dave Canton, Bill Benson, John Akare Aden, Leonard Moore, Germaine Jackson, Damon Scott, Christine Shaw, Scot Brown, Peter Kweku Pletcher, Howard Robinson, Beth Furuno, Kelly Tucker, Edward Pavlic, Michelle Williams, Karen Chow, Hasan Jeffries, Regina Deil, Daryl Harris, Roxanna Harlow, Samson Abraha, Felicia Bell, Nataki Goodall, Kim Searcy, Eric Anderson, Hilda Ivette Llorens, and Andrew Warren. Special thanks to Erin C. St. Onge and the entire St. Onge and Daly families for being so wonderfully supportive. Dornita LeCount, Ligiah Villalobos, Chandra Martin, Richard Walker, and Kell Shrivers certainly made my research trips to Los Angeles enjoyable. My graduate career was enriched by conversations and friendships with Joseph Heathcott, Crystal Keels, Jeremy Rich, Roxanna Harlow, Charles Chubs Peterson, and Geoffrey Coats.

Richard Brown, Amii Omara-Otunnu, Frank Costigliola, Altina Waller, Karen Spaulding, Sue Porter-Benson, Ronald L. Taylor, and Rose Lovelace have been tremendously supportive in so many ways. Vincent Southerland, Melanie Brown, Ryan Shanahan, Carlton Smith, Big Buff Dan Perkins, Ada Gonzalez, Mark Beasley-Murray, and Emily Morse have been very special students who helped me have fun and take pride in being a teacher and friend. Thanks to Dan Simmons, Rick Borque, and Abe DeLeon for helping me to mature as a graduate teacher, advisor, and scholar.

The ephemeral conversations and interactions at conferences and elsewhere with Earnest Allen, Robin D. G. Kelley, Komozi Woodard, Timothy Tyson, Charles E. Jones, Ward Churchill, and Manning Marable have added to the contours of my work. Jeff Chang, Kevin Powell, Elsa Barkely Brown, Vijay Prashad, Eddie S. Glaude Jr., Nikki Taylor, and Yohuru Williams enjoy my appreciation. Big shout to the Black Panther Party, Black Power, and black nationalism dissertation cohort ('96–'03): Akinyele Umoja, Scot Brown, Robyn Spencer, Tracye Matthews, Angela D. LeBlanc-Ernest, Michelle Mitchell, Hasan Jeffries, and Charles McKinney Jr. I eagerly await all books.

My undergraduate career at Morehouse College helped spawn my interest in academia. I have a deep and profound appreciation for the History Department there and am grateful for the guidance, support, instruction, and friendship of my undergraduate advisor, Alton Hornsby Jr. The discipline, high standards, and expectations of Marcellus C. Barksdale shape my own pedagogical standards. Giles Conwill helped me cut my teeth on my first real research project. Leroy Davis takes the credit for originally converting me to history. My graduate advisor, Richard J. M. Blackett, has always offered sound advice and substantive observations of my work. I will always have deep gratitude for his constant support and direction. He is the gold standard of graduate advisors. The advice of John Bodnar, Chana Lee, and C. R. D. Halisi is greatly appreciated.

Robert J. Brugger, my editor, recognized this as a viable project for the Johns Hopkins University Press and carefully worked with me through to the end. Thanks for the attention, care, important questions, and eye for structure, form, and substance.

Black Power

For the People and of the People
Black Nationalism, Identity, and Popular Culture

The tumultuous 1960s produced great changes in how Americans negotiate issues of race and identity. Bolstered by the legal successes of the civil rights movement, African Americans transformed the way they saw themselves and expected others to see them. More than thirty years later, members of the Congressional Black Caucus wield considerable influence in congressional politics. New York, Los Angeles, Chicago, and Atlanta have had black mayors. Harvard University proudly promotes its renowned Institute for African and African American Research. Corporate America deftly markets its products to the $500 billion African American consumer market, exploiting Black History Month, Kwanzaa, and other cultural celebrations. From music to fashion to mainstream politics, the cultural landscape of America significantly reflects not only the presence of African Americans but also a general and pervasive understanding that black people are far more than background characters in an ostensibly white drama. Nor are they subsumed in an ethnically indistinct Americanness. In fact, Americans at the end of the twentieth century celebrated diversity in ways never imagined two generations earlier. America had become neither the idyllic world Martin Luther King Jr. dreamed of nor the racially separate utopian community envisioned by Elijah Muhammad. It no longer practiced blatant and legally codified forms of white supremacy. However, African Americans still lagged behind whites by most positive socioeconomic measures and led whites in most negative indicators. Still, pervasive change—superficial and substantive—was palpable.

How could a country with explicit white supremacist policies at the federal, state, and local levels for most of its history make such significant changes in so short a time? What brought about such wide-reaching cultural transformation? Beyond revision of the law, these cultural shifts included wholesale rejections of old notions of racial etiquette. What challenges to racial suppression prompted many Americans to view racial diversity as a good thing? How could the African American effort to integrate with whites bring about a proliferation of "black" professional societies, associations, and student centers in an age with unprecedented white acceptance of black people? Answers lay beyond the scope of the civil rights movement, which, while dismantling the pervasive legal underpinnings of racial subjugation, expressed no profound concern over the psychological consequences of being black (or white) in a virulently antiblack society.

In trying to explain the development of a new African American identity in the second half of the century, one has to understand the Black Power movement, and to explain Black Power, one must came to grips with the Nation of Islam (NOI) and the Black Panther Party (BPP), organizations that did the most to foment the cultural shifts that reconfigured politics and identity in America. The NOI was the chief inspiration and benefactor for the Black Power movement. The Panthers raised the bar of radicalism and resistive politics, while influencing society far beyond what many expected from its small cadre of members. Both organizations built on the traditions of the black freedom struggle, which had deep roots, but the Panthers and Muslims in the 1960s forced conflicted discussions within the black community, which gave rise to Black Power and expanded radical discourse.

Black Power affected African American identity and politics as much as any speech, march, or legal victory of the civil rights movement. Its thrust was "black nationalism," though Black Power was not necessarily nationalist. Black Power employed—even co-opted—the activism typified in civil rights struggles and operated on basic assumptions of rights and privileges. In essence, it demanded inclusion while advocating autonomy and self-determination. It asserted black access to full citizenship rights while conspicuously cultivating pride in much that was not American. Black Power was many things to many people and an enigma to most. Two fundamental themes, however, were widely celebrated among proponents: black pride and black self-determination. From the traditions of black nationalists (and some integrationists) there developed a fundamentally new system of beliefs that shaped the political currents of the late 1960s and beyond.

In general, nationalism pulls from many belief systems, with many manifestations and types found throughout the world. Black nationalism in America is simply one subset of this very diverse structure of ideas. In many aspects, it reflects the rhetoric of nationalist movements that have swept across the historical landscape of the last three centuries, demonstrating theoretical continuities with them.

A juxtaposition of European and American forms of nationalism immediately brings into sharp focus the saliency of racial contrasts. Unlike virtually all nationalist movements, black nationalism embraces a highly racialized agenda. The racialized terms of the agenda reflected the racialist policies of the United States. The Nation of Islam, for example, believed in the universal deviltry of white people, whether they were American or not. The NOI simultaneously embraced all people of color (Asians, Indians, etc.) as kindred "blacks." This reflected the prevailing thrust of white supremacy in America. It simply inverted the doctrine of white supremacy. It was, in fact, a declaration of white inferiority. Race, not ethnicity, has been the cornerstone to black nationalism. The same cannot be said for nationalism elsewhere, where ethnicity overrides virtually all other variables.[1]

The most viable definition of black nationalism is one that includes group consciousness among black people and the belief that they, independent of whites, can achieve liberation by the creation and maintenance of black institutions to serve the best interests of black people. Territorial separatism and/or racial exclusivity are essential to this definition. Thus, the distinction is made between integrationists like Martin Luther King Jr., who galvanized racial solidarity in grassroots struggles, and separatists like Marcus Garvey, who also advocated racial solidarity but in the context of self-determination and separation from white society. Accordingly, the NOI is in the strictest meaning a nationalist organization. It demanded land, either in North America or Africa, for the development of a black nation-state. In the meantime, the NOI built a veritable nation with a network of businesses that included farms, a cannery, apartments, supermarkets, schools, and other staples of nationhood.

The NOI and the BPP, like their black nationalist predecessors, considered themselves the true representatives of the interests of the African American masses. Unlike integrationist, middle-class-led organizations like the National Association for the Advancement of Colored People and the National Urban League, the NOI and the BPP systematically recruited from the poorest segments of the black community and developed rhetoric that appealed to many poor blacks, particularly males. They also fully recognized the important role that culture played in popular movements yet developed drastically different interpretations of black popular culture. The NOI vilified black popular culture while the Panthers not only celebrated it but extolled some of the crudest elements of what they called "lumpenproletariat" culture. The Panthers simultaneously excoriated cultural nationalists who insisted that a cultural renewal of black America was essential for black liberation. Although it made overt appeals to the socially and economically displaced majority of the black community, the Nation made virulent attacks against black folk culture.

African American rhetoric always has concerned itself with questions of identity. Free blacks widely used the term *African* up to the 1830s, when white supremacists increasingly argued for "repatriation" to Africa for free blacks. *Colored* and *Negro* suddenly grew in popularity because they downplayed any association with foreign lands. By the early twentieth century, nationalists avoided "colored" and more fully embraced *Negro* (always capitalized) as a more fitting and proud term. Some, like Noble Drew Ali, insisted that *Moor* and *Asiatic* were the correct terms. For Ali, these labels inherently connected black people to their rightful place of origin and their history as great conquerors and builders of civilization. Not until 1930, however, did any organization reject *Negro* and *colored* and fully embrace the term *black*. The Nation of Islam's embrace of the term *black* shocked many African Americans, who continued to see the word as pejorative. In virtually all cases, nationalists before the 1960s refused to consider black people as "Americans." To call attention to being American undermined the fundamental arguments of the nationalists, who insisted that their citizenship had never been fully recognized by America. Identity formed, thereby, an essential part of the black nationalist program. It conveyed important symbolic meaning and bolstered the nationalist agenda.

A study of black nationalism necessarily begins in the eighteenth century with protonationalist emigrationism. It was from the inchoate nationalist desire to return to Africa that a lucid, intellectual black nationalist dogma developed in the mid-nineteenth century. One of the chief differences between emigrationists and later nationalists was the former's belief that the settlement of blacks in Africa would largely be to the benefit of indigenous Africans who could adopt the "virtuous" characteristics of Anglo-American civilization. By the mid-nineteenth century, the agenda of emigrationists was less concerned with indigenous Africans' salvation and more focused on establishing a symbiotic relationship between Africans from the continent and the Diaspora. In fact, it was necessary to evoke a cultural rebirth in Africa, according to emigrationist nationalists. Nationalist leaders from Martin Delany to Henry McNeal Turner and Marcus Garvey promoted Christianizing missions into Africa to rid the

continent of traditional religious beliefs and open it to "civilization."
Certainly, many of these emigration nationalists aimed, albeit indirectly,
to impose European cultural hegemony on Africa. Black nationalists were
generally interested in "civilizing" Africans. This theme of "civilizing" the
"wretched" Africans was particularly salient in the early-nineteenth-century
efforts of Paul Cuffe, a successful sea captain from Massachusetts, who
attempted to uplift West Africans by carrying free blacks from the United
States to the region so that they could spread the Christian gospel.[2] Later
in the century, Martin Delany emerged as the "father of black nationalism" and an outspoken advocate of Western civilization.

Delany, in his affirmation of blackness, promoted incongruent messages, on the one hand stressing that the historical glory of Africa had
been systematically denied by Europeans to reinforce white supremacy,
while on the other hand insisting that it was necessary for African
Americans who have been "despoiled of our purity and corrupted in our
native characteristics" by whites to "regenerate Africa morally, religiously,
socially, politically, and commercially." Delany also warned that it was
the task of African Americans to bring Christianity to Africa, for white
missionaries were crippled with racist agendas that ultimately would
result in Africans being "doomed to see [themselves] sink right back into
their old habits," while the continent would "continue in the same condition, without the beautiful improvements of the white man." It is strik-
ingly clear that Delany held elements of European culture in high esteem,
even as he denounced Europeans for their traditions of oppression and
incivility. After all, it was the "beautiful improvements of the white man"
that Africans needed. Yet how could black people who had "inherited
[white people's] vices" while living among them in America regenerate
Africa? European civilization was, according to Delany, "the most advanced
civilization ever attained to, and wherever propagated in its purity, to be
effective, law and government must be brought in harmony with it."[3]
Should government and law not be infused with Christian truths and
praxis there would be potential for the corruption and duplicity that
characterized Christian society in the United States. His message was
clear: Hold true to the principles of Christianity; otherwise, civilization of
Africa would be impossible. Delany's Christian missionary zeal to civilize
the people of Africa was identical to the agendas of his nationalist con-
temporaries, as well as those of the early twentieth century.

In the 1920s Marcus Garvey appealed to both the self-determination
values and economic interests of most African Americans. Garvey created
the Universal Negro Improvement Association (UNIA), the largest black

mass organization ever. The UNIA, founded in 1914 in Jamaica, was incorporated in the United States in 1918, two years after its founder immigrated. Predicated on a mix of militant black nationalism and Booker T. Washingtonian ideals of self-reliance, Garvey created a massive organization headquartered in Harlem but extending to forty-one countries and including millions of members.[4] Evidence of the UNIA's influence can be seen in the NAACP's decline in membership after peaking at 91,203 in 1919. Its decline, according to some historians, was directly related to the actions of W. E. B. Du Bois and other prominent integrationists who unleashed a series of attacks on the UNIA in the press.[5] Even those who did not set integration as the cornerstone of their political activities had a difficult time competing with Garvey and his rhetoric of "race first." Black leftists had particular difficulty attracting a mass following.

Labor leaders A. Philip Randolph and Chandler Owen appealed to many through the *Messenger* to join unions and work under socialist principles, but most blacks in the period were skeptical of unionization because most unions were antiblack. Most black people had trouble viewing their oppression in class terms. Explicit laws systematically oppressed them because of their race, not their class. A college-educated black man was denied municipal jobs, entry into corporate America, or housing in white areas as easily as a poor uneducated black man. Furthermore, the naked racism of many poor whites worked against class unity. It was Garvey who articulated the distrust that many blacks had of white-controlled institutions. He warned against involvement with any white people who appeared to be friends of blacks. The white liberal, according to Garvey, was just as prone to join a lynch mob as a Georgia Klansman.

Garvey was highly critical of the behavior of black people, or at least what he perceived as their behavior. Garvey warned against the staunch fatalism he saw everywhere among black people. The sickness and diseases that many black people experienced were preventable. Sickness, he argued, was "a direct violation of the code of God in nature." The people who often fall ill "are people who are ignorant of the laws of Nature." These people eat the wrong foods, live the wrong lifestyle, and die young, and the survivors remark "God took him early." Garvey stated that this erroneous conception of God made Him into a murderer. "Negroes, your concept of God is wrong! Trace the causes of premature sickness and death and you will find that God had nothing to do with it." He further derided black people: "Negroes won't take medicine for 10 years and expect to be well, and when they get sick . . . they say 'God's spirit has left me.' What spirit wouldn't leave you? You ignorant good-for-nothing lot."[6]

While Garvey's condemnation of irresponsible health habits is not an explicit attack on black folk culture, his condescending and paternalistic tone reflects a hyperbolic rhetorical tradition that characterizes the language commonly used by black nationalists. He, like his black nationalist predecessors and successors, often derided black people as desperately uncouth and unsophisticated. In his speeches and writings, Garvey often depicted black people as gullible and misled sheep who have consistently chosen to follow corrupt leaders. Not only were black leaders a shady lot, they were "the biggest crooks in the world."[7] For Garvey, black people were products of a dysfunctional culture, since he argued that there were no biological differences between races. Although there were "backward peoples," they were not inferior, Garvey noted. "As far as humanity goes," he remarked, "all men are equal."[8] Garvey's condemnation of black popular culture reveals a peculiar tradition of self-effacing rhetoric that is common in the black nationalist tradition.

During Garvey's era, many blacks embraced nakedly antiblack propaganda promoted by white society at large. The racist images in popular media, movies, and cartoons had psychological consequences among black people, and scholars studied their pernicious effects on levels of self-esteem and identity.[9] Advertisements in black publications routinely encouraged black people to whiten their skin in order to be more beautiful. Black-owned clubs refused to hire dark-skinned women as waitresses or dancers and antiblack colloquialisms were commonly promoted among black people.[10]

The manner in which Garvey participated in the tradition of self-effacement is paradoxical. Garvey may have used the popular antiblack notions held by blacks to promote black nationalism and ultimately black pride. After all, it could be argued, black people were in such troubled conditions because they were dependent on hostile whites for food, clothing, housing, employment, education, government, and health care. Blacks were born, raised, and conditioned in a hostile, antiblack society. Their culture, therefore, could not be healthy; it was dysfunctional by design. It was imperative, then, for African Americans to extricate themselves from the conditions that created the archetypal confused and ignorant Negro. Independence and knowledge of self would lead to total emancipation and cultural rebirth.

Many nationalist organizations of the interwar years were highly critical of behavior they considered self-destructive, including hard drinking and other pathologies often associated with ghetto life. The African Blood Brotherhood (ABB), founded by leftist black nationalists in Harlem after

World War I, was one of these organizations. While there have been no definitive studies of the ABB, some historians have offered cursory remarks about the country's first revolutionary nationalist organization. Created in 1919 by Cyril Briggs (a journalist and Communist), the ABB was composed of men from throughout the United States, many of whom had served in the war. They embraced direct action self-defense and, while all black, were sensitive to the need to work with radicalized whites. The members of the group considered their semiclandestine, paramilitary organization the "Pan-African Army" of the black world. Membership ranged from three to five thousand at its zenith, including a large number of Caribbean people. Briggs's monthly magazine, *The Crusader,* became the official organ of the ABB and reached a peak circulation of nearly twenty thousand.[11]

The revolutionary nationalist body was represented in fifty branches, including Chicago, Baltimore, Oklahoma, West Virginia, Africa, and the West Indies. Much like its successors in the 1960s, the ABB utilized a Marxist class analysis that emphasized working-class consciousness. While its rhetoric regarding popular culture is largely unknown, it is clear that the ABB did not denounce popular culture as inimical to the interests of black liberation. Neither did its rhetoric glorify "ghetto life." In fact, the writings and speeches of its leaders clearly reflect a preoccupation with affecting fundamental systemic change. Heightening class consciousness, mobilizing workers, and establishing alliances with radicalized whites and "small oppressed nations" were the chief concerns of the ABB. Furthermore, it embraced notions of uplift, military efficiency, and other ideals that would characterize the Nation of Islam and other nationalists in the years following World War II.[12]

By the 1950s a convergence of events gave rise to mass movements of resistance to white supremacy and a renewal of black nationalist activity. Building on the legacy of organizations like the UNIA and Noble Drew Ali's Moorish Science Temples, the Nation of Islam emerged as a central player in the politics of race and resistance, ultimately engendering a transformation of America. In a matter of twenty years, Americans witnessed profound challenges to racism from the civil rights and Black Power movements. High profile black leaders such as King, Roy Wilkins, and Whitney Young Jr. disagreed with Black Power, yet the term eventually dominated the thrust of the black freedom movement by 1970. How did such a marginalized slogan become so powerful for so many so soon? There are also serious questions about who comprised the rank and file of the Black Power movement and its leading organizations like the Black

Panther Party and the Nation of Islam. How did the machismo revolutionary chic attract so many women into the movement? Did women within the Panther Party or Nation of Islam offer real challenges to patriarchy? If so, how did the male leadership respond to these challenges? Ultimately, some of Black Power's most vocal critics were Panthers and Muslims. What explains their critique? Was Black Power co-opted? If so, by whom and how? How were the fruits of Black Power evident in African American cultural politics and expression at the end of the twentieth century? What role did consumerism play in the rise and decline of Black Power and the formation of African American identity in the late 1960s and early 1970s? These questions bring attention to the significance of Black Power and will help us understand the cultural transformation that substantively altered American politics and culture.

CHAPTER 1

An Organization of the Living
The Nation of Islam and
Black Popular Culture

The Nation of Islam (NOI) developed out of a nexus of political, cultural, and social tumult. Like any social phenomenon, it was a product of its time.[1] America in the early twentieth century was a country with a huge cultural investment in the theoretical construct of white supremacy, and while white supremacy was obviously inimical to all people of color, its primary focus was to secure for whites exclusive access to a wide range of democratic (social, political and economic) pursuits and to affirm black inferiority. In all areas of life, African Americans endured incessant attacks against their humanity. On the federal, state, and local levels, laws and customs pushed black people into the periphery of American citizenship. That black people lived in a country that celebrated freedom, democracy, and equality caused double frustration, since most African Americans were banned from voting or serving in the country's military on an equal basis with whites. Movies, radio shows, postcards, and popular sayings ridiculed black people, even making light of black suffering and death. Lynch mobs, poor housing, inadequate education, and job discrimination meant that being black in America was both dangerous and unwise. To be sure, black people were enveloped in a virulently antiblack society. That black people, too, could be affected by antiblack sentiment was essential to white supremacy's efficacy. Even black organizations that were ostensibly pro-black struggled with reconciling their own contradictions with black self-love. The Nation of Islam was one of them.

Many African Americans organized to resist the legal trappings of white supremacy by demanding desegregation and equal access to schools, housing, and jobs. The National Association for the Advancement of Colored People (NAACP), founded in 1909, had devoted itself to realizing a country that truly embraced its creed of democracy. To that end, the NAACP challenged racial segregation as anathema. In a similar vein, the National Urban League, founded in 1911, sought to uplift African Americans with self-help

activities, while also challenging the legally sanctioned system of racial subjugation. The Universal Negro Improvement Association (UNIA), incorporated in America in 1918, emerged as a black nationalist juggernaut before
splintering in the 1930s. When the Nation of Islam was formed in 1930, its
founder, W. Fard (pronounced Fah-RARD) Muhammad, developed an organization that at once appealed to the rage and defiance that African
Americans long held in the face of white supremacy, while pandering to the
ignorance and self-hate with which many black people struggled. It was this
ironic fusion of lure and loathing that provided an ideological and cosmo-
logical foundation for the Nation of Islam, ultimately making it a major
organization during the civil rights movement.

The Nation, as it was called, largely existed as a small cult until the
mid-1950s, when a convergence of factors made it the fastest growing
major black organization in the country, altering the way race and racial
etiquette are understood. The modern civil rights movement, the meteoric popularity of national spokesman Malcolm X, and the organizational
skill of NOI leader Elijah Muhammad made the Nation the largest black
nationalist organization by the late 1950s. Much of its popularity was
dependent on how the Nation viewed black people and how they, in turn,
responded to it. Despite its black nationalist rhetoric, the Nation was
deeply influenced by the popular currents of white supremacist thought,
as were most African Americans. On many levels, this proved to be a curious strength in its appeal to black people, many of whom were searching
for an organization to extricate them from the bowels of racism.

The Nation's message of cautious and pragmatic resistance, frugality,
and cultural regeneration dominated the era of "modern black nationalism."[2] Through the 1950s, the NOI's position on black popular culture
was in most respects a continuation of black nationalist movements that
dated to the mid-nineteenth century. Like its nationalist predecessors, the
Nation viewed popular culture with a certain level of disdain. In many
ways, the nation was on a civilizing mission to rebuild, redeem, and reju-
venate a downtrodden and backward people. Still, the Nation considered
itself an organization of the masses, the people's true representative, even
if the people did not know it.[3] The NOI embraced traditions and symbols
of white middle-class status in an attempt to create an image for itself as a
viable organization of black uplift. The antipathy toward black folk culture and appreciation of significant elements of white American culture
demonstrate that the Nation was able to deconstruct the popularly
accepted ideas of race—and tangential notions of history—and culture.
This deconstruction of racial theories was done with the ironic use of

white supremacist language. Racial essentialism, innate virtue, images of ignorant, lazy, and indolent Negroes coexisted with the story of Yacub, which explained the inherent wickedness of Caucasians and their moral, physical, and intellectual inferiority to black people.

The Founding of the Nation

In 1930 a mysterious clothing salesman appeared in the black ghettoes of Detroit with a message of black liberation. Calling himself various names, including Wallace D. Fard and W. F. Muhammad, the itinerant entrepreneur told his clients about a hidden history and hidden religion—Islam. The "so-called Negro," he told them, was really the Asiatic black man—the founder of civilization and Original Man, created in the image of God, whose proper name is Allah (ah-LAH). Interested people helped Muhammad form a study group where they listened to lectures on the true nature of black people. It was in these lessons that followers learned the story of Yacub.

Yacub is the eschatological centerpiece of the Nation's dogma. The story explains the inborn evil of whites, who are the progeny of mutants genetically manipulated or "grafted" into existence by the wicked scientist Yacub and his dutiful servants. According to the teachings, humanity was originally dark as the color black and lived in an Edenic state of peace and brotherhood in Asia. Yacub, a genius who lived 6,000 years ago, took it upon himself to challenge Allah's righteous world by performing genetic experiments and mutations with black and brown "germs." He started a colony and systematically killed all of the darker babies while mating the lighter ones with each other with the intention of ultimately creating a race of people who were physical and spiritual anathema to the Original People. Although Yacub died before he could see his efforts come to fruition, his laborers continued his efforts until brown, red, yellow, and finally white people were spawned on the Mediterranean island of Patmos (also called Pean). From there, the "pale-skinned, blue eyed whites" freely practiced decadent values and immorality. They were morally weak by nature, incapable of doing good for its own sake.[4] Eventually they were driven out of the vicinity of the Original People and forced to live in the caves of the Caucasus Mountains where they crawled on all fours and developed amorous relations with canines. In fact, dogs are the "closest relatives to the white man," argued Fard. That is why modern white men refer to the dog as their "best friend"; it also explains the "dog-like" hair of whites and "canine odor" that they emit.[5]

The word *Negro,* they were told, is a misnomer, created by whites to affirm their domination over the Original People. *Negro* was derived from the Greek word *necro,* Fard said, meaning "dead." When whites called Original People "Negroes," they were surreptitiously calling them mentally and spiritually dead. Negroes were those who lacked knowledge of self. They were the deaf, dumb, and blind masses that believed what white supremacists told them about the world. They accepted the notion that blacks were without history, that Africa was a land of barbarism, devoid of empires or civilizations. They embraced white supremacy and its dependent variable, black inferiority. Negroes lived in awe and fear of whites. They hated everything black and desired nothing more than to be white. Self-hate was the cornerstone to the Negro's dilemma. Once the so-called Negro received knowledge of self, he was transformed into a black man. Black was the proper name of Allah's chosen people.

In an age when *black* was a derogatory epithet, Fard's message was particularly powerful. While some used *black* interchangeably with *Negro,* none had rejected *Negro* or argued for *black* as a label for people of African descent.[6] While the Original people were black as the color itself, blackness included not only people of African descent but also indigenous people from Asia, the Americas, Australia, and the Pacific islands. Whites, alone, were outside the brotherhood of humanity. It was ironic, therefore, that Muhammad looked like a white man.[7]

According to NOI tradition, Fard was God incarnate and assumed a white appearance to appeal more effectively to black people who had been enamored of whiteness. Nonbelievers, however, have long researched the mysterious Fard. Karl Evanzz, a journalist and author of two books on the Nation of Islam, builds on the FBI's argument that Fard was a white con man who discovered a way to exploit gullible blacks into unwavering devotion, making himself plenty of money in the process. As expected, the FBI story has been dismissed by the Nation as a continuation of the bureau's ruthless assault on black organizations. Evanzz argues, rather convincingly, however, that the mysterious Fard Muhammad was actually the very mortal Walli Dodd Fard, son of a Maori father, Zared Fard, who had Pakistani roots. His mother, according to Evanzz, was Beatrice Dodd, a white woman who lived in New Zealand. Though Evanzz considers this finding a contradiction of the Nation's lessons, the Nation has always insisted that Fard had a black father and a white mother (a "she beast") and that he was born in "the East," or Asia. Strictly speaking, neither story contradicts Evanzz's new revelations. The findings that undermine much of what has been known about the Nation's founder, however, come from files that suggest that Fard was also known as Wallace Dodd Ford and was arrested for drug selling in Los Angeles in 1926. Ford was not the Oxford University alumnus that NOI ministers have praised. He was, according to Evanzz, an unlettered restaurant owner who typically embellished his past. Although he initially self-identified as white, Ford grew critical of white supremacy and aligned himself with black nationalists and others who challenged white global domination, such as the pro-Japan, black-oriented Society for the Development of Our Own. There is even speculation that Ford was a member of the Moorish Science Temple of America (MSTA), the UNIA, as well as the Ahmadiyya movement.[8]

W. Fard Muhammad embodied the paradox of racial identity. Race was perhaps the most important factor in influencing a person's life, yet there was nothing biologically absolute about race. Socially, however, race determined whether one was fit or unfit, qualified or unqualified, worthy or unworthy. Still, Fard ventured into the white world undetected to "see the devil up close" and understand his ways.

According to Fard, only whites were excluded from the Islamic fold. In essence, he reversed the U.S. tendency to accept all whites but reject and legally sanction the oppression of people of color. Although white ethnics were open to some forms of discrimination, they, too, benefited from white supremacy throughout the country. In no branch of the military were units segregated into completely Polish or completely Jewish formations. European immigrant children attended American schools (even in segregated areas like the South) with native-born white children. White privilege always afforded Irish, Italians, Greeks, and others municipal jobs as police officers, clerks, and firemen. From all-white policies in union memberships to major league sports, Italians, Jews, and all other whites enjoyed access, even if they were sometimes victims of ethnic slurs. Even the most maligned white ethnics could vote and hold office. No white ethnic group had ever been systematically bared or segregated from the political, economic, military, social, and educational arenas as people of color were. As late as 1950, most African Americans (the majority of whom lived in the South) were denied their right to vote.[9]

The Nation of Islam's decision to form an open and inclusive position on blackness reflected the popular ideas of race in the United States, as well as Fard's early political development. Although passing for white was not uncommon, most blacks embraced the "one-drop" rule, which declared that any known African ancestry made a person black. The hypodecent rule that created a myth of white "purity" proved functional for those who benefited from enslaving mixed-raced people. While it propagated racist myths of purity and taint, the Nation extended this belief to welcome Asians, Native Americans, and other people of color into its fold. Their interpretation of the rule provided an element of psychological and emotional camaraderie that transcended traditional black nationalism. A popular Muslim saying declared that "one drop will make you black and will also in days to come save your soul."[10]

Indeed, the struggle against white supremacy had global dimensions. Elijah Muhammad was careful to explain that black people around the world have suffered at the hands of whites who "have covered the earth and sea with their death-dealing rule over the aboriginals of the earth since they left the confines of Europe."[11] Over 95 percent of Americans in 1950 were either white or black. Until 1965, laws restricted immigration from Africa, Asia, and other countries, resulting in negligible (and largely localized in California and the Southwest) numbers of Asians and Latinos. For the average African American who understood race as a binary of black and white, Muhammad clarified the position of the NOI: "We shall never again permit white people to sit in our meeting—armed or unarmed. This does not include the Turkish people, Chinese, Japanese, Filipinos, those of Pakistan, Arabs, Latin Americans, Egyptians and those of other Asiatic Muslim and non Muslim nations . . . [And] all black Americans, even those who have a few drops of black blood in them, must unite under the crescent to try and save ourselves from the doom of the enemies."[12]

Fard Muhammad taught that all people of color were members of the brotherhood of humanity and that African Americans had a special relationship with Allah. African people in America were victims of the most pernicious exploitation and brutality at the hands of Yacub's progeny. They alone languished under such tyranny and injustice. If their burdens could be overcome, then every other group would be given a model of resistance to follow. Furthermore, black people in North America, or the "Lost Tribe of Shabazz," had drifted so far from righteousness that their spiritual redemption would be a harbinger of the redemption of humanity and the restoration of peace on earth.[13] The ultimate significance of this universalization of blackness was the effect that it had on boosting self-esteem and faith in the NOI membership. It assured them that their struggle was broader than the confines of the United States. Moreover, they were not minorities outnumbered seven to one by hostile and vicious enemies; they were the majority. The struggle of the righteous majority against a minority of oppressors could only be victorious, the NOI concluded. Finally, this universalism reflected the humanistic qualities of the Nation that rarely characterize most types of nationalism. For example, all major black nationalist exponents have embraced a Pan-Africanist affinity with black people beyond the borders of the United States. They have not, however, promoted a common history and identity with indigenous peoples of Asia, Australia, and the Americas. This more universalist nationalism of the Nation is unique among nationalist organizations and a direct outgrowth of Fard's personal worldview.

Fard's New Zealand and Pakistani background and activities in various black nationalist and pro-Japanese circles provide him with a historical context. Though ethnically ambiguous, Fard would have been familiar with the daunting forces of white domination throughout the country. For an immigrant in early-twentieth-century America, any accent or other cultural markers may have relegated him into the unenviable category as "Other" and evoke outrage at the consequences. The early 1920s saw a rise of violent nativism, manifested in anti-immigrant riots, legislation and terrorist campaigns led by the Ku Klux Klan, which reached its zenith of popularity during the decade. Fard's friendship with other people of color such as his best friend, Edward Donaldson, a Chinese American, would have provided opportunities to explore the effects of racism emotionally and intellectually. In addition, the popular activities of the UNIA, and Islamic variants like the MSTA, granted Fard an opportunity to witness black people's hunger for spiritual and physical respite from oppression. These organizations proved to be models of what could be done to mobilize African Americans. They did not rely on traditional (white) interpretations of history, race, religion, and civilization; rather, they built on the premise that whites were deceptive, unethical, and hostile to black people. The cosmology of the Nation reflected this thrust, while also imbuing its form of black nationalism with a wider internationalist perspective. It explicitly associated African Americans with all people of color around the world. Black people in America became part of an organic unit of all non-European people. Fard's early associations with Asians, blacks, Chicanos, and others convinced him that the struggle against white supremacy was strengthened by being as broad as possible.

Though viewed as a pathologically corrupt con man by some and God by others, Fard was most likely a man who was a true believer in his campaign to resist white supremacy. He did not deny his involvement in nationalist organizations when arrested in Detroit in 1933. Under the threat of further arrest, he continued to organize around national and international causes that challenged white supremacy.[14] Whether these causes simply were meant to enrich Fard is unclear. He had much more to lose than to gain by engaging in such activities in the virulently racist and violent climate of 1930s America. Ultimately, however, political oppression could account for his departure from political organization in 1934.

Fard's curious teachings raise concerns. They were not orthodox radical platforms. To be sure, the fanciful tales of germs, mad scientists, and race appeared outlandish. That Fard relied on creative myths to bolster his agenda is evident. Not all followers embraced his lessons either. Malcolm X biographer Bruce Perry suggests that, while national spokesman for the Nation, Malcolm did not take all of the stories of the Nation literally.[15] For Malcolm and many others the lessons were metaphoric tales with powerful practical meaning. There is no doubt, however, that many others took the stories at face value. With all religions, as Fard must have observed however, a foolish belief to some is well-deserved faith for others.

The internationalist perspectives that shaped the early development of the Nation engendered confidence that the black struggle had important agents worldwide. It also became a cause for alarm for the State Department during World War II. Leading up to and during World War II, Muslim ministers warned against fighting "the devil's war" against Japan, a fellow black nation. Though the Germans and Italians were devils acting as they were genetically programmed, the Japanese were simply reacting to the wickedness of white invaders of Asia. A Japanese agent, Satokata Takahashi, spoke at NOI temples in Detroit and Chicago, imploring listeners to resist attempts by the American government to recruit them to die for white supremacy. Echoing the language of Marcus Garvey, Japanese imperialists demanded an "Asia for Asians."

Despite being out of step with the great majority of African Americans about serving in the war, Muslims actually shared a popular black affection for imperial Japan, at least up to the attack on Pearl Harbor. The power and industrialization of Japan, many African Americans believed, was a direct refutation of white supremacy. Moreover, some reasoned that the Japanese, as people of color, would be sympathetic to the plight of black people since Japanese in the United States also suffered from racist discrimination. After Pearl Harbor, one-half of blacks in one poll agreed that blacks would be better off or no worse off under Japanese rule. Attempting to galvanize the general sympathy for Japan among African Americans and rejecting the call to arms, the NOI publicly denounced serving in the U.S. military, as long as black people languished under the thumb of white supremacy. Though not activist in nature or even demanding fair treatment per se, Muslims refused to serve and many faced imprisonment.[16]

Elijah Muhammad, who took a tenuous hold of the organization after Master Fard's disappearance in 1934, was arrested with thirty-seven other

Muslims in September 1942. Charged with draft violations, most pleaded guilty. Muhammad was sentenced to one to five years and served most of his time in Milan, Michigan. He emerged from prison a martyr in 1946 and provided a cohesive bond for the heretofore splintered movement. Similar to the Universal Negro Improvement Association and other nationalist organizations, the NOI increasingly saw the value in creating a veritable black nation until black people had their own geographically distinct nation-state. With a new commitment to "nation building" the NOI purchased a 140-acre farm in Michigan in 1945 and began to expand the business holdings in 1947. By the mid-1950s the Nation owned businesses in several states and property worth millions.[17]

By the dawning of the civil rights movement in 1955 the Nation was growing significantly and gaining greater name recognition in black communities. On street corners and on sidewalks, Muslims announced their plan for the tripartite liberation of black people that would free them mentally, physically, and spiritually. The first step was to reveal the heinous nature of the oppression under which black people lived. This was done through speeches and writings on actual acts of brutality committed against blacks by whites. Providing graphic accounts of lynching from antilynching publications, Muhammad spoke about the joy and glee entire white communities experienced when they communally tortured and murdered black men, women, and children. Surely, only a sick, ignorant, and foolish people could participate in such hate, wickedness, and barbarism.[18] As the civil rights movement unfolded, Muhammad had many other stories of white misdeeds to reveal what he called the "true nature of the devil."

The civil rights movement created the social and political climate that precipitated the rapid growth of the Nation. The civil rights movement brought on many examples of white aggression and terror to substantiate the NOI's belief that whites were demons and that integration was the preoccupation of fools, idiots, and enemies of the black nation. No sane person would ever love his murderous, rapist enemy, the Nation insisted. The desire to integrate with whites must be a symptom of the dysfunctional slave culture that black people embraced.[19] The second factor that led to the rapid growth of the NOI after 1955 was the organizational and leadership skills of Muhammad and his chief minister, Malcolm X.

The struggle for civil rights directed considerable attention toward the glaring injustices, inequalities, and suffering experienced by millions of Americans who were victims of legally sanctioned white supremacy. The efforts of nonviolent men, women and children who directly challenged de jure oppression were televised worldwide. The brutal policies of local and state governments repulsed many throughout the United States— black and white. Sympathy for civil rights workers grew among white liberals who helped give birth to a vibrant public intellectual discourse on race and oppression in the country. Black and white intellectuals met at conferences, published sundry books and articles, and lauded the activities of those who nobly fought to end white supremacy.

The heightened consciousness of racial oppression and the burgeoning movement against it provided an arena of discourse for the Nation that it had not previously enjoyed. The images of vicious attack dogs tugging at the flesh of unarmed and peaceful men and women were burned into the memory of millions. The savage acts of terrorists who dynamited black churches, killing children—such as in the Birmingham tragedy in 1963—produced a strong distrust of nonviolence among some blacks. Furthermore, the efficacy of integration was seriously questioned by many blacks who lived in the North and West, in cities and states without legally sanctioned racial oppression but where de facto policies were nonetheless brutal, direct, and efficient in subjugating black people.

Out of this tumultuous period emerged the charismatic, verbose, and defiant Muslims of the Nation, ubiquitously called the "Black Muslims" by the white media. It was the NOI's chief assistant who helped spread and popularize the teachings and accomplishments of the Honorable Elijah Muhammad and the Nation and, for many, contextualize the struggle for black liberation in a manner not done before, helping to build a black nation.

When Malcolm X was released from prison in 1952, there were four Temples of Islam, one each in Chicago, Detroit, Washington, and Milwaukee. Malcolm X, a passionate and zealous Muslim, was a very effective recruiter when he joined the Detroit temple. After the young minister tripled the membership of the Detroit temple, Muhammad took it upon himself to personally train Malcolm in Chicago. He was appointed minister of Temple Number Seven in Harlem in June 1954. In Harlem he sharpened his oratorical skills by, among other things, competing with other soapbox preachers. In Harlem, Malcolm's charismatic style attracted scores, then hundreds and thousands to street corners. Malcolm was also appointed head minister to temples in both Boston and Philadelphia, while simultaneously working on the formation of temples in several other cities, including Miami, Pittsburgh, Newark, and Los Angeles. By 1957 there were twenty-seven temples across the country. Within two years, the number jumped to forty-nine.[20]

Malcolm's appeal was multifaceted. He had a number of characteristics that immediately made him appealing to audiences: his good looks, verbal skills, intelligence, and personal history. Standing at six feet four inches, Malcolm was a commanding sight. He was clear and accessible to the people in his language and choice of words and expressions. He adeptly used black colloquialisms in speeches, providing humor with strong political and social commentary. According to many, he could also favorably represent himself, the Nation, and black people in general during his interactions with the white media.

In 1959, CBS reporter Mike Wallace was made aware of the growing Muslim movement when a black reporter proposed a story on the NOI. Wallace and millions of other whites were shocked at the Nation and its rhetoric. Any similarly vitriolic rhetoric against blacks made by southern whites "would set off a federal investigation," complained Wallace.[21] In the five-part CBS special, "The Hate That Hate Produced," Malcolm appeared calm, bright, disciplined, and knowledgeable. Within months after the show aired, NOI membership doubled.[22] Malcolm was also an embodiment of Muhammad's message and ability to reform, build, and radically change the most vile, violent, and downtrodden members of the black community. Malcolm always took the opportunity to explain his previous life as a "Negro." Of his life of criminality, he noted that "I am not ashamed of this because it was all done when I was a part of the white man's Christian world. As a Muslim I would never have done these awful things that caused me to go to prison."[23] It was Malcolm's prior life as a street hustler and thug that made him bigger than life.

His life as a prisoner was so vicious that he was named "Satan," unquestionably creating an element of respect among other criminals and street toughs whom the NOI attracted. To many, the Muslim leader was a true black man. He was upright, strong, defiant of white supremacy, and intelligent. He was not a privileged Ph.D. from a middle-class background who insisted that true manhood (and womanhood) meant allowing whites to beat, maim, and attack black people. Without doubt, Malcolm spoke to many of those whom Martin Luther King Jr. failed to reach. In addition, Malcolm spoke to those who were growing more disenchanted with King's message of integration and nonviolence.

For those who lived in black communities outside the South, racial oppression was very real. In Chicago, headquarters of the Nation, blacks who attempted to move into all-white areas such as Marquette Park or Cicero in the late 1950s and early 1960s were met with bombings and arson from hostile whites.[24] Nationally, the police were popularly known for their harassment and brutality of blacks.[25] Closed housing, job discrimination, and police brutality were universal experiences in every major black community in 1960. Blacks outside the South often doubted the efficacy of the struggles against Jim Crow. For this reason, many of them gravitated toward the Nation and its attempts to build black institutions, instead of integrating white ones. Too, the NOI's bold rhetoric had a potent appeal. As a Harlem cab driver stated in 1963: "I dig [Malcolm] the best. He's the only one that makes any sense for my money . . . I'm too busy makin' a buck to join anything. But those Muslims or Moslems, 'ever what you call 'em, make more sense than the NAACP and the Urban League and all the rest of 'em put together. They're down on the good earth with the brother. They're for their own people and that Malcolm ain't afraid to tell Mr. Charlie, the FBI or the cops where to get off. You don't see him pussyfootin' around the whites like he's scared of 'em."[26]

To be sure, the appeal of the NOI was not confined to the northern poor or working class. Members of the black middle class grew warm to black nationalism as the efforts of civil rights workers were met with considerable violence by whites. Photographer Gordon Parks writes: "It came as a shock, one afternoon at a chic outdoor party, to hear well-to-do Negro women extolling black nationalism. One matron threatened to join the New York mosque of the Muslims. I heard another berate a blond woman for the Caucasians' treatment of 'her people.' 'You mean "our people,"' retorted the fair-skinned lady. 'I happen to be Negro too.' The hostess laughed and nudged me. 'Neither she nor anyone in her family would have admitted that 10 years ago.'"[27]

Despite the attraction that some middle-class blacks felt for the Nation, the average recruit was usually poor and often—in the case of men—a former criminal. Although it is difficult to fully assess, as many as 90 percent of the adult male members of the Harlem Temple Number Seven had criminal records in the early 1960s. Recidivism, however, was virtually nil.[28] A. Philip Randolph observed that the NOI attracted the black person "lowest on the totem pole" because of its ability to relate to the poor masses. Unlike the NAACP and the Urban League, the Muslims, according to Randolph, have "hour-to-hour contact with people . . . who suffer the same problems every day."[29]

Much of this appeal had to do with the nature of the message: "Clean yourself, stand up and do something for yourself." The tone of the Nation was unequivocally meant for the most downtrodden elements of the black community who seemed the most in need of the cultural and spiritual rebirth advocated by the Muslims. Because of the nature of the message, poorer blacks were the most open to the scathing critiques of black popular culture. They appealed to the desire for betterment and uplift, as well as empowerment. Furthermore, the harsh condemnations of black culture fit comfortably into the popular notions of hard work and personal responsibility, which often overlooked systemic inequalities and institutional injustice.

The NOI and Mass Black Culture

Culture, popularly defined as the rituals and customs of a people—all learned behavior—was central to the Nation's struggle to push back the boundaries of oppression and attract members. Inheriting parts of its beliefs from Booker T. Washington, the Nation was a staunch proponent of self-help and advocated little agitation or direct resistance to white supremacy after World War II.[30] The power to uplift, the NOI argued, rested in the hands of the oppressed. It was therefore essential to reform the way of life of the oppressed. Their dysfunctional culture needed to be destroyed and a new, more moral, practical, and industrious one put in its place.

The Nation's strong arguments against the life-styles and culture of most black people spilled over into the rhetoric against the civil rights movement. In its attempt to convey the message that black people were victims of white devils, the Nation used vitriolic language to describe how whites oppressed blacks in virtually every way. This oppression created a nation of deaf, dumb, and blind Negroes who celebrated a slave culture of violent pathology and self-destruction.

The Nation's cartoons, articles, and speeches found in the *Muhammad Speaks* newspaper and other NOI publications reveal the derisive views toward black popular culture that the organization promulgated. These critiques of black people are multifaceted and can be categorized into criticisms of (1) popular culture, (2) religion, and (3) politics. Latinos, Asians, and Native Americans were generally spared the vitriol of the Muslims, chiefly because they were not the target audience for the Nation's agenda of redemption, nor were they considered the oppressors of black people.

Defining Black Popular Culture

Discussions and debates over the nature of African American popular culture and the viability of integration were not confined to the nationalist community. Radical leftists, liberal integrationists, and an array of academics had engaged in this vigorous debate throughout the years of the civil rights movement. Intellectual Harold Cruse took a position similar to that of the Nation when he declared that if culture is the "soul of a race, nation, people or nationality," the soul of black people in America had "lost its power of communication," retarded by the "idolatry" of white people "in the arts, abandonment of true identity, and immature, childlike mimicry of white aesthetics."[31] He suggested that black people needed a cultural renaissance in order to secure liberation for themselves.[32] Cruse's position was a formidable critique of the integrationist struggles led by the NAACP, the Congress on Racial Equality, and leaders like King who proclaimed that "cultural integration" was the "promised land" of black people.[33] Many took umbrage at Cruse's writings. Saunders Redding attacked Cruse's position on culture as "not only wrong, but wrong-headed." Moreover, Redding went as far as to say that white and black Americans possessed a "single identity, a oneness of thinking and doing." This fundamental cultural commonality among whites and blacks in America was evidenced in the "values and value judgments, ideas and ways of thinking about these ideas, customs, costumes and manners, images and symbols—all these and more, both abstract and concrete, are the same for Negro Americans and for whites."[34]

Cruse was not alone in recognizing the cultural differences—both subtle and obvious—that marked white and black America. Sociologist E. Franklin Frazier had engaged in a popular debate with anthropologist Melville Herskovitz over the expanse of the cultural chasms that separated blacks and whites in the United States. Herskovitz argued that African cultural retention was palpable among African Americans. Frazier insisted that no significant African cultural traditions survived the Middle Passage, thereby making whites and blacks culturally identical.[35]

W. E. B. Du Bois and others had long discussed the cultural dimensions, and dynamic nature of African American music, food, dance, family structures, and religion.[36] Rarely, however, had the debate over culture been focused on a hierarchical system of cultural values that encouraged black people to extricate themselves from their love affair with white culture. Some middle-class integrationists in the South and elsewhere semiprivately complained that many black people were obstreperous and embarrassing. They were crude and unsophisticated and needed to be culturally "refined" if the civil rights efforts were going to be successful.[37] The aim was not, however, to celebrate a more virtuous African cultural renaissance. The efforts of these integrationist leaders reflected a tacit support and promotion of what was considered white normative culture and behavior. The NOI's position on popular culture was in some respects similar to those of Du Bois, Frazier, Herskovitz and others. The Nation supported the integrationist adherence to white, middle-class norms while simultaneously advocating a cultural renewal that was not dependent on white symbols and traditions. To the Nation, black people had been made into self-hating slaves. As a result, the cultural rebirth of blacks was linked to a paradoxical withdrawal from white society and a replication of select qualities of white middle-class culture, such as culinary traditions, dress, and public decorum.

Elijah Muhammad, the theocratic leader of the NOI and its messenger of Allah, commonly referred to the average black man in both sympathetic and derisive terms. "The so-called Negro," Muhammad writes, has been viciously oppressed by white "beasts" who are "the only people who live like savage beast[s] without human civil actions of love and sympathy for human beings or righteousness."[38] The so-called Negro is actually the Original Man, created in the likeness of God. In fact, the Original Man is godlike. He is "the owner, the maker, the cream of the planet earth, father of civilization, God of the universe."[39] Because of the evil nature of the whites, who enslaved, raped, and terrorized black people, black people have been made into virtual slaves. This condition of slavery did not end with the Thirteenth Amendment. Muhammad often called the black man the "Black Slave."[40] This condition of slavery created a degenerate type of black man, a "Negro." It is the Negro who ostensibly represents the most confused and self-hating of all black people. He apes white people, obsequiously submits to the will of whites and works—consciously or not—against the interests of black people. Negro leaders taught blacks to beg whites for integration. It was the Negro leader who told black people that they had no right to defend themselves against terrorist attacks, and it was the Negro minister who told blacks that they will achieve freedom after death.

The NOI derided the "Negro" masses for embracing a cultural world that was not in their best interest. Religion, diet, fashion, music, love of sports, and liberal political leanings were routinely ridiculed in speeches, articles, and cartoons. The black church was the most frequent target of its criticism. Like Karl Marx, Muhammad vilified Christianity as an opiate of black people, but, unlike Marx, Muhammad did not characterize all organized religion as flawed. Islam was innately liberating, according to Muhammad. It was the religion of the righteous and those who sought to realize freedom, justice, and equality, the cardinal points of the Nation's theology.

The Theology of the Nation of Islam

The Nation was very cynical about Christianity, castigating it as a "grave-yard" for black people.[41] As a religion, Christianity could not adequately serve as the spiritual base of any black liberation struggle. "Wherever you find non-white people today," announced Malcolm X in 1960, "they are trying to get back their freedom from people who represent themselves as Christians . . . And if you ask these [subject] people their picture of a Christian, they will tell you 'a white man—a slave master.'"[42] Yet, NOI tenets did not consider Christianity to be inherently foul. What whites and blacks in America practiced, according to the Nation, was a Westernized form of Christianity that has been corrupted by deceivers to suit their odious agenda.[43] The true religion for black people, however, was Islam, which can transform deaf, dumb and blind Negroes into black people. Islam and "knowledge of self" were what "the white man hates most."[44] It was by design that whites had so assiduously promoted Christianity among the black people whom they enslaved. Religion was unequivocally the most important part of the process of making a Negro. With a Bible in one hand and a whip in the other, white enslavers tortured African people into submission and proceeded to inculcate the enslaved and broken people with the decadent values and hypocritical tenets of a bastardized Christianity. Thus the Negro Christian was born in the wilderness of North America:

> As "Negro Christians" we idolized our Christian Slave master, and lived for the day when his plurality of white gods would allow us to mingle and mix up with them. We worshiped the false beauty of the Slave master's leprous looking women . . . We regarded them with the utmost respect, courtesy and kindness, bowing, and tipping our hats, showing our teeth. We perfected the art of humility and politeness for their sake . . . but at the same time we treated our own women as if they were mere animals, with no love, respect or protection.
>
> Fear ruled us, but not fear of God. We had fear of the Slave master, we had no knowledge of truth and we were apparently afraid to let him see us practicing love and unity toward each other. . . .
>
> Is it a wonder that the world laughed at us and held us [up] to scorn? We practiced love of others, while hating ourselves . . . unity with others and disunity with our own kind. We called ourselves "Negro Christians," yet we remained an ignorant, foolish people, despised and rejected by the white Christians. We were fools![45]

In this statement Malcolm X presents Christianity and its effects on black people as an inexorable evil. He gives little attention to resistance movements that found a comfortable niche in Christian rhetoric, most notably Nat Turner's rebellion or the many militant struggles of black Christians from David Walker to Marcus Garvey. It was the aim of Malcolm and other NOI ministers to present the plight of black people in exaggerated rhetoric, even accusing them of capitulating to white supremacy. Malcolm's hyperbolic language is what historian Sterling Stuckey identifies as the black nationalist "tendency to exaggerate the degree of acquiescence to oppression by the masses of black people."[46]

Reference to African Americans as ignorant, foolish, and senseless sheep at once appears to be an axiomatic expression of white supremacy. Yet denigrating blacks was a common modus operandi of the NOI in its struggle for black uplift. The Nation, in a sense, embraced the prevailing stereotypes of the Negro, which were celebrated by white American popular culture. From D. W. Griffith's *Birth of a Nation* through *Gone with the Wind*, from *Amos 'n' Andy* to Aunt Jemima and Tarzan, white popular culture had copiously maligned, ridiculed, and degraded Negroes as ignorant, lazy, criminal, and uncivilized. Black people were not oblivious to the attacks against their humanity. The psychological ramifications of being black in a virulently antiblack society have been well studied and documented. Black nationalists were well aware of the strong antiblack sentiment that was ubiquitous in the United States, and in their attempt to resist racist propaganda most nationalists abandoned their identity as "Negroes" altogether. The term used to describe people of African descent became a term of contempt for virtually all black nationalists by Malcolm's departure from the Nation in 1964. The Nation led the way in the nationalist deconstruction of the term *Negro*.

Most black people were essentially "Negroes," the Nation's leaders argued, in that they did not think independently of whites. They were far from the intelligent, spiritual, peaceful, and industrious Original People of ancient Asia. Indeed, black people were made into veritable "zombies"— the walking dead: "You are the people that are dead in the body. You are the people that must be reassured in the dead. It doesn't mean getting up in the graveyard among dead bodies. It means that the power and authority and wisdom of God goes up and the understanding of God rose up from a dead people—from a mentally dead people that's all it means."[47]

It is the tendency of classical black nationalists to depict the plight of black people in extremely desperate terms. They, "more than any other group of Afro-American ideologists," writes historian Sterling Stuckey, "have been able to combine in terrible and uneasy tension the most devastating criticisms of, and the most sublime faith in, their people."[48] On one hand, such depictions convey to black people that their struggle is in dire need of radical change, one that can only come with a disavowal of the prevailing practices and notions regarding race in the United States. On the other hand, they also suggest a paternalistic "tough love" that implies faith and confidence in the abilities of black people. In addition, classical black nationalists, like the NOI, insist that black people are, in no uncertain terms, oppressed and denigrated by white people. Moreover, this oppression can only be effectively challenged by extricating themselves from white society. Moral suasion and other attempts to appeal to white people have been futile. The only available option, nationalists argued, is separation. Otherwise, black people will always remain beggars to whites, pleading for handouts in the form of welfare and other government-supported programs for the poor.

Malcolm X spoke to the frustrations of many blacks by pointing out the very palpable inconsistencies in the popular notion of violence and its use in the United States. Whites took great pride in their violent past, Malcolm argued. They were not ashamed of picking up arms to fight for their liberty during the American Revolution. They did not hide the fact that they killed Native Americans. White Americans are proud that they defended themselves against Japanese attack at Pearl Harbor and dropped bombs on civilians in Hiroshima and Nagasaki. Furthermore, whites do not hesitate to send blacks to kill people in other countries. But when it came to self-defense in Alabama, Mississippi or California, black people were told that violence was wrong. "You bleed for white people, but when it comes to seeing your own churches being bombed and little black girls murdered, you haven't got any blood. You bleed when the white man says bleed; you bite when the white man says bite; and you bark when the white man says bark. How are you going to be nonviolent in Mississippi, as violent as you were in Korea?"[49]

Contrary to Christianity, Islam supported self-defense, according to the NOI. Self-defense, the desire for protection for family and community, was natural, Muslims insisted. Furthermore, Islam was the natural religion of all peoples, except, of course, whites. By extension, the ideals of Islam—justice, righteousness, and equality—were natural to all black people. Christianity, however, allowed whites to oppress, murder, and exploit other Christians because it was based in "falsehood."[50] Ultimately Allah would destroy this spiritual falsehood. Blacks, Muhammad explained, could avoid destruction with whites if they accepted Islam their "true religion [and] salvation."[51]

But as long as blacks "begged" whites for acceptance and integration they were destined for doom. Genocide would be the fruit of integration because whites were incapable of living in peace with blacks and would continue to beat, maim, and oppress those too foolish to refuse self-defense and separation and to "do something for themselves."[52] This type of praise of strength and self-defense undoubtedly attracted many.

For members of the Nation, Islam was redemptive. It offered a standard of civilization, respect, community, and achievement not easily accessible for the poor people attracted to the Nation. It also freed black people from their spiritual dependence on whites, instead grounding its members on a religious nationalist foundation that placed black people at the center of their spiritual analysis and synthesis. Christianity was "the grave" of spiritual ignorance, and Islam was salvation, truth, and knowledge. It was the harbinger of freedom, justice, and equality—ideals alien to the world of Caucasians who systematically oppressed black people. Moreover, the Nation's religion was promoted in direct contrast to the teachings of leading Christians, who sought integration and racial reconciliation. For Muhammad, integration would inevitably welcome widespread intermarriage and further erosion of the moral and spiritual fiber of black people. This course of action was suicidal. "Why would any black man in his right mind want to marry a lyncher, a murderer, a rapist, a dope peddler, a gambler, a hog eater . . . a devil . . . for that's just what the white man is." Truth, Muhammad argued, hurts. "That is why whites hated the Muslims so much."[53] Islam was the answer to the despair experienced by black people worldwide, but the rejection of Christianity also marked the Nation's rejection of the "slave culture" of black people as well as thoroughly Eurocentric Christian churches in black communities.

Gender

The Nation of Islam clearly embraced traditional views of gender. Patriarchy was divinely sanctioned, Muslims insisted. Women were meant to be submissive, domestic, and "the man's field to produce his nation."[54] While the rhetoric of patriarchy was no great deviation from the predominant views of gender in much of the world, the NOI managed to offer a peculiar slant to its brand of male domination. The Muslims' patriarchal language was couched in the Nation's typical condescending vitriol against Negroes. Especially before the 1960s, black women were particularly maligned. They were blamed for being the "greatest tool of the devil." Minister Malcolm X asked, "How do you think this black man got in this state? By our women tricking him and tempting him, and the devil taught her how to do this." In fact, Malcolm explained, "the trickiest in existence is the black woman and the white man."[55] The Nation's sexism was tempered by the mid-1960s as a nascent women's liberation movement developed, but the affirmation of male domination was always obvious. Still, numerous women found the Nation more appealing than the larger society.

For many women, the NOI's patriarchal arrangement was not substantively different from the Christian church, although the rhetoric was more explicit. Indeed, white and black Americans embraced sexism in most of their institutions. The civil rights movement's leadership was clearly male-dominated, despite the formidable efforts and activities of women throughout the country. Women such as Fannie Lou Hamer, grassroots organizer in Mississippi, and Ella Baker, executive director of the Southern Christian Leadership Conference (SCLC), as well as Dorothy Cotton, Septima Clark, and others in the SCLC, had met with incessant confrontations of sexism in the movement.[56] The black church had long been a bastion of patriarchy. That the Muslims also practiced male domination in a clearly male-dominated society meant little to some women, who felt affirmed in their black womanhood in ways not found in the larger society.

Elijah Muhammad often referred to the black woman as the "mother of civilization." She was God's wonderful creation and "until we learn to love and protect our woman, we will never be a fit and recognized people on the earth." Muhammad explained that the black woman "is your first nurse. She is your teacher. Your first lesson comes from your mother. If you don't protect your mother, how do you think you look in the eyes of other fellow human beings?"[57] While the rhetoric of "protection" suggested that women were incapable of protecting themselves or were weak and defenseless, it must be reiterated that Muhammad merely reflected ideals that were ubiquitous in African, Muslim, and Western societies. He was careful, however, to relate the message to the unique situation of African Americans, who had long been victimized by white sexual predators.

Muslims always expressed outrage at the thought of white men married to, or engaged in intimate relations with, black women. Hundreds of years of rape at the hands of devils, according to Muhammad, indicated the danger of allowing a white man near a black woman. It was the scared and foolish Negro man who did not have the wisdom or courage to resist the devil rapist. Black women "cannot go without being winked at, whistled at, yelled at, slapped, patted, kicked and driven around in the streets by your devil enemies right under your nose. You do nothing about it, nor do you protest."[58]

The Muslim leader vilified the ignorant and confused Negro masses that lived outside the righteous community of Islam. These Negroes, Muhammad taught, had developed a culture that failed to recognize the importance of its women. Negroes taunted black women with vile language and flirtations on the streets of America. "There is no nation on earth that has less respect for and as little control of their women as we so-called Negroes here in America. Even animals and beasts, the fowls of the air, have more love and respect for their females than have the so-called Negroes of America."[59] The Nation offered its alternative to this dysfunctional "slave culture." To foster proper gender relations within its own ranks, it developed Muslim Girl Training and General Civilization Class (MGT-GCC) for female members. Males were members of the Fruit of Islam (FOI).

The MGT-GCC was the "name given to the training of women and girls in North America how to keep house, how to rear their children, how to take care of their husbands, sew, cook, and in general, how to act at home and abroad." Women were taught proper hygiene, "English, spelling, penmanship, refinement, beauty [and] art" among other things. A female supreme captain ran the MGT-GCC, and all women over thirteen were required to report to a monthly weight check. Obesity was contrary to the standards of health as outlined by the NOI. Into the early 1960s MGT administrators charged women a fine of a penny for every pound they were overweight. The group also maintained a Sick Committee and Poor Committee to visit and assist the poor and infirmed membership.[60] Women were expected to work at home, unless the family was unable to survive on one salary. In the case that women were single and unemployed or otherwise in need of work, job notices were available at each mosque. Members were instructed how to prepare for job interviews. They were told to use proper diction and dress.[61]

Many women, as Cynthia S'thembile West relates, enjoyed employment in NOI-owned establishments. West, who studied one of the largest mosques in the country in Newark, New Jersey, explains that despite the media image of Muslim women as "submissive women who were confined to the domestic sphere," they "played an active role in the community as well as on the home front." Women in the Nation found employment and authority in many of the twenty-five NOI operations, such as day-care facilities, schools, and businesses. Women were encouraged by the teachings of Elijah Muhammad to acknowledge their role as "the central most important figures in domestic life [and] the key to the black man's success." Most women were employed through home-based ventures but still found a sense of autonomy, worth, and significance.[62]

In most respects, the NOI supported assumptions about womanhood that were conventional to America into the 1960s. Muslims lauded practices and notions that affirmed the cult of domesticity and traditional gender roles. Males were the protectors; females were the purveyors of culture and civilization to the children. Women were to be adored, protected, and respected. While the Muslims affirmed sexist and at times misogynist ideas, such ideas were not in stark contrast to the sexism of society at large. Many women enjoyed the affirmation they received as black women who were told not to mimic the "leprous" looks of white women but take pride in their own black beauty. Black women and men who joined the Nation, especially into the early 1960s, were largely from the poorest sections of the community. In the NOI, men and women were able to construct their own world, complete with all of the staples of middle-class life. Cities like Newark, Chicago, New York, and Los Angeles provided black-owned and operated businesses that gave worth, dignity, and a modicum of power to many heretofore impoverished and powerless blacks. While many urban blacks languished in poverty, the self-help ventures of the Nation provided socioeconomic status and an arena of authority that was elusive in their world as "Negroes." Men were able to assume a greater sense of manhood, as it was understood by the larger society. Women, too, found a higher sense of womanhood, despite the obvious confines and limitations of patriarchy.

The NOI was able to reveal the fundamental limitations of African American gender relations (such as female objectification) without fundamentally deconstructing the traditional framework of sexism and male domination. In their pursuit of the western bourgeois standard of civilization, the Muslims necessarily supported both patriarchy and the cult of domesticity that relegated women to the home as important figures of domestic family affairs, but many women, long familiar with naked and crude sexism, appreciated the new status as homemakers and important and esteemed mothers of civilization.

Music

The NOI considered black popular music, like other cultural traditions of the African American masses, unworthy of appreciation. Black musical creations such as the blues, jazz, rock and roll, and rhythm and blues were criticized for promoting "indecency and slave ways." Dancing to such music was part and parcel of the evil practices of a decadent society.[63] The stiff, military-type exercises of the Fruit of Islam and Muslim Girls Training-General Civilization Class were the only types of dancing permitted.

E. U. Essien-Udom, while researching the Nation, observed of its parties: "There is usually no program and no speech. Men and women sit together at long tables and chat. Occasionally three or more people stand and chat. On the whole the atmosphere appears rather subdued. Conversation is carried on in low voices. The party is orderly and Muslims are particularly cordial to visitors."[64] Muslim poets, playwrights, and musicians conducted organized entertainment. The music generally had religious and political messages, such as Minister Louis X's popular song "The White Man's Heaven Is a Black Man's Hell."[65]

Popular R&B entertainers such as Smokey Robinson and the Miracles, the Supremes, and Chubby Checker were ridiculed for their "zealous love" for their "open enemies." Their conks, perms, and short dresses were examples of how they had been deceived by white "tricknology."[66] The popular groups of the 1960s were simple products of a confused and lost people.

The NOI's rejection of black popular music was but one of its attempts to separate itself from the popular culture of black people. The NOI developed its own cultural world, complete with its own mores, customs, and folkways. Music, a central expression of a people's culture, was one of the more powerful mediums of African American expression. It was, to the NOI, an expression of a morally and spiritually flawed people. Any celebration of this "slave" culture ran the risk of tainting the virtuous world of the Nation of Islam, which incessantly buffered itself against Negroes and the devil. A complete rejection of black popular music facilitated this protection from the outside world of sin. Furthermore, it helped the NOI rely on itself to create and develop its own new and unique culture to prepare itself for full nationhood.

The NOI introduced some curious and enigmatic interpretations of black popular culture. Its condemnation of popular culture and its characterization of it as hostile to the well-being and salvation of black people is not entirely surprising when historically contextualized. It would be inaccurate to suggest that the Nation's position on popular culture should be anticipated, given the traditional black nationalists rhetoric. It does, however, help us understand the overall theoretical framework of the Nation's arguments. In addition, the Nation, for all intents and purposes, is organizationally *sui generis*. Cultural relativism was not very pervasive in 1930. It certainly was not popular in the mid-nineteenth century, during the time of Martin R. Delany.

The Nation embraced the prevailing standards of culture known in the United States, in many respects. It also rejected much of the popular culture of black people in America and promoted strict codes of conduct and decorum that were more Victorian than anything else. Traditional Muslims in northern and eastern Africa have strict dress codes. The NOI, however, did not adopt the Arabized garments of these societies for men. They instead proudly wore Western suits—symbols of middle-class status. Despite this, Muslims refused to adhere to cultural traditions promoted by white Americans, which, like deference, submission, and obsequiousness to whites, were born of racist traditions. While the Nation taught its members to respect all people, even whites, it claimed never to tolerate any violent acts perpetrated against a Muslim. The Arabized dress of Muslim women was also a departure from the Western dress worn by Muslim men. Why conservative Western dresses were insufficient for black women was never addressed. Furthermore, its rejection of West African–inspired clothing and certain foods reveals some inconsistencies in the Nation's rhetoric of racial pride. Much like its classical black nationalist predecessors, the NOI straddled the fence of racial consciousness.

The Nation developed a theology that explicitly promoted racial pride and dignity among black people. It affirmed black people as the Original People long before Louis and Mary Leakey announced their discovery at Olduvai Gorge in Kenya. It argued against the white supremacist Christianity that was promoted throughout the Western world and in many black churches. NOI teachings did, however, historically detach African Americans from their West African roots by emphasizing Arabia and Asia. It did not fully recognize the accomplishments of black people in Africa who were not Muslim. It pandered to the ignorance of most black people by downplaying West Africa while promoting North and East African histories and peoples. White people oftentimes validated North Africa as having produced high civilization. The Nation, in turn, sought to claim the same locale as the heritage of black people in North America, while simultaneously capitulating to the racist ideas surrounding West African history.

The Nation's attacks on black popular culture reflected an attempt, on one level, to gain respect and admiration in the black community by adhering to middle-class status symbols and cultural mores. The NOI presented itself to a very desperate people as a vehicle of salvation and liberation. In order to legitimize its mission, it described the state of black people as terribly bleak. To paraphrase one observer, a once great people who built huge monuments and studied the sciences had been reduced into self-hating, ignorant, lazy, and indolent eaters of pig bowels.

While the NOI would never go as far as to blame black people fully for the conditions in which they found themselves, it was very sure that black people had more power to improve themselves than generally thought. Many of the pathologies that black people embraced, its leaders argued, were rooted in the wickedness and manipulation of white people. Still, blacks had been taught to perpetuate these pathologies. In a sense the so-called Negro was an American creation that was a result of a systematic process of destroying the hard-working, moral, intelligent, and industrious Asiatic black man. The cultural developments made by black people in North America were invariably a by-product of 400 years of slavery and oppression that left black people deaf, dumb, and blind. It was not the nature of the mentally dead masses to create redeeming traditions. Religion, dress, and music were simply the creation of people who were lost and not yet found. The Nation wanted black people to know this. Furthermore, it wanted black people to know that the Nation was the righteous alternative to the decadence and despair in which many found themselves.

CHAPTER 2

"There Go My People"
The Civil Rights Movement, Black Nationalism, and Black Power

By 1960 the Nation of Islam (NOI) had become a national organization with name recognition in every major black community. It was one of the fastest growing black organizations and posed a peculiar threat to the civil rights establishment. The Nation, primarily during Malcolm X's membership, provided a visible contrast to civil rights organizations. The vilification of whites and endorsement of self-defense was anathema to the humanistic language of the Southern Christian Leadership Conference (SCLC), Student Nonviolent Coordinating Committee (SNCC), and Congress on Racial Equality (CORE). On one level, the NOI brought attention to the ubiquity of white supremacy and its effects on black people, such as unemployment, police brutality, and housing and job discrimination outside the South. It also made organizations like the National Association for the Advancement of Colored People (NAACP) and the SCLC seem attractive alternatives to white America, which recoiled at the vitriolic attacks made by the NOI. By 1963, concessions from the white power structure were more common, partly (but by no means chiefly) because of the fear of the Muslims, and the civil rights leadership knew this.

The NOI was the chief benefactor of the Black Power movement. While it did not adopt the slogans of the movement at its mosques or temples, it assiduously promoted the staples of Black Power: a rigorous affirmation of blackness and racial pride and an insistence on the economic and political liberation of black people, independent of whites. The Nation, however, was much more rigid and explicit about its nationalism than the general Black Power movement, whose organizations varied on the issue of territorial separatism.

Civil rights organizations experienced the threat of black nationalism in two major stages. The first was the meteoric rise in popularity of Malcolm X and the Nation of Islam, which lasted from 1957 until his defection from the NOI in 1964. Malcolm X, minister of the Nation and its national spokesman, helped the organization grow from around 400 members in 1952 to an estimated 100,000 to 300,000 in 1964.[1] After Malcolm's departure, the organization no longer captured the media spotlight or grew as rapidly. The second stage of the black nationalist challenge to the civil rights movement was the explosion of urban rebellions and the call for Black Power in the mid-1960s. This stage began with the Watts rebellion in 1965 and included the emergence of the Black Power militants of SNCC and dozens of other organizations in the late 1960s.

Strange Fruit

It is generally agreed that the modern civil rights movement had its origins with the landmark court case of *Brown v. Board of Education* in 1954 and the Montgomery bus boycott of 1955–56, though civil rights struggles had endured for decades before the 1950s.[2] There was, however, another event that fueled what has come to be called America's Second Reconstruction—the lynching of Emmett Till. In August 1955 fourteen-year-old Emmett Till, visiting relatives in Money, Mississippi, was kidnapped, beaten, tortured, and shot in the head for whistling at a white woman. His assailants then tied his body to a cotton-gin pulley and dumped it in the Tallahatchie River, where it was found three days later.[3]

John William Milam and Roy Bryant, the two men who had kidnapped Till, were arrested and tried before a traditional all-white male Mississippi jury. Despite blood in the kidnappers' pick-up truck, eyewitnesses, and other evidence, the jury returned a verdict of not guilty. The Tallahatchie sheriff, H. C. Strider, insisted that the NAACP "planned and plotted" the murder of Till for its own nefarious purpose of challenging white supremacy. The killers later told their story of kidnapping and murder to a northern reporter.[4]

Mamie Bradley, Emmett's mother, chose to have an open casket service for her slain son. Ten thousand people passed his casket at the Roberts Temple of the Church of God in Chicago. His bloated and disfigured head and contorted face, missing an eye, testified to the heinous crime committed by a party much larger than two or three people. Indeed, the majority of white people in Mississippi sanctioned Till's murder. They provided the means and apparatus that would facilitate such a gruesome crime. In 1955, to murder a child was socially acceptable among enough white Mississippians that Milam and Bryant joked and laughed during the one-hour jury deliberations, showing little concern that they would be convicted. The Till case was but a recent addition to the long history of racist terror directed at black people who dared to violate the written and unwritten laws of white supremacy.[5] It would not be the last. Black America knew this.

Jet magazine, the country's leading black news magazine, made a bold and controversial decision to publish pictures of Till's open casket. The image of Till's savagely disfigured corpse was etched into the memories of many black people in every region of the country. It was a testimony to the brutal nature of white supremacy and its tacit acceptance among many whites. It magnified the salience of racial oppression like no single event in recent times had. The anger among black people at the blatant miscarriage of justice made many clamor for social action. Years later, veterans of the black freedom movement like Amzie Moore, Cleveland Sellers, and Ann Moody would mark the Till incident as an impetus to action. James Forman, the first head of SNCC, said that Till's murder made "black people all over the country . . . angry . . . but also frightened."[6] For African Americans, the Till case was a powerful example of the barbarity of an intractably racist system. According to the Nation, the case was indicative of the bestial nature of whites and a lesson for foolish black people who desired integration with their "open enemies."[7]

The visibility of white supremacist violence fomented militancy from activists and sympathy from many whites. It also hardened the positions of nationalists, who viewed such violence as an affirmation of the impossibility of integration. The bombing, arson, beating, jailing, and killing suffered by civil rights activists did not stop them from agitating. Moreover, such violent reactions worked against white supremacist agendas by evoking federal support and international pressure. The violence also propelled the most basic thrust of black nationalism, particularly the Nation's cosmology that argued against whites' humanity. No moral or ethical people could find joy and pleasure in such acts of brutality. For the Nation, racist violence only strengthened its position that integration was a doomed and misguided effort.

Similar to the development of most cosmologies, the NOI's theology provided a spiritual explanation for the immediate physical environment in which people found themselves. Moreover, it adapted Islam to meet the physical, psychological, and spiritual needs of black people. Paradoxically, the barbarism of white supremacy often benefited the Nation. Each time whites lynched a black person, NOI leader Elijah Muhammad hyperbolically noted that "we get 100 new recruits the next week." Racial terror convinced many that black nationalism was an effective way to resist racial oppression. These continuous acts of racist brutality also affirmed the notion that whites were, indeed, immoral. The Nation was careful to exploit racist violence to its fullest.

Stories about lynching alone could not convince black people that whites were devils or that Islamic black nationalism was a viable alternative to Christianity and integration. Lynching, although not confined to the South, was largely a southern phenomenon. Also, most blacks in the 1950s were not confronted with the kind of naked and barbaric racism practiced in Mississippi. Nevertheless, a harsh and brutal form of racism had long confronted blacks in northern cities. There was, for example, widespread support for housing restrictions that excluded people of color from living in white areas. When those restrictions were challenged, there were immediate reactions, sometimes violent as in the case of Trumbull Park in Chicago, where the homes of black families were bombed.[8] California voters, in 1964, repealed a state law prohibiting housing discrimination rather than allow all citizens equal access to housing.[9]

Housing, of course, was only one facet of the institutionalized oppression blacks experienced outside the South. Virtually all white-owned corporations in the 1950s had tacit policies of white-only hiring for upper-management positions. Corporate America had long resisted meritocracy in hiring. In 1955, people of color earned 55.35 percent of the median white income. Four years later the ratio had dropped to 51.69 percent.[10] With similar educational backgrounds, blacks earned significantly less than their white counterparts.[11] While job discrimination was one of the most significant concerns for black people, they were also confronted with the ugly practice of police brutality. Police officers in some communities regularly preyed on black people by beating, intimidating, and even extorting money from their businesses.[12] The daily confrontations with police brutality, housing discrimination, segregation into poor schools, and job discrimination were universal experiences for black people in the United States.

It was this ubiquity of oppression that helps explain the tenets of NOI theology. The Nation not only produced a new and unique interpretation of the nature of racial oppression, but its proposed solutions were also, by nature, anathema to the civil rights movement and substantively different from those offered by any other nationalist organization. The Nation rejected the overall thrust of the civil rights struggle to realize equal rights for black people in the United States. Equal rights before the law would amount to little more than a more insidious and opaque form of racial oppression, argued NOI leaders. The most important characteristic of the NOI was its unwavering assertion that black liberation would never be realized by integrating with or living under the domination of people who were considered innately evil. This type of racial essentialism was not characteristic of any of its black nationalist predecessors, and it offered a peculiar interpretation of oppression that was routinely denounced by civil rights leaders.[13]

The Nation of Islam's rapid growth in the late 1950s offered an implicit challenge to the civil rights movement in several ways. Many observed the growth as a portentous sign of the failure of the southern-based movement to meet the fundamental needs of poor urban northern blacks.[14] Others were particularly disturbed by the Nation's racial proclamations and insistence that black people should defend themselves when under violent attack, an ideal that many in the civil rights leadership did not wish to proclaim as boldly and widely in public. The various civil rights organizations approached the Nation with both caution and disdain. The general position among the NAACP, CORE, and the National Urban League was to avoid mention of the NOI as much as possible. This policy, however, could not last long.[15]

Nonviolence and Civil Rights

For civil rights organizations, the Till tragedy was a clarion call to action. Community organizations sponsored Mamie Bradley to speak in Harlem, Chicago, and other cities. The lynching also created a climate that helped make the Montgomery bus boycott successful. Not only did the local black population almost universally support the boycott, it had the blessings of millions of blacks who were eager for an organized and effective challenge to white supremacy. Out of the boycott emerged the SCLC and its leader, Martin Luther King Jr., who became known as a staunch supporter of nonviolent grassroots action and a proud follower of Gandhian ideals of morality and social action. Initially, however, King's embrace of nonviolence was more tactical than philosophically absolute. When he began to receive death threats and after his home was bombed, King purchased a firearm. He also accepted an offer for armed protection from volunteers who served as sentinels at his home. Though King embraced nonviolence, he also believed that he had a right and an obligation to protect and defend his wife and child. King, or any other black person, could not expect Montgomery's notoriously racist all-white police force to protect and serve the black community. Indeed, King fully understood the importance of strategic actions that were peaceful. He instructed black youth to resist any attempts to violently take to the streets after his home was bombed. He also viewed peace as coterminous with Christian ethics. Still, there was a practical limit to his concept of nonviolence. King's interaction with long-time pacifist Bayard Rustin, however, helped alter King's notion of nonviolence.[16]

King developed a belief in nonviolence that understood the power of violence and hoped to manipulate it for social and political justice. Inherent in King's activism was a resilient faith that moral fortitude and nonviolence could and would fundamentally and drastically reconstruct the collective psychology of white people. Nonviolence, King argued, can "save the white man as well as the Negro."[17] For King, nonviolence was empowering; it helped bolster the cause of the activists who made strong displays of morality in the face of stubborn racist brutality. Ultimately, the racists would be forced to recognize the humanity of black people and permit liberation, which King insisted, was inextricably linked to racial integration. King promoted his notions of nonviolence throughout his public career, even when under increased criticism from black nationalists and others in the larger black community.[18]

King's philosophy anticipated violence and exploited it. It also rejected direct action self-defense.[19] For example, civil rights activists expected violence from white civilians during marches. The activists prepared for it and trained how to avoid serious injury. They understood the power of the images sent globally of men and women violently attacked and not fighting back. For adherents to King's path, the violent racists were ultimately unable to defend themselves morally, while civil rights soldiers won the moral battle. They also knew that these tactics would elicit sympathy from other whites, nationally and internationally.

It is therefore not entirely accurate to view the SCLC, CORE, and SNCC as purely "nonviolent." Each organization embraced a philosophical commitment to "nonviolence," but it was clearly grounded in the rejection of direct action self-defense. It is indeed ironic that Malcolm X, so often associated with violence, avoided it his entire public career until his assassination. King, conversely, is largely viewed as the apotheosis of nonviolence, though he was often enveloped in violence. Though not simply an issue of semantics, the theoretical discussion of nonviolence is important in that the civil rights movement is viewed as strictly nonviolent while black nationalists like the NOI are rarely, if ever, viewed as nonviolent. White Americans generally embraced direct action self-defense for themselves. A black man who advocated anti-self-defense positions against white violence was clearly more acceptable to whites than one who advocated armed defense against armed attack. In time, King and other leaders would recognize how they grew more attractive to white America as Malcolm X and the Nation grew more popular to black people.

The Nation of Islam took particular offense at King and his message. For the Nation, King was the archetypal "deaf, dumb, and blind" Negro Christian who had been duped and confused by the devil. King was a white man's best ploy to undermine black liberation. Indeed, many of King's beliefs were in direct contrast to the Muslims'. He was a Christian minister who implored his followers to love their racist oppressors and to turn the other cheek when physically attacked by whites. Moreover, his ultimate aim was to secure black liberation by integrating with white people. Initially, Elijah Muhammad directed ministers to refrain from publicly denouncing King by name.[20] His decision to withhold public attacks against the civil rights movement's leaders may have been a cautious attempt to avoid isolation by the majority of black people who admired King and the struggles that he and others led. By the early 1960s, however, the Muslim leader would allow ministers to rebuke the leading civil rights activist.[21] By 1959 it had become apparent to Muhammad that Muslim criticism of the civil rights movement did not isolate the Nation from enjoying widespread support in black communities. In fact, the Nation continued to grow at unprecedented levels the more the media brought attention to its nationalist positions and its disdain for whites.[22] A growing segment of the black community gravitated to the Nation— attracted to its apparent radicalism and defiance. Muslim ministers articulated the anger evoked among African Americans after seeing black churches destroyed and children murdered across the country.[23] Increasingly, nonviolence lost adherents, and the most prominent purveyor of nonviolence fell under increased criticism.

In 1963 Malcolm X denounced King as a "chump" for the decision to use children in the Birmingham campaign, which resulted in mass arrests and brutality inflicted on the young demonstrators. Malcolm derided the March on Washington as a "Farce on Washington" and King for being a "clown" who allowed whites to water down the more militant posture of some of the march's speeches. King's belief in nonviolence confirmed for Muslims that he was a "traitor" to black people.[24] Elijah Muhammad also vilified King, calling him a "fool" and compared him to a dog that "just waddles all around the door" obsequiously waiting for its master to bid a favor.[25] Initially, King tried to ignore and dismiss these attacks. The civil rights establishment tried unsuccessfully to portray the Nation as an insignificant group of hateful black supremacists who had no real presence in any black community. Of course, this portrayal belies the reality.

The Nation by the end of 1959 had fifty mosques in more than twenty states and the District of Columbia. The *Pittsburgh Courier, Amsterdam News,* and *Los Angeles Herald Dispatch* had been publishing weekly articles from Elijah Muhammad and Malcolm X for several years, and in May 1960 the Nation launched its own newspaper, *Muhammad Speaks. Muhammad Speaks* soon grew to become the largest circulating black newspaper in the country, publishing more than 500,000 copies a week, surpassing the *Pittsburgh Courier's* weekly circulation of 300,000.[26] In addition to the successful NOI newspaper, Malcolm X was often in the media spotlight, commanding thousands to New York street corners for public speaking engagements. King could not dismiss the Nation as insignificant. In fact, the Nation became King's bane in the black community, and he grew alarmed at its rapid growth and was determined to resist the spread of its nationalist gospel.

In a 1959 *Pittsburgh Courier* article, King attacked the Muslims for their "hate." He saw the NOI's belief in the demonization of the white race was unhealthy, dangerous, and equal to the racism of many whites. During his address to the National Bar Association in that year, King condemned the Nation for being a "hate group arising in our midst which would preach a doctrine of black supremacy."[27] Contrary to the language of the Muslims, the Nation offered only a "philosophy based on a contempt for life. It is the arrogant assertion that one race is the center of value and object of devotion, before which other races must kneel in submission."[28]

King, like many other NOI detractors, refused to differentiate between the offensive racism of white supremacists, which hated and oppressed all nonwhites, and the defensively xenophobic ideas of the Nation, which supported universal brotherhood for all people of color, including those who were not popularly considered black (Asians, Native Americans, Latinos, etc.). For King, the Nation's racialism led to little more than "spiritual or physical homicide." Despite his attacks on the Nation, King could not overlook the success of the Muslims in promoting self-esteem, pride, and enterprise in downtrodden black city dwellers. During a Detroit lecture in 1963, King praised the efforts of nationalists who were effectively promoting pride in blackness. King valued the affirmation of blackness. In reference to the Muslims, however, he warned that black pride is not a prerequisite for hating whites. This "doctrine of black supremacy," he insisted, overlooks the white people who "are as determined to see the Negro free as we are to be free." Moreover, King claimed that he understood the evolution of "black supremacy" in the Nation. "I can understand from a psychological point of view why some caught up in the clutches of the injustices surrounding them almost respond with bitterness and come to the conclusion that the problem can't be solved within. And they talk about getting away from it in terms of racial separation." Still, King insisted, "black supremacy is as wrong as white supremacy . . . God is not interested merely in the freedom of black men and brown men and yellow men. God is interested in the freedom of the whole human race."[29] Of course, the Nation dismissed any possibilities of white moral salvation, at least in any significant way.[30]

Malcolm X, who at times derisively referred to King as the "Reverend Dr. Chicken Wing," explained that whites love "these old religious Uncle Toms" to teach blacks not to defend themselves when beaten by racists. Their philosophy of nonviolence was used "just like [a dentist uses] Novocain" so the victim will suffer peacefully. Black people should never be duped into resisting their natural urges for self-preservation, Malcolm noted. "How can you justify being nonviolent in Mississippi and Alabama when your churches are being bombed, and your little girls are being murdered, and at the same time you are going to get violent with Hitler, and Tojo, and somebody else you don't know?" For Malcolm, it was simple logic and consistency: "If it's wrong to be violent defending black women and black children and black babies and black men, then it's wrong for America to draft us and make us violent abroad in defense of her. And if it's right for America to draft us, and teach us how to be violent in defense of her, then it is right for you and me to do whatever is necessary to defend our own people right here in this country."[31]

Indeed, the white press excoriated Malcolm X as "violent" and "a preacher of hate" because of his exhortations of self-defense and vilification of whites. In 1959, *U.S. News and World Report,* generally hostile to the civil rights movement, led the way in attacking the Nation as "violence-prone black supremacists."[32] Even King admitted that those same whites believed in self-defense for white people. The racist double standard was not lost with either leader. King, however, carefully and consistently denounced what he called "defensive violence" and "retaliatory violence." When asked if self-defense and nonviolence were incompatible, King retorted that "I don't think we need programmatic action around defensive violence . . . The minute you have programmatic action around defensive violence and pronouncements about it the line of demarcation between defensive violence and aggressive violence becomes very thin."[33] Here, King avoids using the more innocuous term *self-defense.* Even he must have known that it was difficult to explicitly denounce a people's right to self-defense, especially when law enforcement agencies refused to protect the victimized. Terms like *retaliatory violence* implied a more ominous confrontation, suggesting avoidable destruction and subtly equating the moral nature of all forms of violence. Violence, King explained, "deepens the brutality of the oppressor and increases the bitterness of the oppressed. Violence is the antithesis of creativity and wholeness. It destroys community and makes brotherhood impossible."[34] There was nothing redeeming about violence, King argued, even when used by the victims of violence.

King embraced an unwavering faith in the power of love and nonviolence. His humanism meant that he had to reject the Nation. Opposition to such views was necessary if King hoped to maintain a following and thwart challenges from organizations and philosophies he found repellent. He firmly rejected the nationalist notions that the survival of the races was predicated on separation. For King, humanity was bound together in a common destiny of salvation or destruction. It was the stubborn traditions of racism that threatened the unity of humanity. The Nation was part and parcel of this racism. It had to be rebuked in the most explicit terms.

An Eye for an Eye

King was not, of course, the only vocal critic of the Nation during the period of Malcolm X's popularity. The oldest civil rights organization, the NAACP, was adamantly opposed to the Nation for several reasons. Chief among these were the Muslims' racialist notions. Roy Wilkins, executive secretary of the NAACP, stated that his organization "opposes and regards as dangerous any group, white or black, political or religious, that preaches hatred among men." In a more virulent denunciation, the chief consul for the NAACP, Thurgood Marshall, told Princeton University students that the NOI was "run by a bunch of thugs organized from prisons and jails and financed, I am sure by . . . some Arab group."[35] The level of disdain for the NOI was palpable. The NOI, of course, conflicted with the fundamental aims of the NAACP: realized constitutional rights for black citizens and integration of black people into the full fabric of the United States. Furthermore, the association was founded on a fundamental belief in universal humanity. The NOI rejected the liberal pluralism of the civil rights movement and even the U.S. government, which to the Muslims was part of the devil's making. American citizenship was no honor to the Muslims. For the NAACP, citizenship and its universal acceptance was essential to black uplift. While the NAACP flatly dismissed the Nation's racial theories and nationalist analysis, it could not so easily reject its positions on self-defense.

The call for armed self-defense caused discomfort for NAACP leadership, although the NAACP was not as disturbed as King had been. Wilkins asserted that self-defense was not immoral or wrong. Unlike King, he fundamentally agreed with the Nation on the principle of self-defense. The NAACP was not, however, particularly vocal about its opinions, although at its fiftieth annual convention in 1959, it resolved that "we do not deny, but reaffirm, the right of an individual and collective self-defense against unlawful assaults."[36] Still, the NAACP avoided the types of grassroots organization and aggressive activism that had historically provoked racist mob terror, such as the Freedom Rides and sit-ins. Wilkins and other NAACP national officials did not usually put themselves in situations where they would be forced to physically defend themselves or turn the other cheek. The rural local chapters of the NAACP, however, had different experiences as the civil rights movement gained momentum.

Throughout the South, NAACP activists were confronted with vicious retaliation for activities. In 1955—the year that Emmett Till was lynched—NAACP leaders Reverend George W. Lee and Lamar Smith were murdered in Mississippi on May 13 and August 13 for their efforts to register blacks to vote. Southern states had passed laws to repress the activities of civil rights organizations like the NAACP, and local law enforcement agencies often worked in conjunction with local terrorists to facilitate raiding parties on black people. After Mississippi field secretary Medgar Evers was assassinated on June 11, 1963, the state NAACP chapters were pushed to greater militancy by more firmly and boldly affirming their rights to self-defense.[37]

Evers's brother, Charles, who relocated from Chicago with a bold zeal and passion to carry his brother's struggle forward, filled the position of field secretary. Evers fully embraced the philosophy of self-defense promoted by the Nation and other militants, many of whom were Christian and southern-based. Indeed, Evers promoted self-defense among NAACP members who eagerly formed armed units of security forces trained with handguns, shotguns, and rifles. His residence was under constant armed protection from community volunteers after his arrival in Jackson in 1963 and continued until he became mayor of Fayette, Mississippi, in 1969.[38] Evers helped form a Jackson-based paramilitary group with ties to the Louisiana-based Deacons for Defense. Despite the rhetoric of King and others who were hostile to the formal organization of armed units for self-defense, Evers's organization provided security for King, Wilkins, and other leaders during their visits to Jackson.[39] Contrary to the belief of many who predicted escalating interracial violence with the birth of black armed defense groups, attacks from racists declined. A former activist who worked with Evers noted, "He encouraged it [an overt armed presence]. The fact that I think folks knew that there was a possibility if they [white supremacist terrorists] did something to Charles; someone was gonna get hurt. That was beneficial to the whole effort down there [southwest Mississippi]."[40] In the most violent state for civil rights activists, Evers's armed guard had only one shootout, with racists who attempted to assassinate Evers in 1968 when he ran for U.S. Senate. No one was injured.[41]

Whether or not Charles Evers was directly influenced by the rhetoric of the Nation is unclear. For several years he had lived in Chicago, where the Nation had a very visible presence, the city serving as its headquarters. Evers's views on self-defense were identical to the Nation's. Whether the NOI actually influenced his decision to practice self-defense is uncertain. Clearly, many who were southern, rural, and Christian fully embraced the belief that black people should arm themselves to defend their communities from terrorist attacks. Even King and other early activists were advocates of firearms for self-defense in the early stages of the modern civil rights movement. The activities of the Mississippi NAACP under Evers's leadership were not entirely unique to southern civil rights struggles. There were, in fact, members of King's organization, the SCLC, who fully embraced the philosophy of armed defense.

In Alabama, local SCLC members, including Rev. John Nettles, state director, and Rev. Fred Shuttlesworth, a leading activist in Birmingham, were aware of and supported armed SCLC agents. On more than one occasion, armed SCLC men escorted King through the state and provided protection for local leaders and other activists. In 1962 an informal organization, known as "Eleven Brave Men," with ties to SCLC met at Anniston, Alabama's only black-owned gas station, Morris and Ray. Ku Klux Klansmen who opened fire on the meeting were shocked to be met with returned gunfire. The exchange of gunfire resulted in a shot gas pump but no injuries on either side. Though the racist attackers fled once the black men returned fire, all black defenders were arrested by law enforcement within minutes. The incident disturbed some SCLC members but encouraged others, who believed that the defense of Morris and Ray expressed the courage of black people to resist terrorism and defend their lives and property the same ways whites would. Though southern blacks were familiar with the message of Malcolm X and the Nation, the local efforts were indigenous. Local people did not need anyone to instruct them the principles of self-defense. Nor did they find being armed incongruent with being members of SCLC. Of the several armed escorts through Alabama, King instructed his closest advisers to direct local SCLC agents to remove weapons on only one occasion.[42] Alabama was not the only direct confrontation that King and others had with indigenous eruptions of armed defense within the civil rights struggle.

During the Albany, Georgia, campaign of 1962, civil rights activists were brutally and savagely attacked by local and state law enforcement. The police chief, Larry Pritchett, was typical in his abusive reign of power as a frontline enforcer of white supremacy. Though not as notorious as J. C. Saxon of Panola County, Mississippi or Bull Conner of Birmingham, Pritchett's officers often attacked and brutalized men, women, and children at will.[43] Their brutality knew no bounds; even a visibly pregnant woman with a child in her arms was not immune from attack. In August 1962, Marion King, wife of leading activist Slater King, went to the county jail to visit the daughter of her maid who was jailed for participating in demonstrations. When police ordered her to move from an outside visitor's area, she was struck in the face for not moving quickly enough. Her three-year-old child, Abena, fell from her arms onto the concrete. The sheriff hit her again in the face and a deputy kicked her in the shins, knocking the six-months-pregnant woman to the pavement. The officers proceeded to kick her several more times, as black on-lookers, including her one-year-old child, Du Bois, could only shriek in horror. King later had a miscarriage. No officer was charged with a crime.[44]

For the leaders of the Albany movement, descriptions of brutality against activists were often told and retold because they helped forge the unity and passion required for prolonged struggle. The Marion King incident, however, was so savage that leaders chose not to discuss it at rallies. For many, the story was such a naked abuse of a high-profile woman of Albany that the leaders feared violent reactions from the people. Many of the nonviolent leaders expressed concern over their ability to control the passion and frustrations of the people that they led.[45] Indeed, many in Albany never supported the nonviolent philosophies of King and others. As news of the Marion King beating spread, more people saw nonviolence as futile and self-defense necessary.

In the wake of the Marion King beating, cases of self-defense grew more common at Albany churches, which were attacked by groups of whites welding guns and bricks. Some black street toughs who did not embrace the movement's nonviolent theories created informal "protection groups" at churches. These mostly poor youths packed knives, collected bricks, and congregated outside churches waiting for racist attacks. On more than one occasion they stoned the cars of racist thugs. Word of the determination of blacks to protect themselves eventually got around, and as a result, the number of attacks sharply declined.[46] Despite their rhetoric of nonviolence, many SNCC activists in Albany admired and appreciated the unsolicited service, which helped influence their own notions of self-defense. Indeed, the militant language of Malcolm X also increasingly influenced these young SNCC activists, although he was not their only source of inspiration. They also found inspiration in the activities of fellow civil rights activists, such as covert groups within the NAACP, SCLC, and SNCC. Across the South, activists found lessons in the indigenous examples of armed struggle.[47]

In July 1965 a group of four hundred civil rights marchers were met with racist taunts and spittle as they knelt in prayer in Bogalusa, Louisiana. When the peaceful group attempted to continue its procession, rocks were thrown at them. A seventeen-year-old girl was struck in the head and stumbled in search of help as blood poured from her wound. She had been taken inside a car for attention when a white man charged the car and physically assaulted two black men in the front seat. Henry Austin, twenty-one years old, grabbed his .38 caliber handgun and shot his attacker twice in the neck and once in the chest. The wounded attacker lay on the ground outside the car, squirming and gasping for breath. Austin, as well as the other black man in the car, was a member of the Deacons for Defense and Justice. Though the white press lamented that his actions "made Bogalusa's civil-rights struggle look more grave than ever," many blacks were proud of Austin.[48] The Deacons for Defense inspired many young activists on the eve of Black Power and made veterans of armed defense like Robert F. Williams proud.

Several years before the Deacons had formed, Robert F. Williams, president of the Union County, North Carolina, chapter of the NAACP in Monroe, urged members to form gun clubs in order to defend the black community against the assaults led by terrorists like the Ku Klux Klan. Williams's language, passion, and ideals were indigenous and Christian. He once sent Christmas cards with militant Christian rhetoric: "I commend myself unto the ruins of Jesus Christ that the hand of no man might be able to seize me, or beat me, or imprison me, or overcome me."[49] Williams took pride in his faith and his militant affirmation of his humanity. Unlike many in the civil rights struggle, he admired the efforts of the Nation. In fact, he frequently spoke at Mosque Number Seven in Harlem, which was led by Malcolm X. Malcolm X and Williams had a mutual appreciation for each other's militancy and tenacity, although the latter may have had reservations about the Nation's avoidance of activism.

Malcolm was drawn to Williams because of his ability and willingness to put into practice what the Muslims had long preached. Malcolm called Williams the "first brother to take up arms and fight." The North Carolina freedom fighters allied with Williams were "facing death for all of us," Malcolm stated at the Nation's largest mosque. There is no evidence that Malcolm ever tried to influence his southern Christian counterpart, but the Muslim minister was clearly eager to promote Williams's armed guard of Monroe, North Carolina. Malcolm even helped raise funds for Williams to purchase arms.[50] Furthermore, Williams's suspension from the NAACP for violent rhetoric was, to many militants, indicative of that organization's conservative policies, which aimed more to make white liberals feel comfortable than to resist racist terror. All whites, the Nation insisted, opposed the black right to self-defense. It was, however, the white liberals like those who helped lead the NAACP who were particularly hostile to blacks acting independently. The NAACP opposed armed defense because it was empowering to black people. The NAACP, Malcolm concluded, was a "white man's conception of a black man's organization."[51] It was not a true organization by, for, and about black people. Williams, who attempted to defend himself in front of the executive body of the NAACP, was surprised to see the extent of white influence, including the president, Arthur B. Spingarn. Wilkins, Williams inferred, was only a figurehead, since the executive director was often seen peering over at the stoic and silent Spingarn to make sure his comments were "to the approval" of the president.[52] Any "real" black-led organization, Muslims noted, would have heralded Williams's courage to resist terrorists, instead of pushing the "suicidal" philosophy of nonviolence.

Many blacks who followed the Williams case thought that the NAACP lacked the integrity and the courage that was expected of an organization truly committed to black people's uplift. For some, the suspension of Williams weakened organization's image in black communities where people were forced to survive by similar self-defense tactics. Wilkins, however, was careful to explain that he was not in ideological agreement with King over the use of self-defense. "Like Williams," Wilkins explained, "I believe in self-defense. While I admire Reverend King's theories of overwhelming enemies with love, I don't think that I could have put those theories into practice myself."[53] Still, conflicts like that between Williams and the NAACP bolstered the position of the Nation of Islam among many blacks who admired the strength and will of militants like Williams and grew increasingly critical of the white influence in the NAACP.

Many blacks saw the NOI as outside of the control of white liberals who either funded civil rights organizations or, as in the case of the NAACP, enjoyed direct organizational influence. Malcolm X was careful to denounce the white liberal leaders of the country's oldest civil rights organization. All of the presidents of the NAACP had been white; most were Jewish. Malcolm quipped that it will be a cold day in hell before black people lead the Anti-Defamation League. Jews, he explained, would never tolerate black people at the helm of their organizations directing the Jewish struggle; why should blacks be dependent on Jews for leadership? Crowds, by the thousands, laughed and cheered at Malcolm's witty attacks on civil rights leaders. By 1960, Malcolm X was actively seeking debates with integrationists.

The Tongue Is Mightier than the Sword

Between 1960 and 1963 the Nation of Islam's national spokesman was active speaking and debating civil and human rights issues across the country. Malcolm is believed to have been the most interviewed black person on radio, television, and in newspapers during this period.[54] His opponents in debate ranged from white intellectuals like Monroe Berger of Princeton University to representatives of prominent organizations such as Constance Baker Motley of the NAACP Legal Defense Fund; James Farmer, president of CORE; and Bayard Rustin, head of the A. Philip Randolph Institute and organizer of the March on Washington. While Malcolm welcomed debates, many black intellectuals and those in the civil rights establishment felt trepidation when meeting him in such arenas.

When Malcolm X debated Kenneth B. Clark, a psychology professor who testified on behalf of school integration during the *Brown v. Board of Education* case in 1954, the Muslim minister was called a "giant killer." According to journalist James Hicks of the *Amsterdam News*, "Malcolm X figuratively murdered Ken . . . and Ken virtually confessed at the end of the program." The NOI spokesman also "slew" John Davis, another college professor; Rev. Milton Galamison; and Gloster Glover of the Urban League at the same debate. They, according to observers, "fared even worse" than Clark.[55]

Malcolm's formidable debating skills proved such a challenge to Roy Wilkins that the executive secretary of the NAACP forbade any staff member from taking up the NOI minister in public debate.[56] Wilkins called Malcolm "a mesmerizing speaker [and] the toughest man in debate that I've ever seen. None of us could touch him, not even Dr. King."[57] Indeed, King refused to accept any debate with Malcolm, despite ample opportunities. In 1962 King threatened to cancel his appearance on the *David Susskind Show* when he was informed that Malcolm would also appear. King's secretary informed one radio station that proposed a King–Malcolm X discussion that King had "taken a consistent position of not accepting such invitations because he feels it will do no good. He has always considered his work in a positive action framework rather than engaging in consistent negative debate."[58] To be sure, King was not alone in his avoidance of Malcolm X.

During a spring 1963 meeting of the "Big Six"—King, Whitney Young, Wilkins, A. Philip Randolph, James Farmer, and John Lewis (leaders of the SCLC, Urban League, NAACP, A. Philip Randolph Institute, CORE, and SNCC)—the leaders attempted to dissuade Farmer from accepting an offer to debate Malcolm X. King warned that he tried his best to keep his distance from the Muslim dynamo. "I was asked to be on that panel with Malcolm X, but I declined and told them that Wyatt Walker, the executive secretary of SCLC, would be there instead of me," King noted. Young affirmed King's position, insisting that the civil rights leaders should make a solemn pact not to debate Malcolm. "I think that all of us should agree . . . that none of the top leaders will appear on a platform, radio or TV with Malcolm X because we just give him an audience." Farmer was unmoved. He stood his ground and resisted the attempts of the others to isolate the NOI by refusing to debate its national spokesman. Besides, Farmer observed, "Malcolm does very well getting platforms and audiences by himself; he doesn't need our help on that." Farmer later wrote that "All looked at me without a word, as though condolences soon would be in order."[59]

During the debate Farmer held his ground, effectively routing Malcolm by carefully describing the brutal and savage nature of racial oppression. Farmer insisted that Malcolm refrain from recounting the evils of racism. "Brother Malcolm, don't tell us any more about the disease—that is clear . . . Now tell us, physician, what is thy cure?" The minister was taken by surprise. "Never before had I seen Malcolm slow to rise and take the microphone."[60] He then went for Malcolm X's weak spot: an effective solution. Civil rights leaders long joked that the NOI lacked any program. By preventing Malcolm from recounting the barbarism of white racists, Farmer no longer put himself in the precarious position of defending the humanity of white people, as many other civil rights leaders had done. Farmer and Malcolm debated each other on a number of subsequent occasions and became good friends, despite their ideological differences. They finally agreed not to have any further debates, since they knew each other's speeches by heart and were not moving to the other's position. Malcolm, Farmer later wrote, "was one of the most feared debaters on the American platform" and despite his vituperative language, was a "civilized gentleman" with whom he shared not only a mutual respect but also friendship.[61] Others who attempted to challenge Malcolm in public debate met with less success, sometimes leaving integrationists who viewed such debates to question their own positions.

In 1962 Howard University invited Malcolm X and Bayard Rustin to debate. Rustin, who had a following at the university, felt comfortable with the mostly sympathetic audience. The civil rights leader detailed the urgency of black integration into the totality of American life. Black people could never effectively realize uplift until the barriers that excluded them from politics, housing, education, and other arenas were removed. The crowd cheered at Rustin's lucid analysis. Then Malcolm spoke. As one observer noted, he "turned the audience around. In an electrifying performance, he articulated many of the things that weren't being said by the black middle class; and he did so in such biting and uncompromising style that he had the audience literally shouting. It was Malcolm's occasion."[62]

Similar stories abound. In 1962 Robert Gore, CORE's assistant community relations director, observed a debate between Rustin and Malcolm X and noted that he left the event with "mixed feelings," which were "the result of the discovery that I was applauding more for Malcolm X than I was for Bayard Rustin . . . There is no question in my mind that Bayard presented the saner attitude, but the amazing thing was how eloquently Malcolm X states the problems which Negroes have confronted for so many years . . . I must confess that it did my heart a world of good to sit back and listen to Mr. X list the sins of the white man toward the black man in America."[63]

For many CORE activists like Gore, Malcolm became a peculiar inspiration. Many—white and black—gravitated to his unabashed rebuke of white racists and his bold yet sophisticated style of oratory. As noted above, CORE's president, James Farmer, deeply admired the Nation's national spokesman. Farmer considered him a "well read and brilliant man with a sharp and exceptionally quick mind." In addition, he noted, Malcolm X was a "perfect gentleman."[64]

In Atlanta, several SNCC activists frequented the local NOI mosque. A few even joined the NOI. Julian Bond, SNCC organizer, admitted to a sense of catharsis to hear Muslim ministers rail against white people for their brutality and savagery. Though they did not hear Malcolm speak, Jeremiah X, the local minister, had a style that was similar to the national spokesman and continued to attract listeners. Malcolm X's appeal among black people was well understood. Some black leaders cautiously noted that if the Nation were a Christian organization, "they might sweep the country."[65] Indeed, civil rights leaders up until 1964 grew weary of the spreading prominence of Malcolm X and the Nation, but they also recognized that the increased popularity of the Nation meant more concessions from the white power structure.

The Muslims were able to generate a new image of black people among many whites. By no means could they in confidence be viewed as buffoonish and cowardly Negroes who would give fearful, bug-eyed looks to whites who threatened them. In fact, neither could they be considered the well-behaved, middle-class blacks who wanted to integrate with whites and who were willing to turn the other cheek if struck while attempting to do so. There were many black people who had no desire to be near whites and who were instructed to be sober and peaceful but, if a white man should attack, to "send him to the cemetery."[66] Black moderate leaders effectively exploited the new militant threat of the NOI. Whitney Young, executive director of the National Urban League, spoke to corporate giants about the need for effective funding for urban job-training programs. Should corporate America ignore the urban black poor, the elite "risk hostility and growing strength from the Muslims." Young's platform worked. "We were able to increase our budget from $270,000 in 1961 to $722,000 [in 1962]."[67] Others used similar strategies.

After Medgar Evers's assassination in 1963, Wilkins warned that law enforcement agencies must protect black people or risk new violence because the "Negro citizen has come to the point where he is not afraid of violence. He no longer shirks back. He will assert himself and if violence comes, so be it." Similar strategies were used during the Birmingham crisis in 1963 when movement organizers made appeals to President Kennedy, virtually quoting Malcolm X. They explained that if the federal government failed to protect black citizens, the militants among black people "would take steps to defend themselves." President Kennedy agreed with this analysis. He implored southern segregationists to realize that if the efforts of moderates are continuously thwarted, "the Negro advocates of nonviolence will give way to extremists who teach violence."[68] The increasing fear of the "violent" Muslims was very palpable in the early 1960s, despite the fact that the Muslims had harmed no whites in any confrontations since their rise to national popularity.

As the influence of the NOI spread, civil rights leaders who had once been criticized and maligned by the white media received more favorable coverage. Integrationists like King, who had once been considered "reckless" radicals by the white press, were promoted as responsible and viable leaders for black people.[69] The three major weeklies, *Newsweek*, *Time*, and *U.S. News and World Report* had been ambivalent toward the civil rights movement from 1955 to 1962. In fact a 1962 poll of 500 Washington news reporters (virtually all white) found that 42 percent believed that "Negro leadership focuses too much [on civil rights.]"[70] *U.S. News* provided the most conservative and inimical coverage of the movement, while *Time* was the moderate and *Newsweek* was slightly more liberal. By 1963 *Time* and *Newsweek* developed much more positive reporting on the efforts of civil rights activists in the South. King, in these two magazines, was often lauded for his humanistic approach to struggle and his unwavering desire for racial reconciliation during the Birmingham campaign. *Time* reported that the city might have fallen to black groups "more aligned to violence," but King "got there first." Malcolm X and the Muslims "could only sneer" at the success of the "gospel of nonviolence."[71] While the white press viewed King more benignly, the NOI national spokesman was routinely demonized and misquoted.[72] For white America, the "Black Muslims," were a veritable black version of the Ku Klux Klan.

The change in coverage of King and the civil rights struggle was coterminous with the meteoric rise of Malcolm X in the public arena of civil rights debate. Malcolm X (along with Senator Barry Goldwater) was the most sought-after speaker on the college circuit in 1963, and the Nation was still growing by leaps and bounds. To be sure, the risk of the Muslims' nationalism and antiwhite positions predominating or significantly influencing popular black thought was a concern among whites. There is no doubt that the brave and tireless efforts of thousands of activists across the South cultivated sympathy for justice and civil rights. However, the fear of "violent," antiwhite black nationalists also caused the white power structure to concede particular demands to moderates. Additionally, efforts were made to promote the moderate leaders as more viable while simultaneously castigating "bad Negroes" for preaching "hate" and "violence."

For many in the civil rights movement, the NOI was a peculiar phenomenon. Activists did not like it because of its inherent antipathy to their struggles for civil rights, yet it helped realize concessions for black people. Moreover, the Nation commanded a level of respect among blacks that was virtually impossible to ignore. It was efficiently run; it attracted the most downtrodden elements of the black community, effectively reformed them, and provided self-esteem and economic opportunities for blacks who seemed in most of need. However begrudgingly, civil rights leaders acknowledged contributions the NOI made to black people across the country. In addition, some leading Muslims respected the struggle for civil rights.

Elijah Muhammad admitted a quiet admiration for President Kennedy for his (largely rhetorical) contributions to the civil rights movement.[73] Despite Malcolm's rhetoric, he secretly respected the efforts and tenacity of black people who challenged white supremacy with staunch conviction, fervor, and morality. Moreover, he knew very well that his "bogeyman" image helped realize civil rights legislation. He once noted that civil rights organizations should give the Nation part of their proceeds for scaring whites into doing what is right. Malcolm's threat of armed self-defense provided a counterpoint to the passive nonviolence of the SCLC, CORE, and SNCC. In other words, if white supremacists did not meet and compromise with advocates of nonviolence, they ran the very probable chance of meeting blacks who rejected nonviolence. "Never stick someone out there without an alternative," Malcolm mused.[74]

While there may have been some unspoken appreciation for the Nation, most civil rights leaders were actively hostile, as noted earlier. However, as the movement evolved, some organizations modified their views on the NOI. Many members of CORE admired Malcolm. Members of the NAACP, such as Williams and possibly Evers, also approved of aspects of the NOI. But the Nation affected no organization in the Big Six as much as it did SNCC.

SNCC members were long known as the most militant figures in the movement. The young and zealous activists confronted white supremacy head on with a tough and forceful dedication and commitment to social change. The organization was founded on the tactic of nonviolence; however, SNCC was never in a state of ideological stasis. When the anti-self-defense strategies were considered inefficacious, SNCC abandoned them for more militant postures, culminating in an organization that was radically different from the one founded in 1960. The process was, of course, not immediate.

SNCC's statement of purpose written in 1960 declared

We affirm the philosophical or religious ideal of nonviolence as the foundation of our purpose, the presupposition of our faith, and the manner of our action. Nonviolence as it grows from Judaic-Christian traditions seeks a social order of justice permeated by love. Integration of human endeavor represents the crucial first step towards such a society.

Through nonviolence, courage displaces fear; love transforms hate. Acceptance dissipates prejudice; hope ends despair. Peace dominates war; faith reconciles doubt. Mutual regard cancels enmity. Justice for all overthrows injustice. The redemptive community supersedes systems of gross social immorality.[75]

By the mid-1960s, SNCC was being pushed toward greater militancy and cynicism regarding the ability of moral suasion to appeal to the white power structure. The urban uprisings of the North revealed, in no uncertain terms, that racial oppression was a national problem of daunting magnitude. The incessant violent reprisals in the South and the duplicity of federal officials made SNCC workers less faithful to the Gandhian principles of nonviolence and more critical of all branches of the government. In 1963 SNCC chairman John Lewis was forced to modify his speech at the March on Washington or face the withdrawal of the Catholic archbishop of Washington. Other leaders followed with objections and forced Lewis to soften the tone of his speech.[76] Surely SNCC's militancy was well known by 1963. President Kennedy had expressed pleasure that SNCC did not lead the Birmingham campaign. "SNCC," Kennedy remarked, "has got an investment in violence . . . they're sons of bitches."[77]

Growing disaffected with the moderation of its civil rights peers, SNCC activists even invited NOI ministers to speak at an Albany mass meeting in 1963, despite Big Six attempts to isolate the Nation. Being close and "up under" white people was only the goal of sick and ignorant Negroes, Muslims argued. Black people needed to free themselves from their dependence on whites. Freedom should not be determined by the proximity and intimacy that the oppressed has with the oppressor. In reaction to this analysis, SNCC chairman Charles McDew explained that his organization's ideological cornerstone was not integration into white America. "We are working for *desegregation,* not integration."[78] Of course, this was a modification of SNCC's 1960 statement of purpose, which explained that "integration of human endeavor represents the crucial first step towards such a society [of justice permeated by love]." The evolution of SNCC continued as members moved further away from the language of love, reconciliation with racists, and nonviolence.

Not Flower Children

Love, nonviolence, and reconciliation with racists were intimately held ideals of SNCC's founders in 1960. The rapacious nature of racists, however, and three years of federal, state, and local government antipathy to the efforts of nonviolent activists caused many in SNCC to fundamentally alter some of their beliefs regarding black liberation. The Albany campaign was a brutal experience for those involved. Klansmen, police officers and others terrorized the black community, and despite the language of SNCC and the SCLC, for many of the local people who joined the efforts of the activists, nonviolence had its limitations.

John Washington Cooley was a local resident of Albany who joined SNCC in 1962 and quickly became a local hero for his tireless efforts toward community organizing. After the beatings of C. B. King and scores of others, many, including Cooley decided that armed self-defense was safer than "nonviolence." In the midst of the campaign, fellow SNCC workers who officially disavowed weapons caught Cooley with a handgun in his possession. The incident caused considerable debate in SNCC, eventually resulting in the revelation that several other members secretly carried arms or supported armed defense.[79] Many others, primarily poorer locals, admired SNCC but could not tolerate beatings from whites. These militant locals, however, had a growing number of sympathizers in SNCC.

When the Ku Klux Klan marched through the black section of Albany in late 1962 in an effort to intimidate blacks, the white supremacists were met with militant young blacks with sledgehammers, baseball bats, bricks, and bottles. "We were side by side with the locals, throwing bricks and bottles at the Klan," explains Willie Mukasa Ricks, SNCC organizer. The Klan was shocked and unprepared; some were beaten badly. One racist attacker was pleading for his life as he was pounded with rocks and bats. For SNCC workers like Ricks, this was a victory. For King and others, it was a portentous defeat. King reminded the activists of their ideals, but, explains Ricks, "Theoretically, people believed in the words of the 1960 SNCC statement of purpose, but not practically. Nonviolence was tolerable only to a degree. Love was good, but we were not flower children."[80]

By 1965 SNCC was significantly more militant and more removed from the nonviolent positions of its foundation. The influence of Malcolm X was more palpable; some even began quoting him. Cleveland Sellers, who joined SNCC via its affiliate at Howard University, the Nonviolent Action Group, was inspired by Malcolm's rhetoric of armed self-defense. In Maryland, he and others "stopped extolling the virtues of passive resistance. Guns were carried as a matter of course and it was understood that they would be used in a case of attack. If attacked, we intended to defend ourselves—'by any means necessary.' "[81] Malcolm X's famous quote was popular among the SNCC militants and those in CORE who experienced a similar transformation toward Black Power.

Even while some in the movement became more radical, they did not necessarily grow fonder of the Nation of Islam. Michael Flug, a former member of CORE, explains that "we had great appreciation for Malcolm X's historical analysis while he was a member of the Nation." There was, however, a general skepticism about the Nation, he notes. "We did not dislike the Nation because it was nationalist. We disliked it because it did not do anything. CORE and others were activists."[82] Flug was not alone. Willie Ricks recalls that despite the fiery language of the Muslims, civil rights organizers in the South "were in actuality badder than the Nation, although the Nation had the badder rhetoric." He explained that Muslims "had the rhetoric but they were not facing that cracker."[83] Even Malcolm was critical of the Nation's inactivity, remarking that he knew that many blacks thought the Muslims were a lot of talk and little action. After all, Muslims were not on the frontlines in the struggle. He later explained that the NOI's philosophy was a political "straightjacket" that limited black activism.[84] In addition, it was not until his break from the NOI that Malcolm openly challenged blacks to form armed units for self-defense. It was also in his post-NOI period that he personally armed himself, even taking an iconic picture boldly brandishing an assault rifle while peering through a curtain. This new, more militant, stance was a result of his own ideological evolution that was not possible within the NOI. Malcolm's political evolution, of course, had its beginning with the Nation and Elijah Muhammad, who rescued him from the depths of despair and pathos while he was in prison, but Malcolm's own sagacity pushed him forward, transcending the narrow nationalism of the Nation and developing a broader appeal among militants.

The Birth of Black Power

When Malcolm broke from the Nation in March 1964, he explained that he was "freed" from the conservatism of Elijah Muhammad. Flug and other CORE activists met Malcolm X who spoke at a rally for a rent strike in New York City that spring. Malcolm from that point on, explains Flug, grew in popularity among CORE activists. "We were tremendously drawn to Malcolm. Everyone who was serious was attracted to Malcolm X and Farmer knew this." The admiration of Malcolm was so strong that Farmer discouraged CORE staff from attending meetings of Malcolm's Organization of Afro-American Unity, despite his private and public praise for Malcolm.[85] By 1966, CORE and SNCC were thrust into the Black Power movement as its most visible exponents. Flug is correct to note, however, that the Black Power movement actually had antecedents in the NOI and the urban unrest of Watts and other cities.

It is evident that the Nation of Islam was instrumental in fomenting a climate of militancy, despite its ostensibly conservative character. The Nation was a militantly conservative organization that epitomized classical black nationalism. It embraced many of the traditions of Western culture while failing to offer any direct challenges to the white supremacist power structure in the form of civil rights activism. Malcolm X knew this and moved away from the organization partly because of its antipathy for activism.[86] In many regards, Malcolm X, although a loyal student of Elijah Muhammad for his entire career in the Nation, introduced a new and more militant posture of nationalism that was not wholly characteristic of the organization before and after his membership. Malcolm X's oratory appealed to the masses of urban malcontents, who would later pick up the mantle of black nationalism and militancy. The new black militants of SNCC, CORE, and others in disparate urban organizations sought a niche in the rising black militancy of the middle and latter part of the decade.

In 1966 James Meredith, who was the first African American allowed to attend the University of Mississippi under a court injunction, chose to conduct a one-man march against fear through the state of Mississippi to encourage black citizens to assert their right to vote. Two days into his march he was shot by a sniper. He survived but was unable to continue the march. Civil rights activists mobilized to continue the march. It was during the march that disagreement over civil rights strategy was first publicly aired. Roy Wilkins and Whitney Young, leaders of the NAACP and Urban League, respectively, arrived from New York to support the march and hoped to use the event to raise support for passage of President Johnson's civil rights bill. Stokely Carmichael, chairman of SNCC, disagreed with this focus. Carmichael declared that the march was to demonstrate that the people would no longer cower to racist terrorism; legislation was secondary. It was, after all, a march against fear. Young and Wilkins were unhappy with the militant stance of Carmichael, who was also critical of President Johnson's civil rights policies. Carmichael's rhetoric, the two thought, would make the administration less zealous about civil rights protection. Carmichael did not waver; black people, he insisted, needed to be cleansed of their fear of whites. Moreover, the marchers should make clear that they supported the efforts of self-defense advocates such as the Deacons for Defense and Justice, a Louisiana-based organization that defended civil rights activists.[87] Young and Wilkins left rather than be associated with the march. They were not, however, alone in their discomfort with the growing militancy of Carmichael and other SNCC workers.

During this march, state troopers attacked marchers with tear gas and clubs. In frustration at the incessant racist attacks, SNCC organizer Willie Ricks demanded that black people abandon pleas for white acceptance and adopt a strategy for "Black Power." Stokely Carmichael, head of SNCC, energized the crowd by joining in chants for "Black Power!" CORE leaders chimed in with chants for "Black Power," while SCLC members appeared dismayed. The fissure between the more militant members of SNCC and CORE and the other major organizations was crystallized.

CORE in 1966, under direction from its new national director, Floyd McKissick, fully advocated Black Power. It lauded its efforts to "forcefully" bring forth its activities in urban ghettoes "from Harlem to Watts."[88] McKissick explained Black Power as a "program destined to rescue Black people from destruction by the forces of a racist society which is bent upon denying them freedom, equality and dignity."[89] Reflecting a strong nationalist bent, CORE declared that "White Americans fail to realize that if there is any one goal for all Black People, that goal is self-determination—the right to control one's own destiny."[90] CORE embraced a quasi–black nationalism after 1966 and tried to compete and affirm its legitimacy among the burgeoning nationalists in black communities across the country.

CORE acknowledged that the Nation was widely popular among the poor of the country's urban ghettoes. It was "primarily a religious group" that had "tremendous influence in the ghetto." Moreover, CORE's "Black Manifesto" declared that "the Muslims have propagated a political idea which has wide influence—the concept of separatism."[91] That CORE wanted to tap into the new political direction of the black masses seems clear. It did not want to do this alone, however. CORE was eager to work in coalitions with other militant organizations, including the NOI.

The twenty-third annual CORE conference, held in Baltimore in July 1966, convened only weeks after the Meredith march. Invited guests from other organizations included Stokely Carmichael of SNCC and Fannie Lou Hamer of the Mississippi Freedom Democratic Party, who criticized the "chickeny black preachers" who "sold out" the black masses. She proudly exclaimed that black people were gravitating toward Black Power.[92] Minister Lonnie X of the NOI supported the efforts of the conference with a powerful speech on July 4, the last day of the national gathering. A force of twenty Fruit of Islam guards who provided security accompanied Lonnie X. There were also many other Muslim men and women in full NOI attire.[93] The Muslim minister praised CORE's efforts to instill a greater sense of pride and self-esteem in black people, who had been robbed of their true identity by whites.[94] By virtue of his appearance, the minister set an unprecedented tone of tolerance between a leading civil rights organization and the Nation. Indeed, NOI participation at the national CORE conference indicated the Nation's attempt to signify its new militancy and radicalism. It was a move that revealed to the militant youth, of whom McKissick often spoke, that CORE was a viable organization for the black liberation struggle. It was not a tired, atavistic group run by whites and timid Negroes. It was a staunch advocate for the new black consciousness.

CORE was sensitive to the political climate of the country and considered the increasing frequency of urban unrest, cultural manifestations of racial consciousness, and growing prominence of the Nation to be indicative of the ideological evolution of the black struggle. It observed the new political consciousness of "the young people [who] view the ghettoes as a colony, controlled, dominated and exploited by the white society." This group was a "black bloc" that had learned that "integration was not possible in this society and the only alternative is for Black People to exercise the power over their own destinies."[95]

The Father of Hate

From the call for Black Power in June 1966, nationalist fervor continued to grow throughout the country. Most civil rights organizations denounced the call in the most virulent terms. The cry of "Black Power!" at the Meredith March against Fear was almost immediately denounced by King at the march and by other leaders who issued a statement titled "Crisis and Commitment" in the *New York Times*. In the *Times*, they declared that "we are committed to the attainment of racial justice by the democratic process." They assured the public that not all black organizations spoke such "militant" and "threatening" words as "Black Power." "We repudiate any strategies of violence, reprisal, or vigilantism, and we condemn both rioting and the demagoguery that feeds it . . . We are committed to integration, by which we mean an end to every barrier which segregation and other forms of discrimination have raised against the enjoyment by Negro Americans of their human and constitutional rights."[96]

Wilkins of the NAACP denounced Black Power even more vocifer-
ously than he denounced the Nation and Malcolm X. Black Power was,
according to Wilkins "a reverse Hitler, a reverse Ku Klux Klan" and "the
father of hate and mother of violence." With great alacrity Wilkins publicly vilified Black Power as a precursor to "black death" and inherently
"antiwhite power."[97] Others were nearly as adamantly opposed to Black
Power, including King, who claimed that "it connotates [sic] black
supremacy and an anti-white feeling that does not or should not pre-
vail."[98] Despite his public rebuke of Black Power, King decided not to sign
the "Crisis and Commitment" statement. He did not want to "isolate"
the advocates of Black Power, he claimed. It was, perhaps, his attempt to
maintain a level of cohesion and professional tolerance that many considered necessary in protracted social and political struggle. Black liberals
and moderates were not alone in their excoriation of Black Power. Many
elements in the white power structure, too, expressed their disdain for
the new black militancy.

President Johnson lamented the new "extremism" found among
advocates for Black Power and declared that "we are not interested in
Black Power and we're not interested in white power, but we are interested in American democratic power, with a small d."[99] In a similar vein,
Vice President Hubert Humphrey, considered a respected white liberal
among civil rights leaders, spoke at the fifty-seventh annual convention
of the NAACP. Humphrey criticized what he considered a dangerous turn
toward racism in the civil rights movement. "Racism is racism," he
declared, "and we must reject calls for racism whether they come from a
throat that is white or one that is black."[100] It was clear that the call
for Black Power caused considerable discomfort for whites and black liberals alike. The latter, however, condemned the new militancy with the
greatest fervor.

Almost immediately, the leadership of the NAACP, the Urban League,
and the SCLC declared Black Power a useless and divisive term. That it was
even called a "reverse Hitler" and "father of hate" speaks to the level of
disgust that many leaders had for the term, but Wilkins's hyperbolic
comparison to the greatest mass murderer in history reveals some interesting things about civil rights and black militancy. Black power advocates like Stokely Carmichael and Floyd McKissick were careful to explain
that the term did not mean black supremacy. According to McKissick, "it
does not mean the exclusion of whites from the Negro revolution, does
not advocate violence and will not start riots."[101] In spite of these assur-
ances, the civil rights establishment attacked Black Power in the most

extreme terms possible. The attacks were much more vehement than the attacks on the burgeoning Nation, which did not equivocate on the nature of white people. The Nation did not waver in its assertions that whites should not be allowed in any black liberation struggle. The Nation was very clear in its declaration of the inferiority of whites to all other groups of people. Yet Wilkins and others never thought it necessary to use such vitriolic language to denounce Malcolm X or Elijah Muhammad.

That the chief exponents for Black Power came from the civil rights movement had much to do with the level of condemnation of Black Power. By 1963, it was clear that ideological differences separated moderate organizations from radical ones among the Big Six. The ideological chasm only widened as the movement continued. The obstinate nature of white supremacy in every region of the country gave the Nation of Islam greater voice and popularity, not only among poor black urbanites but even among many in the movement. Furthermore, southern racist terrorists' continued assaults on black people gave birth to indigenous paramilitary organizations, which were either chapters of national civil rights organizations, allied with them, or simply groups of local people. Some of the militant language that had once been almost exclusive to the Nation spread throughout the black struggle.

More moderate organizations that depended on white leadership, as was the case with the NAACP, or derived income from whites, like the Urban League, denounced the rising radicalism because it crept up on the movement from within. Evoking anger and hostility among whites would not be beneficial to the movement, they insisted. In fact, the year of the Black Power controversy saw the total income of all major civil rights organizations decline for the first time since the beginning of the movement. The decline was largely limited to SNCC and CORE, which suffered significant losses. The two most moderate organizations—the NAACP and the Urban League—who most virulently denounced Black Power enjoyed an increase in income. The SCLC, which was critical of Black Power although not as damning as others, also experienced a decline in income. The SCLC's decline, however, is largely attributed to King's denunciation of the U.S. military activities in Vietnam.[102]

By 1966, the civil rights leadership could no longer point the finger at the Muslims for being an ominous alternative to integration. There were prominent elements within the Big Six organizations that now represented this threat, which was what many in the civil rights establishment had feared. Since they could not control the ideological development of SNCC and CORE, Wilkins, Young, and others tried to ensure that their organizations would not suffer a similar decline. They hoped that the movement would not suffer an untimely death from "white backlash."

The NAACP knew that the civil rights movement could no longer use the Nation as a bogeyman to scare the white power structure into making concessions. Whites were incredibly hostile to the call for Black Power, and the civil rights establishment knew this. The moderate leadership had to make every effort to clarify their positions: they wanted integration and wanted it nonviolently. That SNCC and CORE also wanted this was beside the point. The moderates knew that the tenuous support for civil rights in Congress could not be maintained if the masses of whites associated civil rights with antiwhite, violent black supremacy. The Nation and its public derision of white devils and their "dog-like hair, long noses that resemble dog snouts and pink, pig-like skin" surely caused alarm for those whites who feared the spread of this gospel. The movement's survival would be in jeopardy if it ever embraced a philosophy that would drive away white support, argued moderates. The opponents of Black Power often stated that blacks could not "go it alone."[103] In addition, the passage of landmark legislation such as the Civil Rights Act of 1964 and the Voting Rights Act of 1965 was evidence to many whites that the aims of the movement had been met. Many whites had already begun to think that the movement was going too far.

Black people all across the country, however, continued to gravitate to new levels of racial consciousness and militancy as Black Power took shape and gave rise to its own movement. To be sure, this more militant trend in political and cultural consciousness predated the Meredith march. In fact, the call for Black Power by Ricks and Carmichael was a reaction to and acknowledgment of this new and emerging consciousness. Despite the denunciations made by most black leaders, the appeal of Black Power grew in virtually all segments of black America, even giving birth to revolutionary organizations that flowered in the late 1960s and early 1970s. Unlike the NOI, many of these new radicals would offer biting criticism of capitalism and embrace activist politics. Of these new organizations to emerge from Black Power, none captured the attention of America like the Black Panther Party. Eventually, moderate leaders who once denounced Black Power found themselves trying to catch up with the spirit of the masses who were moving further to the left as the decade came to an end. As Wilkins and others advocated integration into the (white) American mainstream, black people increasingly abandoned their European names, chemically straightened hair, and skin-whitener ointments; donned Afros and dashikis; and created black holidays and black-academic-themed houses on white college campuses. The moderates by the end of the decade would be forced to reassess their positions on Black Power. As King, the quintessential follower of Gandhi, was apt to quote the Indian activist, "There go my people, I must catch them, for I am their leader."[104]

CHAPTER 3

A Party for the People
The Black Freedom Movement and the Rise of the Black Panther Party

The Black Panther Party (BPP) emerged from the politically and socially turbulent 1960s as the most popular organization of the Black Power movement. Founded in October 1966, the party formed as an ideologically inchoate black nationalist organization borrowing from an eclectic collection of organizations and ideas.[1] The Panthers' sources of inspiration were broad. They found direction from, among others, northern-based organizations such as the Nation of Islam, the Revolutionary Action Movement (RAM), and the California-based Afro-American Association. Robert F. Williams, the Deacons for Defense, and the Student Nonviolent Coordinating Committee (SNCC) represented southern models of activism. Though popular perceptions of the black freedom movement often place the origins of armed defense activities with black nationalist militants from the North and West, the South actually developed an organic tradition of armed self-defense, while the largest black nationalist organization, the Nation of Islam, officially disavowed guns. It is from this larger landscape of black struggle that early Panthers grew to appreciate the dictum "by any means necessary."

Though Muslim ministers like Malcolm X celebrated black people's right to "send an attacking devil to his grave," Elijah Muhammad forbade Muslims from carrying guns; even knives that could be construed as weapons were banned.[2] In contrast, the Southern Christian Leadership Conference (SCLC), co-founded by Martin Luther King Jr., tolerated some armed defense. Though not a consensus, many SCLC members, including such prominent figures as Rev. Fred Shuttlesworth, were aware of inconspicuously armed SCLC agents who provided protection for civil rights leaders and other activists. On at least one occasion, a shootout erupted between racist attackers and black defenders from the SCLC.[3] Throughout the South, NAACP members had pistols, shotguns and handguns in their homes and on their person, as did many SNCC members.[4]

Although it is difficult to identify an organization that proved most inspirational to the Panthers, SNCC was central to the ontological development of Panther politics. The bold activism of SNCC, in many ways, provided an early model for Panther founders Huey P. Newton and Bobby G. Seale, as did the vigorous defiance to white supremacy and identification with common people. Founded in 1960 by student activists, SNCC was closely affiliated with the SCLC, an adamant defender of the movement's popular notion of "nonviolence." While liberal whites and blacks lauded nonviolence, activists strategically anticipated violence as a viable strategy of resistance and exploited it for the movement's ends.

When civil rights leaders entered Birmingham, Alabama, in 1963 to challenge the rigid customs of the "most segregated city this side of Johannesburg," they expected the repressive arm of the local and state governments. The city's notoriously racist police commissioner, Eugene "Bull" Conner, became a pawn in the larger struggle against white supremacy. Activists anticipated brutal forms of repression from police. They also expected attacks from white citizens who were not officers of the law. Civil rights groups even devised training sessions to teach activists how to position themselves to help minimize the risk of serious injury when physically attacked.[5] For them, this was a necessary sacrifice to win the struggle against oppression. National news reported the efforts of nonviolent men, women and children who were brutally attacked. With these captivating and enthralling images, activists declared a moral victory over the forces of oppression and white supremacy. This was one aspect of the "nonviolent" strategy of King.

Nonviolence in this context has a strong and peculiar rhetorical quality. It represents a belief of passive resistance that not only anticipates violence but also exploits it. Civil rights activists would not use direct action self-defense in their campaigns to dismantle discriminatory laws. While activists were not purveyors of a pathologically masochistic agenda, they knew the weight of images of their suffering in the national and global media. The injustice of Jim Crow appeared more salient in the context of children facing the thuggish tactics of Bull Conner. At the height of the cold war, as the United States claimed to be the leader of the "free world," millions across the globe saw men and women beaten and jailed in America for seeking some of the most fundamental rights. It was the daring strategy to insist on anti-self-defense that won the movement supporters in other parts of white America, which had not been particularly antiracist.

Despite the popular rhetoric of nonviolence, the SCLC, SNCC, and the National Association for the Advancement of Colored People (NAACP) rank and file, as well as leaders, recognized the limitations of nonviolence. Many, if not most, reserved the right to defend their homes and families if necessary. Movement leaders and local activists were aware of men who carried concealed weapons in movement circles. Armed sentinels were placed at some leaders' homes, including King's for a period. Though guns were not entirely uncommon in movement circles, leadership remained critical of weapons, especially conspicuous arms. In 1965 Stokely Carmichael chastised SNCC workers in Greenwood, Mississippi, when he found guns in a local freedom house. He immediately directed SNCC members to remove the weapons. Within a year, Carmichael would embrace armed self-defense. Increasingly, the threat of terrorism caused activists to contemplate arming their homes, even when they simultaneously prepared for and withstood beatings in public from police or white supremacist civilians. They did not consider their willingness to accept physical assaults in marches or sit-ins incongruent with their belief in protecting their own lives or their family's lives.[6]

Though all major civil rights organizations supported nonviolence in theory, the NAACP did not embrace a philosophical position on nonviolence, as had the SCLC, the Congress on Racial Equality (CORE), or SNCC. The NAACP clearly affirmed its commitment to achieving the constitutional rights of all American citizens by peaceful means. It did not, however, argue against black self-defense. In scores of cases across the South, NAACP members either armed themselves or publicly advocated arming themselves in self-defense against racist terrorists. Yet no case of indigenous armed struggle is as celebrated as that of Robert F. Williams.

In 1957 Robert Williams, president of the Monroe, North Carolina, chapter of the NAACP, organized a group of black men to defend themselves against terrorist attacks from the Ku Klux Klan. Advocating the creation of gun clubs, Williams and others dispersed a group of Klansmen who paraded through the black section of town shooting guns and calling black women "whores." By shooting their guns in the air, the armed black men scattered members of the most violent and notorious terrorist organization in the country. Williams also provided armed sentinels at the home of Dr. Albert Perry, a prominent black activist who received numerous death threats for his efforts to allow blacks to use a public swimming pool. Williams's defiance of the nonviolence exhortations of the civil rights establishment resulted in his suspension from the NAACP in 1959.[7] Under pressure from local supporters Williams was allowed back into the organization; however, he never denounced the right of black people to defend themselves against terrorist attack. His book, *Negroes with Guns,* influenced many young activists, including Huey Newton and Bobby Seale.[8] In his book, Williams outlined the legitimacy of self-defense for black people, which, he argued, was a natural right of human beings and an American tradition. When the established forces of law and order refuse to provide protection from the forces of terror, it is the right of the terrorized to arm themselves in defense. Wanton violence, he insisted, was wrong. Random attacks on whites would not only be militarily unwise but immoral. Blacks, he clarified, could not stoop to the low level of morality widely embraced in the white South.[9] Williams helped establish a foundation of direct action self-defense within the civil rights struggle. Years later, a significant number of other civil rights activists would grow sympathetic to Williams's ideas, ultimately giving birth to the Black Power movement. This new movement had its roots in the traditional activities of the southern-based civil rights movement, as well as in the rhetoric of northern-based black nationalism.

The Student Nonviolent Coordinating Committee

It was the 1966 March Against Fear, led by CORE, the SCLC, and SNCC, where the fissure between the traditional civil rights rhetoric and the language and ideas of Black Power emerged. That summer, SNCC was the leading organization advocating the new militant slogan. Stokely Carmichael, its chairman, was very active speaking on college campuses around the country, promoting and explaining the black liberation struggle and its new dimensions of discourse and militancy. Many young members of the Nation of Islam (NOI) were encouraged by the tenacity, dedication, and, above all, activism of SNCC during this period. SNCC workers boldly confronted the most crude, brutal, and vicious forces of white supremacy with grassroots activism. SNCC's promotion of Black Power was an affirmation of militancy, as well as a challenge to the psychological effects of white supremacy. Carmichael and others believed that black people needed to free themselves from their deeply ingrained fear of white people. For many in SNCC, chants of "Freedom Now!" were ineffective. "That don't scare white folks," Carmichael asserted. "The only thing that's gonna get us freedom is power."[10] This was, indeed, an extension of the Nation's challenge to white supremacy. While the NOI was not the only organization to advocate black pride, self-defense, and antiwhite rhetoric, it popularized these themes as no organization in history had. Many SNCC workers, despite their commitment to desegregation and nonviolence, were drawn to the speeches of Muslims.

Though the Nation had no real southern presence, it did have a foothold in major cities of the South, including Atlanta, which had a number of SNCC workers who visited the city to party or vacation from the trying activities of the movement. Many others were students in the city's four black undergraduate colleges: Clark, Morehouse, Morris Brown, and Spelman. In Atlanta, some SNCC workers visited the local mosque of the Nation of Islam to hear minister Jeremiah X offer a black nationalist interpretation of history and current events. As Julian Bond explains, the Muslims were not particularly admired for their vituperative language against whites. "It was easy stuff to say in [all-black communities]." There was a peculiar appeal that Minister Jeremiah X offered in Atlanta, however. The message of black manhood resonated among the SNCC staff who knew of the emasculating nature of white supremacy. Moreover, the excoriation of whites had a cathartic allure for many who had experienced the most brutal forms of oppression. By 1965, John Churchville, Curtis Hayes, and a handful of other SNCC staff had joined the Nation of Islam.[11] Most SNCC workers, however, remained critical of the Nation's defiant talk but conciliatory behavior. For many who were attracted to the bold nationalist language of the Nation but discouraged by its lack of activism, Black Power was particularly appealing. Ron Wilkins was one such person.

After leaving the moribund Community Alert Patrol (CAP), Wilkins and other local activists who were attending a Black Power rally in San Diego decided to form a Los Angeles chapter of SNCC.[12] Brother Crook, as Wilkins was called, met Angela Davis and soon after organized the chapter in January 1968, with Wilkins serving as director.[13] SNCC, for many radicals in southern California, was the organization needed to galvanize and cultivate the energies of local militants. It had the charismatic and militant iconoclastic leaders of Black Power: Stokely Carmichael and H. Rap Brown. Members organized against police brutality, holding forums and various workshops, and in doing so helped change the scope of the civil rights organization. A similar trend toward new strategies and goals also emerged in southern branches of SNCC.

In the spring of 1966, SNCC's Atlanta Project emerged as a Black Power juggernaut, promoting a new direction, which did not include white membership. The Atlanta Project was driven by a few influences, including RAM, which by 1964 systematically attempted to steer the ideological direction of the civil rights movement by working within SNCC and CORE. RAM's intentions were to influence "bourgeois reformers" through infiltration and coalition-building while maintaining an essentially underground movement.[14]

Infiltrated by RAM and former (and current) members of the NOI, the Atlanta Project heralded a nationalist agenda that also set grassroots organization as central to its course of action. Atlanta had a very pronounced class chasm that only appeared more palpable as the civil rights movement dismantled Jim Crow laws. In the Ben Hill area of southwest Atlanta, middle- and upper-middle-class blacks enjoyed spacious homes and good schools. The Vine City section, less than two miles from downtown, had one of the highest concentrations of poverty in Fulton County. Residents lived in cramped, dilapidated homes that, in some cases, were crumbling. By organizing in Vine City, the Atlanta Project hoped to highlight the dilemmas of class and race, pushing the movement's leaders to consider the complexity of economics and racial oppression. The debates over the primacy of race or class were actively waged in SNCC. While the project staff was influenced by the nationalist rhetoric of the Nation of Islam, SNCC and RAM workers also recognized the limitations of race-only analysis. Capitalism, they argued, could adjust to absorb some blacks into the bourgeoisie and capitalist classes; however, the effects of white supremacy and class exploitation would remain as virulent in a post-civil-rights era.[15]

Project workers also recognized the ubiquitous effects of white supremacy and knew that a class-centered agenda was insufficient to address the daunting challenges of racial oppression. For project organizers, it was crucial to free black people from material and psychological dependence on whites. This meant that they reject the labels used by whites to describe black people. Project staff regularly used the term *black* to refer to people of African descent by early 1966. Use of the term *Negro* was banned or used derisively to refer to those who were too conservative, timid, or ignorant to help the black cause. Echoing the mantra of the Nation, SNCC chairman H. Rap Brown declared that "Negroes have a hard time accepting anything Black unless it's been legitimized by white people."[16] Organizers also grew critical of the ideal of racial reconciliation, which, in action, meant that black people incessantly forgive whites for atrocities committed against them. Many began to criticize whites openly. Organizer John Churchville, who joined the NOI after he was in SNCC, remained active, despite the Nation's dismissal of activism. "All whites," Churchville argued, "are racists; that is no white person . . . can stand to deal with black people as humans, as men, as equals, not to mention superiors. They can't stand the thought of black people ruling over them or ruling independently of them."[17] In March 1966, the Atlanta Project sponsored a vote to expel whites from SNCC. The chairman Stokely Carmichael and most members did not support the purge.

While the distrust of white involvement had some roots among southern-born-and-bred SNCC members, many of the project militants were former members of the Nation and roughly half were from the North.[18] Indeed, the project demonstrates that Black Power was derived from many sources and was an organic response to the political, social, and cultural circumstances of the black freedom movement.

King and other SCLC members expressed consternation with self-defense organizations like the Deacons for Defense, claiming that their activities were "illogical."[19] Their position against direct action self-defense, however, grew less popular as the militancy of CORE and SNCC bloomed during the 1966 Meredith March Against Fear, culminating in the historic cry for "Black Power."

The persistence of racial oppression precipitated new militancy and nationalism in the aftermath of the Meredith march. Both Carmichael and King knew this, but their analyses of the Black Power phenomenon were quite different. For King, black nationalism and Black Power were part and parcel of a "nihilistic philosophy born out of the conviction that the Negro can't win. It is, at bottom, the view that American society is so hopelessly corrupt and enmeshed in evil that there is no possibility of salvation from within."[20] Carmichael, however, asserted that Black Power was the proper articulation of the needs of the people. "Black power," Carmichael explained, "means the coming together of black people to elect representatives and to force those representatives to speak to their needs."[21] In addition, "it is a call for black people to begin to define their own goals, to lead their own organizations and to support those organizations. It is a call to reject the racist institutions and values of this society."[22] The Lowndes County, Alabama, Freedom Organization (LCFO) was a true manifestation of this idea, he claimed. The Lowndes County Freedom Organization was an independent political party founded in 1965 in reaction to the all-white Democratic Party of Alabama. The LCFO was also a militant reaction to the failure of civil rights activists from the Mississippi Freedom Democratic Party to gain recognition from the 1964 Democratic National Convention in Atlantic City. The LCFO advocated armed self-defense and the bold slogan "move over before we move over on you."[23]

The LCFO adopted the black panther as its symbol, which was, according to Carmichael, "a bold, beautiful animal, representing the strength and dignity of black demands today." To LCFO members, the black panther was a positive, brave and militant symbol; however, it struck fear in the hearts of whites and black moderates and "added insult to injury" by helping to widen the country's racial divide, some argued.[24] Despite the spirited and indelible reactions to the new mascot, the impetus behind the selection of the mascot is shrouded in myth.

Willie Mukasa Ricks recalled that when SNCC members who formed the LCFO met and searched for a mascot, members thought of several possibilities and during a meeting someone pointed at Mrs. Moore, of Lowndes County, remarking that she appeared strong and powerful like a panther. "That's it," they remarked. "We will be strong and powerful like Mrs. Moore—a black panther."[25] Identification with the people was an intrinsic part of SNCC organization by 1965. That a peasant woman, Mrs. Moore, had risen against white supremacy and its many manifestations to organize politically was in and of itself a powerful act of defiance and courage. Her strength was all the more salient when viewed against the backdrop of gender and class dynamics.

To be sure, she embodied the qualities that SNCC workers wanted in a mascot; however, it is not universally agreed that Mrs. Moore was the immediate inspiration for the panther. According to SNCC member Ruth Howard Chambers, she and others were asked to design a mascot for the LCFO. "I came up with a dove. Nobody thought that worked and someone said I should look at the Clark College emblem . . . That's where the panther came from."[26] In this case, a less romantic story suggests that the general gravitation to greater militancy persuaded the organizers to reject the dove, a conspicuous symbol of peace. The dove's image as soft, small, non-threatening, and white ran against the new mood among SNCC workers. In contrast, the panther was big, black, and suggestive of the power of the organizers. Yet another explanation suggests that the decision to adopt the panther was taken from Alabama history. James Forman, former executive secretary of SNCC, explains that the LCFO discovered that panthers once roamed Alabama hills. Much in the way cities adopt athletic mascots from local history or character, the panther seemed suitable.[27] This strong indigenous animal was selected as an appropriate mascot for a strong indigenous movement.

While the origin of the mascot is in dispute, there are some common themes that run through each story. In all cases, the panther represents the most esteemed qualities that organizers hoped to realize in the movement. Moreover, the symbol simultaneously evoked militancy and an ostensibly black character. The decision to adopt the panther coincided with the rise of militancy and Black Power that had begun to take root in the movement. Whatever its origins, the black panther came to symbolize for many "a bold and beautiful animal, representing the strength and dignity of black demands."[28]

The black panther had a wide-reaching effect on black militants who searched for a symbol of resistance. For Black Panther Party co-founders Huey Newton and Bobby Seale in Oakland, the panther was ideally suited for their new organization. The big black cat was very much like the righteous spirit of the black masses, militants argued. "The Panther," Newton explained, "is a fierce animal, but he will not attack until he is backed into a corner; then he will strike out."[29] Like Newton and Seale, other young militants around the country found inspiration in the LCFO and its powerful symbol, forming their own Black Panther Parties, at times oblivious to the existence of each other.

Carmichael lauded the efforts of independent political bodies that organized under the black panther symbol across the country. This, he explained, was a natural process of political evolution. Blacks had become tired of asking whites for acceptance and inclusion. They were intolerant of appeasing white liberals with language that whites approved. It mattered little if whites liked the phrase "Black Power." "For once, black people are going to use the words they want to use—not just the words whites want to hear," explained Carmichael.[30] The fear of antiwhite violence the cry for Black Power evoked was not merited, according to Carmichael; whites should expect blacks to defend themselves if attacked. It was clear that a new period of political consciousness had emerged, and it took the form of action in the South and the urban unrest that hit many northern cities.

Explaining why people took to the streets during these urban rebellions, Carmichael stated that the civil rights activists were partially to blame. "Each time the people saw Martin Luther King get slapped, they became angry; when they saw four little black girls bombed to death, they were angrier; and when nothing happened they were steaming. We had nothing to offer them that they could see except to go out and be beaten again. We helped to build their frustration." He went on to say that "we cannot be expected any longer to march and have our heads broken in order to say to whites: come on, you're nice guys. For you are not nice guys. We have found you out."[31]

For many SNCC activists, the call for Black Power was a natural process of ideological refinement wrought by experience. The civil rights movement had failed to speak to the fundamental needs of African Americans, especially those outside the South. Much like the appeal of the Nation of Islam, the more militant call for Black Power spoke to those who were not confronted with Jim Crow laws. It did not take Jim Crow laws for white police officers to brutalize blacks in Los Angeles and Chicago. Jim Crow laws were not needed to sustain job or housing discrimination. These types of racial oppression were very real, and black people outside of the South knew it. In Oakland, African Americans faced pervasive job and housing discrimination. The city's black unemployment rate was more than four times the national average, and although suffrage was universal, blacks into the 1960s were politically disempowered in Oakland.[32] When blacks were confronted with police brutality they had little recourse besides filing lawsuits in white courts with white judges, juries, and lawyers, who were often apathetic to complaints of police brutality in black communities. Gaining admittance to a white university was of little concern to the economically destitute segments of the black community. SNCC workers hoped to galvanize these malcontents who were hungry for radical change. While SNCC hoped to infiltrate urban hotbeds, self-described revolutionaries were attempting to infiltrate SNCC in an effort to direct the black freedom struggle toward revolutionary tactics and away from reformist programs. RAM members fanned out across the movement's landscape, operating in various capacities influencing and shaping the political climate of the era.

The Revolutionary Action Movement

The first organization to embody the popular synthesis of northern black nationalism, southern activism, and Third World revolutionary theory was the Revolutionary Action Movement. RAM never attracted the media attention of SNCC or the Panthers, although its significance cannot be overlooked. It helped steer SNCC toward black power and provide an early base for the political education of the founders of the Black Panther Party.

In 1961 a group of black members of the largely white Students for a Democratic Society (SDS) began developing a black nationalist consciousness that was significantly influenced by the Nation of Islam and Malcolm X. Donald Freeman, a student at Case Western Reserve College in Cleveland, established contact with several black students at other colleges who had been familiar with the SDS in Ohio, and together the students formed Challenge in the fall of 1961. Challenge was composed of students primarily from Central State University in Ohio. Several of the members had been expelled from southern schools for participating in civil rights demonstrations. Others were members of the Nation of Islam and other black nationalist organizations. The background of these students helped push the organization in a political direction with a focus on off-campus activity. In the spring of 1962, Freeman encouraged members of Challenge to examine and discuss "Revolutionary Nationalism and the

Afro-American," an article published by Harold Cruse in a radical quarterly, *Studies on the Left*. Influenced by Cruse's article, Challenge resolved that it must develop a northern movement "similar to the Nation of Islam, using the tactics of SNCC but outside of NAACP and CORE."[33] Beginning with Central State, Challenge students infiltrated various student organizations and formed a slate for student elections, RAM. Successful at the student polls, RAM expanded activities off campus.

By the beginning of 1963, RAM began calling itself the Revolutionary Action Movement and members Max Stanford, Wanda Marshall, and Donald Freeman had established contact with veterans of the civil rights movement such as Marion Barry of SNCC, Ella Baker of the SCLC and NAACP, and black leftists like Bill Davis, leader of Philadelphia-based Organization Alert. Stanford even got in touch with Malcolm X, who dissuaded him from joining the Nation. "You can do more for the Honorable Elijah Muhammad by organizing outside of the Nation," the national spokesman insisted. Malcolm X's directive was a portentous sign of his growing cynicism over the NOI's ability to address the problem of white supremacy. Encouraged to develop an independent, activist-oriented black nationalist organization, RAM developed study groups and published a bimonthly newspaper, *Black America*. Through *Black America*, it established contact with nationalist-oriented intellectuals across the country.[34] In the summer of 1964, a former member of the Afro-American Association, Ernest Allen, traveled to Cuba where he met Max Stanford; Robert F. Williams, the exiled former NAACP leader; and General Baker, who was active in labor organization in Detroit. With direction from Stanford, Allen formed a West Coast RAM cell in early 1965.[35]

In New York, members of the Revolutionary Action Movement began working with the Five Percenters in an effort to radicalize them with leftist political education. While the group, founded in 1963, had a fluid membership with little hierarchy, members were devoted to its leader, Clarence 13 X (Clarence Smith), a Korean War veteran who was affiliated with the Nation of Islam. Known as Father Allah to members, Clarence 13 X carried the cosmology of the Nation to street toughs who then modified it, creating a philosophy that postulated that all black men are gods and all black women "earths." Members adopted both Arabic names and English words that were considered attributes of Allah, such as Knowledge, Sublime, Wise, and Intelligent. Membership remained largely young and male, although there were female members, who adhered to a strict dress code that forbade skirts and uncovered hair. Lessons from the Five Percenters included mathematics, astronomy, and geology. Each member, for instance, was obliged to know the square miles of the earth's surface, the earth's distance from the sun, as well as a system of numerology and the "Supreme Alphabet," among other things. The organization prided itself on its wisdom and understanding of physical sciences, but it was not activist in nature. Its ties to gang life were still strong. Members who were not familiar with the lessons often received a reprimand, which could include a beating. RAM believed that the nationalist, street-based group was ripe for politicization. According to RAM documents, RAM was successful in leading Five Percenters to form the Black Panther Athletic and Social Club. The social club, however, was short lived, as members generally lacked the discipline expected of revolutionaries.[36]

Following the Meredith March Against Fear, SNCC representatives in Harlem, working with local nationalists, formed a coalition to serve as a support apparatus for the LCFO and operate an independent black political party. With the support of Stokely Carmichael, Stanford and other organizers suggested the Black Panther Party as a name for the new organization. By August 1966, the Black Panther Party, operating as a coalition party, was formed in New York. The mission of the New York party was to provide a political alternative to "the capitalist racist Democratic and Republican parties and also exhaust the legal political means of protest."[37] For Stanford, it was important to ultimately achieve revolution. Political parties and voting, even in an all-black party, would not realize revolution. These efforts, however, were important and necessary steps, they reasoned, to demonstrate the limitations of the electoral process. The larger political structure was corrupt and would remain so until there was a fundamental overhaul of the economic system that undergirded the political apparatus. This Marxist reasoning was textured by black nationalist dogma and had inherent limitations in a country where blacks were outnumbered by whites seven to one. Nevertheless, the mood was optimistic among the young black left.

Despite the initial enthusiasm, the New York Black Panther Party did not last a year. A faction of the party, led by Larry Neal, a leader of the black arts movement, wanted to picket and pressure black organized crime to support the party financially. Other members disagreed with Neal's focus. Accusations were made that members were "counterrevolutionary" or agents of the state, causing increased factionalism in early 1967. According to RAM officials, other Black Panther Parties, established in several other cities, similarly struggled with factionalism.[38]

Though there were occasional conflicts among the various black nationalist groups in New York, the rich black nationalist community of

Harlem significantly shaped the political expressions of RAM leaders such as Rolland Snellings, a writer and activist who gravitated to the city's nationalist community shortly after his arrival to the city in the late 1950s.The community of elders in Harlem reflected a diverse ideological spectrum, which included Garveyites like Audrey "Queen Mother" Moore and Major Thornhill, intellectuals such as J. A. Rogers and John H. Clarke, leftist radicals like Daniel H. Watts, and nationalists like Abdul Kareem and Eddie "Pork Chop" Davis. Others like Elombre Brath, Carlos Cooks, Oba O. Adefumi, and members of the Nation interacted with each other in various informal networks and social and political contexts.

By 1964 Snellings began writing for *Liberator* magazine as a staff writer with Harold Cruse and Larry Neal. After joining RAM, Snellings, who would rename himself Askia M. Toure, operated through Umbra, a nationalist front for RAM activities. Following the assassination of Malcolm X, Toure went underground following unfounded accusations that RAM was involved in the killing. Surfacing in Atlanta, Toure infiltrated SNCC activities and joined efforts to foment radicalism among SNCC workers. In 1967 he relocated to San Francisco at the behest of James Garrett, head of the Black Student Union at San Francisco State College. There, Toure met other RAM agents who worked through the Black Panther Party of Northern California with Ken Freeman, the top-ranking RAM member on the West Coast. Soon after his arrival Toure was introduced to the fledgling group of a similar name across the bay. It was one of dozens of nationalist groups with which Toure had worked. The Black Panther Party for Self-Defense, however, was different from any other organization that he had ever seen, though the party was influenced by many of them.[39]

The Founding of the "People's Party"

Huey Newton and Bobby Seale were influenced by several phenomena: the Nation of Islam, the civil rights movement, RAM, and the rise of revolutionary struggles in Africa, Asia, and Latin America. For Newton and Seale, the Black Panther Party was a result of a careful and deliberate process of politicization and ideological development. Both came into political consciousness slowly. Seale and Newton met while attending Merritt College in Oakland. They joined the Afro-American Association, led by Donald Warden, a lawyer who promoted the study of black history. Newton was one of the first ten members to join the organization, but he grew dissatisfied with Warden, whom Newton later considered "up to no good."[40]

As national spokesman for the Nation, Malcolm visited the local mosques in Oakland and San Francisco in the early 1960s. Newton and Seale attended the mosques to listen to the charismatic firebrand. Newton found a particular affinity with Malcolm's past as a street hustler, but he was more inspired by the minister's ability to transcend pathos and develop into a disciplined and militant leader. In his discussion of Malcolm X, Newton echoes the sentiments of other Panthers and advocates of Black Power: "Malcolm impressed me with his logic and with his disciplined and dedicated mind. Here was a man who combined the world of the streets and the world of the scholar, a man so widely read he could give better lectures and cite more evidence than many college professors . . . He knew what the street brothers were like, and he knew what had to be done to reach them." Newton considered joining the Nation, but "I had had enough of religion and could not bring myself to adopt another one."[41]

For Seale, the Muslims' national spokesman was "the only one who could really tell it like it is." He explained that "I listened to Malcolm X with mesmerized enthusiasm, having a front row seat and looking around to see the disciplined, ready Muslims everywhere lined against the wall." The Nation sparked a thirst in Seale for political knowledge. "I found myself studying everything about black people and reading *Muhammad Speaks* every week to find out what Malcolm X said."[42] Despite his adoration of Malcolm X and admiration for the Muslims' discipline, their theology "just did not add up." He gave the Muslims considerable thought and examination. "I read *Muhammad Speaks,* spoke to Muslims," but the story of Yacub "was not scientific and did not explain everything around me."[43]

Beyond the theological conflict, NOI membership would have been difficult for Newton and Seale for other reasons. Both reveled in their "lumpen" lifestyle, which included heavy drinking, cursing, and other crude behavior. Seale was a popular barbeque chef who would have had to sacrifice his beloved pork, as well as the "bitter dog" (vodka and juice) that was so popular among West Coast Panthers. Newton would have also been forced to address his violent temper as well. The Nation made behavioral reform central to the conversion to Islam. As some Muslims stated, one could not claim to be black but live like a Negro. The conversion process was a symbolic rebirth that shed behavior deemed anathema to true Islam. For the Panthers, being lumpen carried a particular value that was important to revolutionary behavior, but the lumpen ideal was incongruent with the Nation of Islam.

Journalist and Huey Newton biographer Hugh Pearson argues that Newton was largely an intelligent and manipulative figure with a ruthless and brutal character. Newton's criminal activities, according to Pearson, shaped the direction of the party that he ultimately led into oblivion through corruption and deceit. Though vigorously researched, Pearson's study is myopic. He reduces Newton to a one-dimensional sociopath and erroneously extends this psychological portrait to the organization Newton did not entirely lead. Newton's contradictions and foibles are well known, so are his more laudable efforts to participate in the black freedom movement. Close examination of Newton reveals a complicated man who appears to have been engaged in several battles simultaneously: internal conflicts with himself and struggles between himself and others. Moreover, he was ideologically dynamic, shifting to and developing new theories throughout his Panther years.

Those who were personally familiar with Newton in Oakland knew of his complicated and, at times, violent character. Throughout Oakland, Newton had his share of fights and confrontations. In fact, Seale boasts about Newton's ability to "kick ass" in the Panther biography *Seize the Time*. "The bad cats terrorized the community—and Huey terrorized the bad cats." Detailing Newton's campaigns beating various local toughs of West Oakland, Seale proclaims the street credibility of the minister of defense. To illustrate Newton's lumpen roots, Seale explains that he knew "pimps and hustlers and righteous gangsters on the block who knew and respected Huey" because of his toughness and badass character.[44] Even Seale would admit that Newton was not the quintessential thug, however. Like the organization he led, Newton was complicated and full of contradictions.

According to Ernest Allen, Oakland native and former friend of Newton, the minister of defense had two sides, one that was compassionate, intellectually curious, and sincere. The other was unpredictable, volatile, and roughish. "It simply depended on which Huey you met that day." Similarly, Elaine Brown, former chairman of the party, explains that Huey's brother Walter was a violent hustler who influenced Huey's character. "Huey was sometimes a thug, but he was also a genius," Brown states.[45] In some ways, the West Coast Panthers were an extension of the dual personalities of its leadership.[46] For those who were served by Panther survival programs, the Panthers were veritable servants of the people. From their efforts to end police terror by patrolling the police to giving free medical care and food to poor people, the Panthers in Oakland and Los Angeles were beloved by many. The experience was different for black organizations that differed with the Panther program. On several occasions, ideological disputes ended in beatings and the brandishing of weapons. By 1970, several people would be beaten, shot, or killed in these disputes between West Coast black nationalists. The lionizing of lumpen behavior proved to be a serious liability for the West Coast black nationalist community in general and the Panthers in particular, ultimately creating a siege mentality among black power organizations.

At Merritt College, Newton and Seale were involved in a RAM front organization, the Soul Students Advisory Council (SSAC). Its emphasis on reading and writing various polemics bothered the two, who derided its members as "armchair revolutionaries" who were so enthralled with bourgeois life that they did not want to do serious organization of the black community. In early 1966, the SSAC rejected Newton and Seale's proposal to attend a campus rally with firearms. This, according to Newton, would help recruit "students from the grass roots" who did not identify with intellectual organizations. SSAC members, however, considered such action suicidal.[47] Meanwhile, Newton and Seale were considering the philosophies of such revolutionary theorists as Frantz Fanon, Che Guevara, Mao Tse-tung, and Malcolm X. Like thousands of militant blacks across America, Newton and Seale were attracted to the culturally affirming language of black nationalism and its emphasis on the historical accomplishments of African people in the continent and Diaspora. They were also sympathetic to direct action self-defense against racist terrorists. Unlike rural southerners, blacks in the urban North rarely met with racist terrorism in the form of the Ku Klux Klan or nightriders. Black militants and others, however, universally recognized the police as the most immediate representation of racist aggression. Most of the major urban rebellions of the period were sparked by acts of police brutality.[48]

After working in the SSAC and AAA, Newton and Seale decided to apply many of the principles they had studied. They met with intellectual radicals who admired various revolutionary theorists, but Newton and Seale saw none who applied the revolutionary theories to the urban arena in the United States. For Newton and Seale, it was incumbent on true revolutionaries to study carefully the political and social phenomena and "seize the time." For them, the political landscape was full of revolutionary lessons. Urban rebellion was a major lesson for all.[49]

The 1965 civil unrest in Watts, Newton claimed, was a significant learning experience for black people. "We had seen Martin Luther King come to Watts in an effort to calm the people, and we had seen his philosophy rejected."[50] Watts demonstrated what many others observed: revolutionary struggle must include poor, marginalized, and "discarded" black people. It was the lumpenproletariat members of the black community who heaved bricks at the police and hurled firebombs into the stores of those who refused to hire blacks but charged them exorbitant fees for services. Seale and Newton admired the "[brother] on the block [who] was ten motherfuckers when politically educated and if you got him organized."[51]

From the ashes of the 1965 Watts rebellion emerged the Community Alert Patrol, which was comprised of members from various activist organizations, including Us, a locally based cultural nationalist organization, and SNCC. With cameras, law books, and tape recorders, CAP conducted patrols of the police in black communities.[52] A mood of discontent and radicalism was sweeping ghettoes nationwide.

Admiring the efforts and ideas of CAP, SNCC, and others, Newton and Seale decided in October 1966 to form the Black Panther Party for Self-Defense. On October 16, 1966, using the Nation of Islam's "What the Muslims Want," and "What the Muslims Believe" as models, Seale and Newton drafted the party's Ten-Point Program to outline the goals and objectives of their new organization.[53] The Ten-Point Program and subsequent Panther patrols were implemented, but the party decided on more bold action.

Police brutality was the driving force behind initial party activity. As Chairman Bobby Seale explains, "the Black Panther Party was formed to resist police brutality and the murder of black people in the same manner that the Vietnamese people were resisting U.S. imperialist aggression—by violence if necessary!"[54] In an era of increased levels of resistance to white supremacy, the Black Panther Party for Self-Defense made a conscious attempt to make a psychological break from the mentality that tolerated violence against black life but feared violence against representatives of white supremacy. As followers of Frantz Fanon, Bobby Seale and Huey Newton fully embraced the notion that it was incumbent on the "colonized" to violently resist the "colonizer" in order to liberate themselves effectively from the physical and psychological entrapments of oppression. Violence, according to Fanon, "frees the native from his inferiority complex and from his despair and inaction; it makes him fearless and restores his self-respect." Building on Fanon's revolutionary ideas, the Panthers argued that the peasant of Fanon's writing is the black urban lumpenproletariat in America. "It is clear," Fanon writes, "that the peasants alone are revolutionary, for they have nothing to lose and everything to gain. The starving peasant . . . is the first among the exploited to discover that only violence pays."[55] The participation of local street gangs in the various cases of urban unrest in the late 1960s, such as the Watts rebellion, confirmed the Panthers' theory that the lumpen were ripe for revolutionary resistance, and resistance would be first manifested against the most immediate display of white power, the police.

The long tradition of police hostility and aggression against black people supported the Panther argument that police were an occupying force in black communities. From the beginnings of formalized police in America, black people in northern cities and rural southern areas were not only excluded from becoming officers but also systematically harassed and brutalized. Well into the twentieth century, all southern states had white-only policies for state troopers. Some towns and cities first allowed black officers but did not grant them the authority to arrest white suspects. In effect, white criminals had more protection under the law than black officers.

By the late 1960s, black demands for an end to police brutality had crested with scores of urban rebellions nationwide, most of which were sparked by cases of police brutality, though police aggression was certainly not the sole source for the unrest. The police were on the front line on behalf of the larger power structure. The police, the Panthers noted, had been pawns with the task of protecting the property of the elite while simultaneously providing a palpable demonstration of white power and control. Pulling heavily from the white poor and working class for officers, the state relied on ubiquitous notions of white privilege to assure that the racial status quo was defended, while white officers accrued social currency in the process. White officers, in effect, affirmed their allegiance to the same political, social, and economic apparatus that had marginalized them. In turn, they enjoyed access to arenas of class and race privilege, which was partly derived from knowing that white people did not suffer the humiliations of racial discrimination such as chronic police harassment. Black space, therefore, was violently intruded from time to time for the ultimate purpose of displaying white authority and power.[56]

It was in the context of traditional hostility and aggression between the black community and the police that the Panthers formed. Though many organizations and leaders had long protested police brutality, few groups assumed the task of policing the police. Guns, Panthers noted, were essential displays of courage and militancy. They were of practical importance in that they provided for defense against potential police attacks. In addition, guns demonstrated that there were common black people who no longer lived in fear and awe of white power.

On May 2, 1967, thirty Panthers and sympathizers from the Afro-American Association left Oakland for Sacramento to protest the gun bill introduced by Donald Mulford, a conservative state assemblyman from Piedmont, a wealthy white section of Oakland. The bill was intended to prohibit the armed Panther patrols of the police. The group was composed of six women and twenty-four men, twenty of whom were armed with shotguns, rifles, and handguns. At the state house, Bobby Seale read Executive Mandate Number One, which protested the Mulford bill. Before they could return to Oakland, the Panthers were arrested for various offenses. Most charges were dropped; however, Seale and others remained behind bars for arms violations.[57] This was the first arrest of Panthers and the party's first publicity bonanza. People all across the country heard of the small band of black militants in Oakland.

The Panthers decided early in their development to adhere to keen principles and policies for garnering publicity. The Panthers conspicuously created a media image that, in some ways, relied on a symbiotic relationship with certain elements in the mainstream media who focused on the Panthers as the militants many whites loved to hate. Images of bold, brash, gun-toting, profanity-spewing blacks with clenched fists garnered an array of emotions from the public and sensational news. For some in white America, the Panthers were the perfect justification for their "backlash" against the progress of the black freedom movement. The Panthers' style suggested an unraveling of traditional modes of ethnic pluralism and protest, while simultaneously evoking the most inveterate racist fears of black manhood and racial etiquette breaches. Racists long argued that blacks would ultimately attempt to destroy whites. The Panthers appeared to be the incarnation of that fear. For black militants, however, the new organization was a promising potential ally.

By early 1967 Ken Freeman's Black Panther Party of Northern California established contacts with its counterparts across the bay, but ideological conflict turned the relationship acrimonious. Both groups were armed and supported armed revolution; however, they significantly disagreed on strategy. The Newton-and-Seale-led BPPSD relied heavily on public displays of firearms, which the Freeman-led BPPNC viewed as foolish bravado that invited police attention. The BPPSD also pandered to a street-based image that rejected the decorum normally expected of conventional organizations. Lumpen behavior only affirmed their oppositional relationship with political (and cultural) orthodoxy. Moreover, many Oakland Panthers believed they accentuated their revolutionary character through gun-pulling intimidation tactics that they read as acts of bravery.

In 1967 news of the rivalry between the two Panther Parties reached Stokely Carmichael, whom both organizations admired. Carmichael offered to mediate a discussion to resolve the conflict, but he did not arrive at the designated meeting. In Carmichael's absence the climate was tense. Arguments ensued and a physical brawl erupted. The Oakland party pulled guns on Freeman and his supporters. Carmichael, convinced that the Newton and Seale's group was positioned to carry the Black Power movement to new heights, later advised the BPPNC to change its name. In 1968, the organization changed its name to the House of Umoja.[58]

A similar scenario occurred in Los Angeles, where members of the Black Panther Political Party (BPPP), an organization with ties to SNCC, were told by Oakland Panthers that they must merge or discard the name. Franklin Alexander and Angela Y. Davis, members of the BPPP refused to capitulate to the strong-arm tactics. Instead, they armed themselves, taking the physical threats seriously until SNCC officials encouraged the Los Angeles group to cooperate with Newton and Seale.[59] Some members of the BPPP actually joined the Oakland Panthers, agreeing with the opinion of SNCC officials such as James Forman that the party could "grow where [SNCC] did not."[60] For Forman and many SNCC members, the Black Panther Party of Oakland was the manifestation of political evolution and Black Power. The Panthers, many concluded, were true followers of Malcolm X and among the first to apply the theories of Black Power. They also became a prominent focus of police agencies by mid-1967.

On October 28, 1967, following a party celebrating the Panthers' one-year anniversary, Huey Newton and a friend were stopped by two Oakland police officers. Newton was directed out of his car, and a confrontation erupted between him and Officer John Frey. Shots were fired, mortally wounding Officer Frey and hitting Newton and Officer Herbert Heanes, who was attending Newton's passenger. Wounded in the abdomen, Newton was taken to the hospital by a friend where he was arrested, beaten by police, and charged with the murder of Frey. Convicted of manslaughter, Newton was sentenced to life in prison.

By late fall 1967 it appeared as if the Black Panther Party for Self-Defense would simply be a historical footnote, one among the scores of largely local black militant organizations that emerged during the Black Power era. Supporters feared that Newton might become one of many black men in prison facing a life sentence on unjust charges. There had been nothing particularly remarkable about the party beyond the bold affirmations of armed patrols of police. The efforts of Eldridge and Kathleen Cleaver, however, revitalized the struggling organization. A massive "Free Huey" campaign brought much needed resources to the moribund Panthers by 1968 and made Newton into an icon. Black Power celebrities like Stokely Carmichael, H. Rap Brown, writer and poet Askia Toure, and James Forman spoke out for Newton. Thousands of young people—of various racial and ethnic backgrounds—became acquainted with Huey P. Newton through an aggressive propaganda campaign that lionized him as a strong and defiant defender of justice. The picture of Newton in a wicker chair, holding a spear in one hand and a rifle in the other became famous. He was handsome, strong, and the embodiment of the new consciousness of a generation. Though people argued for Newton's innocence, many surely believed that Newton was justified in defending his life against a police attempt to murder him. Black people had come a long way, and the black freedom movement had a new standard of resistance. The membership rolls of the party expanded precipitously in the summer of 1968.

Part of the rapid expansion of party membership resulted from a growing militancy that was a direct outgrowth of the assassination of Martin Luther King Jr. Young black people rebelled in more than a hundred cities between April 4 and 6, 1968. For many young blacks, the Black Panther Party could harness the anger, rage, and visceral desire for militant action. For law enforcement agencies, the meteoric rise of the Panthers was a nightmarish scenario of black rebellion and revolution. For many young African Americans and others, the party was a harbinger of justice and freedom.

Omar Barbour, who joined the Queens branch of the New York City chapter of the party, explained that the image of Chairman Bobby Seale at the California State Assembly particularly attracted him. It was an image that was unprecedented in the recent struggles for black liberation. While many had advocated the right of blacks to arm themselves against racist attack, no one had had the temerity to commit such a bold act as the Panthers. Black militants, adorned with black leather jackets and berets and armed with shotguns, rifles, and handguns while walking into a bastion of white authority was a compelling image. "The emphasis on *doing*," Barbour said, "was mesmerizing." The Panthers, he was convinced, were not "armchair revolutionaries" but serious and dedicated "soldiers" who were willing to confront the racist and brutal police officers that many, including Barbour, considered an "occupying force."[61]

Black radicals expressed similar sentiment across the country. For those who organized against police brutality, the Panthers were particularly fascinating. During his activities in CAP, Brother Crook, heard of the Black Panther Party for Self-Defense after its entry into the California State Assembly. It was, however, the charges against Huey Newton that grabbed his attention. The day after Newton's arrest, Crook went to Oakland to visit the Panthers. He found their positions interesting but was especially impressed with the party's efforts to resist police terror. So were others, including many in the Los Angeles nationalist community, as well as those outside of California. The Panthers would garner support from many of the country's most prominent Black Power advocates. From a small band of zealous college students and street toughs would emerge a formidable organization that would befriend many and antagonize others.

The climate of the Black Power movement provided the rich political and cultural backdrop to Panther activities. The baby boom generation of African Americans had been reared in an era that embraced a militant optimism of political and social change. The horror of the Emmett Till lynching and the inspiring activism of the civil rights movement were essential to the political maturation of the generation. From emerging nations and revolutionaries in Africa, Asia, and Latin America to the articulations of rage from the Nation of Islam, young African Americans emerged at the precipice of a new era. Heightened expectations, significant cultural shifts, and a generally new conception of the collective black self gave rise to scores of black nationalist organizations. Few, however, would be as distinguished as Oakland's Black Panther Party. A convergence of factors made this organization expand and capture the popular imagination and attention of millions. Whether it generated fear or affection, the party's impact would be indelible.

By 1970 the Black Panther had nearly five thousand members in more than twenty states. From San Diego to New Haven, Panthers and sympathizers were active in scores of programs and service projects. Though the growth of the Panthers was a reflection of the larger popularity of Black Power, the party was not solely a product of a faddish popularity of black militancy. The Panthers made copious attempts to meet people's fundamental needs. More than anything, these programs attracted people to the party. By 1969 the Black Panther Party had free breakfast programs in nineteen locations, feeding twenty thousand children weekly. The Panthers developed liberation schools, as well as the celebrated free health clinics that provided free sickle-cell testing in Chicago, Portland, Los Angeles, New York, and other cities. The Panther-founded National Committee to Combat Fascism brought together an eclectic collection of organizations to resist the Vietnam War, police brutality, and a bevy of other conditions deemed deleterious to the people. To the young, zealous, and determined rank and file of the party, the Panthers were no flash in the pan but the vanguard for the revolution.

The responsibilities of being the vanguard party were vast. The Panthers spread across the country, attracting thousands of young people to commit to the struggle in ways that few organizations demanded. The intellectual arena of Panther politics was complex and dynamic, as members both shaped the party and conformed to the Panther ideal. Different chapters would have different characteristics that reflected provincial sensibilities, while the party at large attempted to develop a national image that never aimed to direct the people toward revolution. The Black Panthers wanted to walk with the people toward revolution, even if this meant that its members must take the first step.

Black Panthers demonstrate at the trial of the Panther-21 in New York City, 1969. Panthers were effective in evoking powerful symbolic gestures of defiance to white supremacy and police brutality in particular. (Courtesy of Roz Payne)

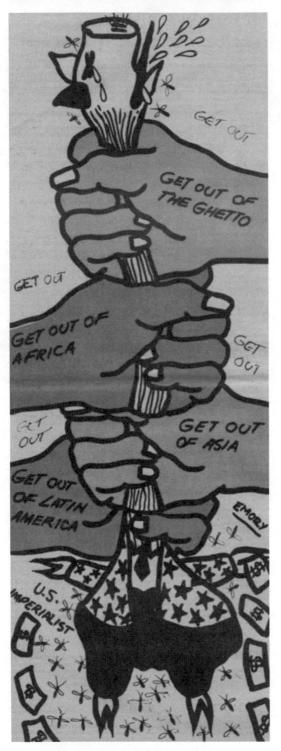

The Black Panther Party relied on the power of art to convey revolutionary and resistive politics, as demonstrated in this 1969 cartoon from Minister of Culture Emory Douglas, published in *The Black Panther*. (Courtesy of the Thomas J. Dodd Research Center, University of Connecticut Libraries)

The *Black Panther* newspaper was a powerful tool of expression and radical media between 1968 and 1972, at its height of circulation. It was the most widely circulated black newspaper after *Muhammad Speaks.* This illustration comes from a 1970 issue. (Courtesy of the Thomas J. Dodd Research Center, University of Connecticut Libraries)

Black Power's Green

Save at Connecticut Savings & Loan Association

616 ALBANY AVENUE (Corner Magnolia) • HARTFORD

As Black Power took deeper root in black communities, even white-owned businesses capitalized on the once vilified slogan to attract black consumers, as seen in this advertisement from 1970. (Courtesy of the Thomas J. Dodd Research Center, University of Connecticut Libraries)

UNTIL THE DAY OF LIBERATION, PROTECTION FOR MY CHILD CAN ONLY BE GUARANTEED THROUGH THE BARREL OF THE GUN.......By: Audry Hudson

The Black Power movement had visible manifestations in various arenas of discourse. This drawing reflects the intersection of international solidarity, deconstructed gender roles, and the importance of students to revolutionary struggle. (Courtesy of the Thomas J. Dodd Research Center, University of Connecticut Libraries)

THE HEIRS OF MALCOLM HAVE PICKED UP THE GUN AND NOW STAND MILLIONS STRONG FACING THE RACIST PIG OPPRESSOR.

Malcolm X was the chief source through which young African Americans learned about black nationalism in the early 1960s. He became the patron saint of virtually all Black Power advocates, despite his status as an outsider to black activist politics. (Courtesy of the Thomas J. Dodd Research Center, University of Connecticut Libraries)

(*top*) Preacherman, field marshal for the Young Patriots, at the United Forum against Fascism conference in 1969. The Young Patriots was a former Chicago street gang composed of poor Appalachian youths. Modeling themselves after the Panthers, they were part of the "Rainbow Coalition," formed by Panther Fred Hampton. The Patriots denounced the cardinal evils of revolutionary nationalists: racism, imperialism, and capitalism. (Courtesy of the Thomas J. Dodd Research Center, University of Connecticut Libraries)

(*bottom*) Jose "Cha Cha" Jimenez (in striped shirt), chairman of the Young Lords, and Bobby Rush (center), deputy minister of defense of the Black Panthers. A former Puerto Rican street gang that was part of Chicago's Rainbow Coalition, the Young Lords became the most visible group of Puerto Rican revolutionaries in the late 1960s and early 1970s. (Courtesy of the Thomas J. Dodd Research Center, University of Connecticut Libraries)

Representatives of the Brown Berets, Asian American radicals, and Black Panther Party rally at a Free Huey Newton demonstration at the Alameda Country Court House in 1968. The Free Huey campaign helped popularize the Panthers and facilitated alliances with other revolutionary organizations. (Courtesy of Roz Payne)

CHAPTER 4

Swimming with the Masses
The Black Panthers, Lumpenism, and Revolutionary Culture

The Black Panther Party for Self-Defense (BPP) considered itself the true vanguard party of the people. It had, since its inception, assiduously promoted itself as a lumpen organization that spoke to the people's fundamental needs, as defined by the people. It was not like the National Association for the Advancement of Colored People (NAACP), which was concerned with enforcing constitutional law, ensuring that black people could attend white schools or live in white neighborhoods. It did not concern itself with the aggressive grassroots mobilization of blacks to resist Jim Crow laws, as did the Southern Christian Leadership Conference (SCLC). Nor did the party occupy itself with efforts to mobilize rural poor to realize black suffrage like the Student Nonviolent Coordinating Committee (SNCC) did. The Panthers were not concerned with the religious emphasis of the Nation of Islam (NOI) and its Booker T. Washingtonian notions of capitalism. Unlike the Revolutionary Action Movement (RAM), the party attempted to practice an aboveground campaign of revolutionary struggle in order to move the people closer to revolution.

Despite its attempt to distinguish itself from other organizations, it is clear that the Black Panther Party was influenced by many of them. It absorbed many of the tenets of SNCC, the NOI, and RAM. It embraced the grassroots and activist nature of SNCC, as well as SNCC's strategic attempt to identify with the people with whom they worked. Identification with the people distinguished the Panthers from other black nationalist organizations such as the NOI and Us. Like other classical black nationalists, these organizations embraced a civilizing mission to culturally reform the masses of black people. Although the cultural nationalist rhetoric contrasted with the praise for European cultural standards, the fundamental thrust of the civilizing mission was similar.

The aim of cultural nationalism was, at its very basic level, to culturally regenerate the mass of black people. Using the NOI's etymological interpretation of *Negro,* cultural nationalists (and other Black Power advo-cates) argued that white oppressors had made black people into *Negroes* who were enamored of everything white and repulsed by blackness. Cultural nationalism was the central thrust of the Black Power movement. In universities, prisons, and community centers, advocates of Black Power celebrated a new blackness that was a rejection of the *Negro.* Maulana Karenga, the leading cultural nationalist, argued that "the *Negro* is made and manufactured in America" and "the only thing *Negroes* produce are problems and babies."[1] Cultural nationalists like the Us organization urged Negroes to become black people by sloughing off Western culture. African names, clothes, rituals, and "sensibilities" were promoted to facil-itate the transition to cultural rebirth. Clearly the majority of African Americans were not willing to abandon their European names, clothes, and customs, though a significant portion did grow warm to aspects of cultural nationalism. Still, for the Panthers, identification with the people did not endorse the separation from black folk culture that cultural nationalism required.

The Black Panther Party was the self-described organization of brothers on the block—the disgruntled urban poor. It was the organization that, according to Minister of Information Eldridge Cleaver, gave "voice to the voiceless." Its members were not, however, ordinary urban poor; they were the lumpenproletariat. These were the poorest of the poor, the "forgotten people at the bottom of society."[2]

Employing Marxist terminology, the Panthers considered the lumpen-proletariat the most open to revolutionary struggle, and an effective mobilization of the lumpen was essential to the Black Power struggle. Huey P. Newton and other leading Panthers viewed the most downtrod-den elements of black communities as the rebellious forces that pushed the movement forward when middle-class organizations were overly cau-tious. Spontaneous urban unrest, argued Newton, indicated civil rights leaders' inability to appeal to significant numbers of black people with integrationist nonviolence. The black people of America's ghettoes had moved beyond turning the other cheek. If there was going to be a viable vehicle of resistance to oppression, Newton and Bobby Seale "had no choice but to form an organization that would involve the lower-class."[3]

Cleaver, one of the more verbose and bombastic leaders of the party, took pride in the Panthers' lumpen character and stressed the significant role of the lumpenproletariat in revolutionary struggle. These lumpen-proletariat, explained Cleaver, "have no secure relationship or vested interest in the means of production and the institutions of capitalist society." They are those "who can't find a job; who are unskilled and unfit; who have been displaced by machines, automation, and cybernation."[4] There was a more sordid character to the lumpen, who also comprise "the so-called 'Criminal Element,' those who live by their wits, existing off that which they rip off, who stick guns in the faces of businessmen . . . Those who don't even want a job, who hate to work and can't relate to punching some pig's time clock, who would rather punch a pig in the mouth and rob him than punch that same pig's time clock and work for him, those whom Huey P. Newton calls 'the illegitimate capitalists.' In short, all those who simply have been locked out of the economy and robbed of their rightful social heritage."[5]

Despite the Panther's Marxist jargon, most Marxists have historically considered the lumpenproletariat suspect. Frederick Engels and Karl Marx referred to the lumpenproletariat as "the social scum, that passively rotting mass thrown off by the lowest layers of old society."[6] Engels warned that this class represents the "scum of the most depraved elements of all classes, which established headquarters in the big cities, [and] is the worst of all possible allies. This rabble is absolutely venal and absolutely brazen."[7] These dregs of society, to Marxists, were particularly open to fascist manipulation because they were the "refuse of all classes" and claimed no affinity or allegiance to a class or principles, beyond personal gratification.[8] Lenin had declared that true Marxism calls for a "dictatorship of the proletariat," not the unpredictable lumpen.[9] Yet, proudly claiming to be Marxist-Leninists, the Panthers asserted their right to develop and add their own effusive analysis of class struggle into the philosophical discussions of class, race, and oppression in the United States and the world.

Cleaver correctly pointed out that Marxism did not develop out of an understanding of the dynamics of race and class struggle in late-twentieth-century North America. "In the past," wrote Cleaver, "Marxist-Leninists in the United States have relied too heavily upon foreign, imported analyses and have seriously distorted the realities of the American scene."[10] It was incumbent on U.S. revolutionaries to break from the limitations of classical Marxism to develop new and relative theories that addressed the fundamental needs of people who were economically, politically, and socially marginalized in the United States. Huey Newton had done this. The minister of defense "gave the Black Panther Party a firm ideological foundation that frees us from ideological flunkeyism and opens up the path to the future."[11]

It was Newton and Seale's desire to attract the lumpen that drew Cleaver into the Black Panthers. Newton was attracted to Cleaver for his powerful writing at *Ramparts* magazine, but his prison record was, perhaps, his most attractive characteristic. Bobby Seale wrote that "Huey related to Eldridge as a Malcolm X, coming out of prison. Huey always respected the brothers that came out of prison. He felt that he could relate to dudes who came out of prison." In reference to Cleaver, Newton exclaimed, "This nigger from prison, this nigger is tired of shit."[12] It was this attraction to the lumpenproletariat that shaped the initial image of the Panthers.

Though the party was never monolithic in terms of class background, the first to join the Panthers were people who closely conformed to the lumpen ideal. Newton and Seale were from working-class backgrounds. Newton had been expelled from high school, engaged in burglaries, and arrested for assault by the time he was twenty. Influenced by black nationalism, he eventually finished high school and enrolled in Merritt College in Oakland, where he met Seale.[13] Newton took pride in having lumpen character and made attempts to attract people of similar background. For many, being a brother on the block evoked toughness and machismo. These very disempowered men in a patriarchal society found ways to affirm their manhood. Coolness was intrinsic to the hyper-male image pervasive among poor urban men. For some, this affirmation of maleness came in the form of an extra cool swagger when they walked. For others, it came in sexual virility. Settling disputes by affirming the stereotypical characteristics of men, like aggressive behavior, was also a feature with which Newton and Seale were familiar.[14] The brothers on the block also were more likely to have disrespect for the law. As mentioned above, Newton admired those who had done prison time. Being from poorer communities helped construct a popular image of the Panthers as more courageous and tougher than the privileged radicals who often formed cultural nationalist organizations. Undoubtedly, the party won more than a few recruits by exploiting its lumpen image.

Alprentice "Bunchy" Carter joined the Nation of Islam with Cleaver while they were incarcerated in San Quentin but left the NOI after Malcolm X's departure from the organization. Once released, Carter and Cleaver had plans to found either a chapter of Malcolm X's Organization of Afro-American Unity or a new nationalist organization. In 1967 Cleaver settled in the Bay area and began writing for *Ramparts;* Carter returned to Los Angeles and quickly connected with his former Slauson gang members.

Carter, a tall, charismatic former leader of one of the largest gangs in Los Angeles, enjoyed acquainting himself with the new political and cultural world of Los Angeles's Black Power scene. He gravitated to various nationalist functions, often alone or with friends who still had strong ties to street life. Carter approached an Us function in South Central and entered into an argument and fisticuffs with members whom he had formerly fought in street brawls. Though known as an able fighter, he did not fare well against the martial-arts-trained Simba Wachangas, the Us organization's quasi-military wing. Carter, the self-proclaimed "Mayor of the Ghetto," left the function and returned with friends. Another brawl erupted and guns were drawn on both sides. While no shots were fired, it was clear that the L.A. gang culture still provided a tense and deadly backdrop to street-level Black Power activities.[15] Soon thereafter, Carter joined the party as the Panthers' new deputy minister of information and extended his hostility for Us into local party politics. The enmity between the new Panther leadership in Los Angeles disrupted the affable relations between Us and the Panthers that Shermont L. Banks, the deputy minister of defense and former head of the chapter, had maintained. Banks and other Panthers attended college with Us members, and the two organizations even engaged in military training together. On February 18, 1968, Ron Karenga, founder of Us, had spoken at the Free Huey rally at the Los Angeles Sports Arena as an ally of the Panthers. Once he had supplanted Banks, Carter, with Cleaver's assistance, undermined the relationship with Us. The tensions between the organizations would ultimately destabilize both groups and reverberate throughout the black nationalist community for years.

Carter's arrival also exacerbated class tensions between middle-class Panthers and lumpen members like Cleaver, Carter, and his "wolves"—recruits from the Slausons gang who served as his enforcers.[16] Carter and others were also skeptical of the middle-class background of many Us members. Their denunciation of other groups' "pork chop nationalism" grew aggressive in 1968. Local Panthers were involved in numerous fights and confrontations in the area. The gangster posturing, coupled with cowboy antics of gun pulling and physical attacks, marred the Panther image for many.[17]

Within the party, Carter agreed with the Panthers' opinions of class despite his enrollment in the University of California at Los Angeles through its High Potential program. Elaine Brown, who worked closely with Carter, recalls that the party attracted the thug element and systematically reached out to it. "Nobody was talking to those people. The Panthers did."[18] Ideas about class consciousness, however, were often inexact and somewhat unconventional. As Charles E. Jones and Judson Jeffries point out, many, if not most, Panthers did not fit the traditional traits of the lumpen. Of the eleven members of the first Central Committee, the

party's primary decision-making body, only one, Eldridge Cleaver, could
be classified as lumpen. Newton and Seale were college students when
they founded the Black Panthers.[19] Further examination, however, reveals
that Panther members who had attended college were from working-class
or poor backgrounds. They were typically first-generation college students, some of whom, like Bunchy, Newton and many others, had criminal records, a strong identification with the streets, and an antipathy for
the "slick black bourgeoisie."

Moreover, the Panther definition of the lumpen was broader than the
traditional Marxist definition. Seale explains that the lumpen "was also
the Black Mother who had to scrub Miss Anne's kitchen floors."[20] Fundamentally, the lumpen was popularly understood to include the criminal
element and those on society's fringes, as well as the working poor. There
was also a clear valorization of toughness that Panthers saw as inherently
absent from the middle class, which had been "softened" by affluence.
Newton described the Black Panther Party of Northern California as "bourgeoisie armchair revolutionaries" who were reluctant to engage in substantive activity in the black community. These "cultural nationalists" were
suspect because they emphasized writing and reading, performed limited
community work, and came from middle-class backgrounds.[21] Newton
and others questioned the tenacity and commitment of these "Paper
Panthers," who "unlike Bobby and me, had not grown up on the block.
They were more privileged."[22] According to one former Oakland Panther,
a prospective member was struck upside the head during an interview
when it was suspected that he was a police agent. His offense: "He talks and
acts too bourgeois to be for real." Chairman Bobby, who prevented further
physical punishment, is remembered as saying "they are all the same:
middle-class bootlicking niggers who can't be trusted."[23]

In stark contrast to the "civilizing mission" of reform of most other
black nationalist organizations, the West Coast branches of the Black
Panther Party often tolerated rouge behavior, including theft, fighting,
and other activities. The civilizing mission was shunned in order to pander to what the Panthers considered the lumpen element. West Coast
Panthers drank hard, partied hard, fought hard, and worked hard. To be a
West Coast Panther was to have no reservations about cursing in public,
fighting, sharing bitter dog, and enjoying an occasional pork rib at a barbeque.[24] Despite the increasing hostility to pork found among nationalists, Panthers made no attempts to encourage modification of the African
American diet.[25] To the Panthers, the Maoist dictum to "swim with the
masses" justified Panther Party culture. The leadership's bias in favor of

lumpen members ensured that leadership (at least on the West Coast) remained in lumpen hands.

This glorification of the so-called lumpen was in direct contrast to the Nation of Islam, which also sought to identify with poor people. In fact, both organizations pulled from similar socioeconomic elements: poor and working-class young inner-city nonsoutherners. More than the Panthers, the Nation recruited from prisons and those entrenched in poverty. With recidivism among its members at virtually nil, the Nation took great pride in its ability to reform criminals and give hope to the poor. Members could not smoke, drink alcohol, gamble, or curse. Dietary restrictions promoted health-conscious living, and fornication was forbidden. The Nation correctly understood that criminality was not the practice of most poor people. Moreover, it tapped into the cultural traditions of African Americans who valued self-reliance, discipline, and hard work. The Nation was very clear in its moral code; however, there were infractions within the Nation. Though Elijah Muhammad had quietly fathered several children out of wedlock, other Muslims were excommunicated for adultery. Other penalties were levied against Muslims for being overweight or being caught using profanity or cigarettes. Such rigid behavioral codes, along with its spiritual foundation, helped strengthen the fabric of the NOI and its general operations, while lumpenism destabilized the Black Panthers.

As obstreperous behavior thrived on the West Coast, many other Panther chapters were much less tolerant of lumpenism, despite the motivations of the national leadership. In 1968, SNCC utilized its national resources to start Panther chapters. In some instances, SNCC chapters simply became affiliated with the Black Panther Party, and members were eventually absorbed, after a formal process. This happened in Chicago, for example, when SNCC leadership contacted Bob Brown, Henry English, and other local SNCC activists about the party. Under the leadership of Deputy Chairman Fred Hampton, the Illinois branch assiduously worked with gang members to end lumpen behavior. Hampton did not use drugs and frustrated the FBI when an informant complained that it was impossible to dig up dirt on the local leader.[26]

The national Panther leadership not only lionized lumpen activities, but it also attempted to regulate them. Point three of the party's "3 Main Rules of Discipline" directed members to "turn in everything captured from the attacking enemy." Newton noted that "many brothers who were burglarizing and participating in similar pursuits began to contribute weapons and material to community defense." It was easy for Panthers to rationalize that goods "liberated" from a capitalist enterprise were revolutionary contraband.[27] Lumpenism went beyond drinking and theft, of course.

Perhaps the most important attraction for the lumpen was the popular use of the gun. Newton and Seale firmly believed that brandishing weapons would help demonstrate that the party was a serious, committed, and, above all, brave organization with which to be reckoned. The gun was empowering; it was the great "equalizer," as the euphemism went. It helped level the playing field when racist police entered the black community. Newton explained that "only with the power of the gun can black people halt the terror and brutality perpetrated against them by the armed racist power structure."[28] The appeal to the lumpen worked. Whether the appeal was the result of machismo posturing, militaristic rhetoric, or strategic circumstance is unclear.

For the Panthers, prospective recruits who were willing to throw Molotov cocktails were naturally willing to be politically disciplined and taught how to use a gun properly in a revolutionary situation. Earlier, Newton and Seale had failed in using firearms to attract "street people" to the Soul Students Advisory Council. Under their leadership, however, the party promoted the gun as a conspicuous symbol of empowerment. They even published a brochure entitled "Organizing Self-Defense Groups," with detailed diagrams and illustrations on how to maintain various types of firearms. Newton wrote that "if the Black community has learned to respect anything, it has learned to respect the gun." According to the Panthers, the gun was their "basic tool of liberation."[29] For some, it became an extension of manhood itself.

Gender Politics

Elaine Brown, deputy minister of information, wrote "You're a man, you see and a man must be whatever he'll be or he won't be free . . . Well then, believe it my friend, that this silence will end. We'll just have to get guns and be men."[30] Here the mantra of manhood seems to transcend gender. Brown, a high-ranking woman in the Black Panther Party, had no problems using the term *man* to refer to all people. The thrust of her writing, however, is to recognize the intrinsic role that maleness plays in resistance movements. Her remarks also reflect what many have observed as the tendency to repress the voice of women in order to place race and class interests first. As Angela Davis remarked, "we said free the Black man because we did not know that we could free the black woman."[31] While the female voice was repressed in order emphasize race and class, it was clear that a salient element of the party's rhetoric equated resistance and manhood, implicitly relegating women into positions of weakness.

Gender dynamics in the BPP were neither static nor precise. As historian Tracye Matthews explains, "one must pay attention to internal conflict as well as agreement; overt as well as covert manifestations of this dialogue; change over time; diversity of individual experiences; internal as well as external influence."[32] Panther members came from a society where patriarchy was widely accepted. As the women's liberation movement gained momentum, feminist critique more bluntly affected Panther rhetoric. While Panthers rhetorically denounced male chauvinism, all members did not reform easily. Throughout the existence of the party, gender and sexism remained contested issues, from the leadership to the rank and file.

When recalling his father's courage and willingness to stand up to racists in Louisiana, Newton explained that his "stand as a strong protector" in the face of racial subjugation taught him a valuable lesson of resistance: "he was teaching us how to be men."[33] In this sentence, "us" included his six siblings, three of whom were sisters. Newton's understanding of resistance as a male quality is particularly noteworthy in his discussion of homosexuality in the California Penal Colony, where he was sent for killing Officer Frey in 1967. "Homosexuals," he wrote, "are docile and subservient." He noted that the prisoners' "sexuality was perverted into a pseudosexuality that was used to control and undermine their normal yearnings for dignity and freedom."[34] Fred Hampton, deputy chairman for the Illinois chapter, also embraced the commonly held association of weakness to femininity when he derided the African *bubas* of "Mamalama Karangatang Karenga" and stated that "if he's gonna continue wearing dashikis . . . he oughta stop wearin' pants. 'Cause he'd look a lot better in miniskirts. That's all a motherfuckin' man needs in Babylon that ain't got no gun, and that's a miniskirt."[35] Despite this remark that equated power and strength with masculinity and manhood, Hampton expressed criticism of the rigid patriarchy of the Us organization: "You think we scared of a few karangatangs, a few chumps, a few male chauvinists? They tell their women 'walk behind me.' The only reason a woman should walk behind a faggot like that is so she can put her foot knee deep in his ass."[36]

The homophobic references are clear. One could not be a true revolutionary and be gay at the same time. There is also a very palpable affirmation of manliness that praised courage, bravery, and militancy. Machismo notwithstanding, the Panthers were not classical patriarchs. As Hampton's statement suggested, the Panthers did not relegate women to cooking and

cleaning while the men took care of "manly" work such as political theo-
rizing and gun practice.[37] Too, as the Party evolved ideologically, it challenged its own sexist and homophobic tendencies.

Though numerous factors influenced the manner in which Panthers
addressed sexism and homophobia, a significant amount of direction came
from Panther leadership, particularly Huey Newton. In 1969 French writer
Jean Genet arrived in the United States to interview members of the Black
Panther Party. Genet, who was gay, was hurt by the relatively common
usage of homophobic language he heard among Panthers. In an audio tape
sent to Newton, Genet expressed his dismay and asked the minister of
defense, "How would you feel being called a 'nigger'? How do you think I
feel hearing these words?" Newton was affected by Genet's message.[38]

In August 1970 Huey Newton reevaluated his interpretation of homosexuality, insisting that the black liberation struggle could be strengthened with an alliance with the Gay Liberation movement. "We must gain
security in ourselves and therefore have respect and feelings for all
oppressed people."[39] Arguing that liberation of women and homosexuals
is intrinsic to the liberation of all oppressed people, he argued "we should
be willing to discuss the insecurities that many people have about homosexuality. When I say 'insecurities,' I mean the fear that they are some
kind of threat to our manhood." Manhood, Newton observed, does not
rest on the ability to oppress people. "We want to hit a homosexual in the
mouth because we are afraid that we might be homosexual; and we want
to hit the woman or shut her up because we are afraid that she might cas-
trate us, or take the nuts that we might not have to start with."[40] Sensitive
to the emerging women's and gay liberation movements, Newton stressed
that these movements "are our friends."[41] Similarly, Eldridge Cleaver
insisted that the Panthers have an obligation to be "the vanguard also in
the area of women's liberation, and set an example in that area." Black
women, he continued, "have a duty and the right to do whatever they
want to do in order to see to it that they are not relegated to an inferior
position."[42] Cleaver explained to men that their freedom could not be
achieved at the expense of women's liberation. "The women are our half.
They're not our weaker half; they're not our stronger half. They are our
other half." Several articles written by women Panthers appeared in the
Black Panther extolling Cleaver's position, while calling recalcitrant male
members to task.[43] This progress, however, cannot overlook bouts Huey
Newton and others fought with sexism even as the party moved into
alliances with feminists.[44] Clearly, the Panthers were not ideologically static or monolithic chauvinists. Many former members are quick to explain

the prominence of certain Panther women and, in at least one chapter, an openly gay Panther.

In the Jamaica Queens, New York, branch an openly gay member operated without obstruction. One Panther explains that "he was truly committed; people knew that." Despite his commitment, not all comrades were pleased. A Panther relatively new to the chapter confronted the gay member with pejorative remarks at the office, and a fistfight broke out between the two. The offending Panther was soundly beaten, and it was the last time that homophobic remarks were made at the office.[45] That a gay member physically conquered the other comrade must have been a shock for some and an affirmation that manliness could not be defined in limited terms of pugilistic skill or sexuality. By extension, the rejection of traditional notions of gender affected how women were treated in the party.

Some former Panthers, men and women alike, emphatically recount that women were in prominent positions of authority when they arrived in Oakland in 1972 to work on the election campaigns of Bobby Seale and Elaine Brown. Ericka Huggins explains that "women ran the Party and men thought they did." Women such as Elaine Brown and Ericka Huggins had college experience and skills that were helpful for daily operations. In the Los Angeles chapter not only were men and women equally engaged in cooking food and feeding children, women were involved in all but one shoot-out with the police. Joan Kelly-Williams, a former member, insists that "at least in the L.A. chapter, women were seen as equals."[46]

Elaine Brown talks about her bouts with sexism within the ranks of the party in her autobiography, *A Taste of Power*, where she describes the recalcitrant men whom she was empowered to lead. This sexism was not, however, unchallenged by women and men. In 1968–69 a group of four L.A.-based Panther women formed "the clique," which served as an informal group to address sexism. Around the same time, Huey Newton read Shere Hite's seminal study of female sexuality, *The Hite Report*. Astounded by the book's analysis, Newton directed Panthers to include the book in its political education readings. The book was important in shifting Newton's and others' views on women and patriarchy. Though it was not until 1970 that Newton endorsed the women's liberation movement, Panthers had already officially denounced patriarchy and openly advocated equality within their ranks.

Many women admired the authority that they held inside the party. Connie Matthews, field marshal; Kathleen Cleaver, communications secretary; and Lauren Watson, deputy chairman of the Colorado branch, were very visible. In 1974 Elaine Brown was named chairman and acting head of the Black Panther Party when Newton fled to Cuba to avoid criminal charges stemming from the death of a prostitute and the assault on a tailor. Brown made significant strides promoting women into high-ranking positions within the BPP, but the organization had been making strides long before Brown's assumption as head.

In 1968 the party adopted the eight points of attention for all Panthers. One of the points that rebuked "tak[ing] liberties with women" was hailed by former Panther Safiya Bukhari-Alston as a "monumental step forward in addressing the issue of the treatment of women." Bukhari-Alston correctly notes that the Panthers were born in a sexist society and not above its predilections, but "the simple fact that the issue was placed in/on the books was a step forward. Now we had to make it a part of our everyday lives, the everyday lives of the lumpen who were the majority element of the Black Panther Party."[47] Elaine Brown echoes this perspective when she asks, "Did these brothers drop from 'revolutionary heaven'? Of course not. We were working through issues [like sexism]."[48]

Clearly there were cases of sexual abuse of women, as Brown mentions in her autobiography, but some Panthers argue that the experiences of West Coast Panthers (such as Brown) were not the norm for the country. Akua Njeri, member of the Chicago branch, recalls that she did not feel marginalized as a Panther. "Men did not try to take advantage of sisters in our chapter. We had respect. Men and women both cleaned and cooked for the children. We also trained together. We were all Panthers."[49] Lee Lew-Lee, a member of the Harlem branch, insists that a woman, Afeni Shakur, "basically led the chapter after the Panther-21 trial [in which twenty-one Panthers were charged with conspiracy to blow up police precincts but were later acquitted]. Women and men worked together without the very rampant type of sexism that was found on the West Coast."[50]

Despite the relative prominence of some Panther women and tolerance that many enjoyed, the party was not free of sexism or patriarchy. Most leaders were men, although women made up over half of Panther membership.[51] Even prominent women such as Kathleen Cleaver experienced macho recalcitrance from their male peers. Ericka Huggins, a celebrated national figure within the party, recalled that "there were men who thought that women were to be slept with. I dealt with male chauvinism." Clearly, women experienced similar sexual encounters outside the party, in places of employment and even churches. This did not, however, excuse abusive actions in the BPP. Elaine Brown and others were not unfamiliar with sexism before they joined the party, but the macho obstinacy from some underlings who had difficultly taking orders from women remained a difficult experience. Former minister of culture Emory Douglas explains that these men had no choice. Rules were rules. They either followed the rules or left the organization.[52]

Although sexism was ubiquitous in America, the lionization of lumpen behavior encouraged sexism to thrive where it could have been more effectively challenged. At the height of the party's popularity between 1969 and 1970, the organization was besieged by state and federal agents sent to disrupt the organization. Some estimates hold that as many as a third of the Panthers were in some way illegitimate—agents provocateurs, informants, or infiltrators. William O'Neal, an agent provocateur in the Chicago chapter, once tied a visiting Panther to a chair and beat him. One can extrapolate and assume that agents were also capable of rogue activities against women. In the end, all influences must be considered, but there is no doubt that legitimate Panthers may have engaged in misogynistic behavior.

Despite myopic approaches that tend to fixate on the BPP as a bastion of sexism, the party made systematic challenges to patriarchy that were rare for its time. The Panther party was the first major black organization to publicly endorse the women's and gay liberation movements. While the major religious organizations of Christians, Jews, and Muslims advocated very rigid patriarchy, women ascended to major positions in the Black Panther Party. They shaped the party in important ways. They led chapters, edited the newspaper, wrote articles, defended offices from police attack, and fed thousands of impoverished children across the country, as had their male counterparts. Kathleen Cleaver, former communications secretary for the party, argues that the narrow focus given to sexism in the party "deflects attention from confronting the revolutionary critique our organization made of the larger society, and turns it inward to look at what type of dynamics and social conflicts characterized the organization." This line of inquiry, she explains, avoids the more important question: "How do you empower an oppressed and impoverished people who are struggling against racism, militarism, terrorism, and sexism, too?"[53]

Ultimately, the Black Panther Party reflected the gender politics of the misogynistic society out of which it emerged. Still, the party was able to address the debilitating effects of sexism in ways that most mainstream—or radical—organizations did not. The Panthers challenged themselves to transcend patriarchy and homophobia in ways the NAACP, Urban League, or the Republican or Democratic parties did not. Kathleen Cleaver asks, "Did the U.S. Congress make any statement on the liberation of women? Did the Oakland police issue a position against gender discrimination?"[54] Though sexism was not unknown to the party, Elaine Brown insists, the Panthers were "absolutely less sexist than society at large."[55] However, they were struggling and working their way around sexism without any significant organizational model. Taken in this context, the strides of Panthers, most of whom were under twenty-five, are particularly remarkable.

Language of the Lumpen

The Panthers were careful in their construction of language to attract lumpen brothers (and sisters) on the block during the first four years of the party's development. The toughness and rough edges of many street people had its obvious manifestations in lumpen vernacular. Many of the Panthers made an art of "revolutionary" speak. Unlike earlier black nationalist organizations like the NOI, many prominent Panthers had no problem using vulgarities in public. It was their belief that they could more effectively speak to the lumpen with colloquialisms that they were used to. In discussing class struggle, Bobby Seale in 1969 warned all "opportunists . . . [and] diseased mother fuckers [that] we will not stop until we have destroyed . . . capitalism."[56] Clearly, Seale and other Panthers believed that utilizing profanity accentuated their speeches.

The very charismatic and popular deputy chairman in Chicago, Fred Hampton, explained that profanity in the Panther's language was an effective way to relate to the people who would otherwise not relate to the message. The former prelaw major stated

> they say Marxist-Leninists . . . don't curse. This is something we got from the slavemasters. We know niggers invented the word mother-fucker. We wasn't fuckin' nobody's mother. It was the master fuckin' people's mothers. We invented the word, you dig? We relate to that. We Marxist-Leninist niggers, and we some Marxist-Leninist cussin' niggers. And we gonna continue to cuss, goddammit. 'Cause that's what we relate to. That's objective reality. Don't nobody be walkin' around in Babylon spouting out at the mouth about a whole lot of academic bullshit, intellectually masturbating, catching diarrhea of the mouth. We say to those motherfuckers if you want to catch a mouth disease, you come and talk that shit in a community where the Panthers are at, and you'll get a mouth disease alright.[57]

While Hampton and others may have been relatively successful using profanity to attract certain people (not just lumpen, of course), into the party, there was not universal tolerance for such language. In November 1969, Chief of Staff David Hilliard, spoke at a San Francisco rally against the Vietnam War. The crowd was estimated at over two hundred thousand, many waving American flags. Hilliard felt uneasy with his audience but made a harsh verbal assault on "American fascist society," and "Richard Milhous Nixon, the motherfucker." Many in the audience started to boo him. This angered Hilliard. "Later for all the people out here who don't want to hear me curse; that's all that I know to do." In anger and desperation, he said, "Fuck that motherfucking man! We will kill Richard Nixon."[58] He was later arrested for threatening the president's life.

Newton warned Hilliard before the rally to avoid profanity because "dirty language alienates us from the community."[59] Such traditions died hard. Despite Newton's public rebuke of profanity, many Panthers continued to use it, most notably Eldridge Cleaver, who enjoyed rallying crowds around the chant "Fuck Ronald Reagan!" To Newton, such language, along with the glorification of violence and the gun, resulted in a "defection" from the black community. Cleaver's use of profanity, Newton explained, "spread like a cancer in our Party and suddenly, we were divorced from the Black community and we found ourselves embraced in the arms of white radicals."[60]

The popular use of profanity deviated from all major black organizations. The Panther's promotion of the gun as the most important tool of political struggle also alienated many from the "People's Party," Newton believed. He explained that the use of the gun was initially important to imbue black people with confidence and courage. "The emphasis on weapons was a necessary phase in our evolution, based on Frantz Fanon's contention that the people have to be shown that the colonizers and their agents—the police—are not bulletproof."[61] Despite the profanity and glorification of the gun, and perhaps in part because of them, the Party found many members during its early stages of development.

In the early days of the party, lumpen members were the norm. Elaine Brown insists that, "most of us come from [the lumpen]."[62] Earl Anthony who joined the BPP in the spring of 1967 was one of the few middle-class members of the organization, which was dominated by men from the ghettoes who were often high school dropouts.[63] Anthony, a graduate of the University of Southern California and a law student at Golden Gate College of Law in San Francisco, was involved with the Black House in that same city. The Black House served as the meeting place for black nationalists in the Bay area, including the Black Panther Party of Northern California. In February 1967, while providing security for Betty Shabazz, widow of Malcolm X, the Newton and Seale-led Panthers, with guns drawn, faced down police during a confrontation. The courage and bold display of militancy made other nationalist groups feel "upstaged," Anthony noted, but it inspired Anthony and Eldridge Cleaver to join.[64]

Emory Douglas, a student at San Francisco State College who was also involved with the Black House, joined the party soon after the Shabazz event. Douglas explains that Seale and Newton were "very serious, articulate and responsible" and that "no organization addressed police brutality [as the BPP did]."[65] In the cases of Anthony and Douglas, the audacious will to defy a brutal extension of the racist establishment attracted them to the party. Anthony noted that his middle-class status had little effect on his desire to resist oppression and police brutality. Despite the appeal of the party to some middle-class blacks in its formative stage, most early recruits were "hardcore," Douglas states. They were pulled from "the gangsters and hustlers of the community" because the party was in direct contact with the poorest elements of the black communities of the Bay area.[66] Even as the organization spread nationwide, the average recruits tended to be street toughs who became politicized by the Black Power movement's ubiquitous influences.

Omar Barbour, who joined the Jamaica Queens branch in early 1968 explains that he and other street toughs, who were not active participants in the black liberation struggle, admired the militant fashion statement of the Panther uniform. The styles were popularly perceived as militant chic and made one appear cool, brave, and strong. Involved in petty crimes while a teenager, Barbour dropped out of high school and became a hustler. Influenced by Malcolm X and the Nation of Islam, he gravitated to black nationalism and enrolled in Harlem Preparatory High School but was not convinced to politically organize until police officers broke up a house party he attended. The officers, calling the people at the party "niggers" and "ninnies," beat a few partygoers and became particularly hostile when they saw him. Noticing his black beret, leather jacket, and sunglasses, they manhandled him, threatened him and dared him yelling "Call me a pig! Call me a pig!"[67] Shaken and disturbed by the brutality, Barbour eagerly joined the organization that, more than any other, challenged what he and his friends considered a "brutal occupying army." Most members of the New York branch had been toughened on the street; however, there were many middle-class members who were just as passionate and dedicated, such as Shirley Booth, the daughter of a prominent judge in the area, who was an active member of the Jamaica branch.[68] Similar stories resonate from other chapters.

Philadelphia had one of the most active branches in the country. In fact, it had two offices, one in North Philadelphia and the other in West Philadelphia. Bobby McCall, who joined the Philadelphia branch in July 1970, was a former Morocco gang member in the city. Like most other Panthers, the Nation of Islam provided him with an early introduction to black nationalist consciousness. Though he read *Muhammad Speaks,* he was not a religious person and could not come to see all whites as demonic. He was, however, increasingly desirous of political involvement. The NAACP, Urban League, or SNCC were not options.

The local Black Panther Party office impressed McCall with its community service efforts. The new father who was working to take care of his baby particularly admired the door-to-door free milk program for children. However, he was not inspired to join the party until the infamous raid of June 28, 1970, when scores of police officers, perched on rooftops and equipped with high-powered arms, attacked the North Philadelphia Panther office. The surrendering Panthers—men and women—were marched outside and forced to strip naked on the sidewalk. A photograph of the nude women and men appeared on the cover of the city's *Daily News,* causing uproar in the black community. "Black people were livid," explains McCall. He was so disgusted that he joined the Panthers the following day.[69]

The Philadelphia branch, McCall notes, was filled with "ghetto niggas. We were soldiers." Wearing combat boots and fatigues, they maximized their militant image. They also had one of the largest free breakfast programs in the country. They gave away ten thousand bags of groceries to poor families and each member sold a hundred copies of the *Black Panther* each day. When a local gang threatened McCall as he participated in a free breakfast program in the local housing project, a young gang member recognized him as a Panther and warned the others not to molest him because "he feeds us everyday."[70] Such cases created the party's popular image among the lumpen and brought them into the organization. The transition was smooth for many but rough for those unwilling to accept the discipline, tedious work, and constant threat of arrest or death.

Steve McCutchen, who joined the Baltimore branch in late 1968, was a college student at Morgan State University. Influenced by *Muhammad Speaks* and the Black Power movement, McCutchen was not willing to support the war in Vietnam and considered the Black Panther Party as a political alternative. Unlike most branches, the Baltimore Panthers experienced difficulty recruiting from the lumpen. The first office, at 1209 Eden Street, was located in a middle-class community. They had to go about five blocks into poorer sections to recruit. Even then, there was resistance when dealing with much of the political terminology. High school students, however, were more receptive. There were also large numbers of working-class and middle-class members who spent considerable time with the party's survival programs, such as the liberation school and free lunch, breakfast, and clothing programs.[71]

The rapid growth of the Black Panther Party was fundamentally a result of the pervasive nature of the Black Power movement and its manifestations in popular culture and widespread activism. To be "black" was a beautiful thing for the first time in African American popular culture. This new black consciousness found its way into the world of African Americans via Afro hairstyles, African clothes, and politically and socially conscious music, which provided a vast backdrop for the cultural experience of black America. The black press and, more specifically, advertisements in the black press provide considerable insight into the ubiquity of black cultural nationalism in this period. Advertisements for skin-whitener nearly disappeared, while products from cosmetics to underwear exploited Black Power iconography. While these cultural and political phenomena inspired many to join or support Black Power organizations, the Panthers were not uncritical of the black consciousness movement. In fact, the party offered biting criticism of much of the cultural nationalism that swept America in the late 1960s.

Music

One of the most pervasive influences of the Black Power movement was the popular music of the era. Rhythm and blues, long the name for the type of music produced by artists such as James Brown, Sam Cooke, and Ike Turner, gained a new name by the mid-1960s—soul music. Soul was a very common, somewhat generic, term for phenomena that reflected the unique qualities of "blackness." For many black artists, its overtly black style safeguarded it against white cooption, unlike jazz and rock and roll. Indeed, the term was synonymous with blackness in that it reflected the new black mood of resistance and self-determination that pervaded black communities after 1966. Still, soul musicians were not universally political or explicit proponents of black nationalism, Black Power, or revolution. In fact, not all soul artists were black. Many were, however, active players in the cultivation and promotion of ideas and culture that complemented the Black Power movement.[72] Moreover, these artists necessarily served as auxiliaries to the efforts of radical organizations such as the BPP. The party was aware of this influence and was cautious about criticizing or praising this form of black popular culture. Socially conscious music reflected and even encouraged political agitation, but the music revealed a strong cultural nationalist bent that was, to the Panthers, ultimately inept. Finding a fine balance of association, encouragement, and critical analysis was important for the party. It did not want to alienate itself from the cultural world of black people, nor did it want to capitulate to the "innocuous" cultural nationalism that suffused black popular music.

Many Black Power organizations considered music an essential complement to the black freedom struggle. From the Us organization to the Panthers, music proved an important outlet of political expression. Black popular music provided a sonic backdrop to the efforts of the new militants who had made a psychic break from the church-based song generally associated with the civil rights movement. For black nationalists, the old Negro spirituals were antiquated rituals of a more passive and inefficacious struggle. The new militancy required a new and relevant sound. Few groups were as celebrated for their militancy as the Last Poets.

The Last Poets, a group of New York–based musicians who delivered rhythmic poetry over African drumbeats, emerged in 1968. Their dashikis and Arabic and African names were reflective of cultural nationalist influence; however, the Poets were not short of scathing political observations and analysis. Like the Black Panthers, they expressed a strong identification with the people and the lumpen in particular. In "Niggers Are Afraid of Revolution" the Poets criticize black people for being proponents of their own despair by gambling, trivial concerns, and frivolous behavior. "Niggas," laments a Poet, "are scared of revolution," but in spite of their faults, "niggas are me."[73]

Of the Last Poets' Panther-like identification with the "brothers [and sisters] on the block," member Alifia Pudim stated that the poetry in their music "is a reflection of the conflicts involved in the different nigger lifestyles, the possibilities, the potentials, the drudgery. I'm from the street, so I don't see how my poetry could come from anywhere else."[74] Of the song "Bird's Word," a catalog of black blues and jazz musicians, Pudim explains that it "praises the recognition for blacks who preserved the nigger sub-culture, while the nigger was going around trying to be other people."[75] It is unclear if the Last Poets' romantic look at the cultural world of the lumpenproletariat is a direct influence of the Black Panther Party. That members of the group admired the Black Panthers is certain.

The Poets emerged when the Panthers were visible and very active in New York City. Local Panthers were very loyal fans. Abiodun Oyewole, of the group, explains that, "They loved us, we loved them." In fact, one Panther, Zayd Shakur, was Oyewole's personal bodyguard.[76] Poet Umar Bin Hassan remarks that Huey Newton, Bobby Seale, and Malcolm X made up his "hall of fame." His admiration for the Panthers came from the party's application of Malcolm X's ideas of black self-defense against racist attack. Moreover, it was the "street element" that appealed to Hassan. The lumpen, Hassan insists, "had to be there, for the heart and for the guts and for the courage to do and attempt to do what these brothers did. No educated bourgeois *Negro* would have thought or even begun to think to do what these brothers did."[77] While the Last Poets agreed with the party's understanding and analysis of the poorest segments of the urban black community, they did not, of course, reflect the Panthers ideology in toto. The race-based analysis of black liberation, for example, was a departure from the party's class analysis. Of course, all soul music that reflected black nationalist influence did not vilify whites, as did some Last Poets songs. Many artists, such as James Brown and the Impressions, praised black people without mentioning whites to any significant degree.

James Brown's 1968 hit "Say It Loud (I'm Black and I'm Proud)" became an anthem of sorts for the burgeoning cultural nationalist movement. "Say it loud," roared the Godfather of Soul, "I'm black and I'm proud." Brown, during this period, abandoned his conked, chemically straightened hair, which most male R&B singers sported before the mid-1960s. His Afro and pro-black songs were a palpable reflection of the spirit of the time and the influence of the Black Power movement on black popular culture. This rise in black consciousness in black popular culture affected many, including some who would eventually join the Black Power organizations.

Michael Zinzun was in prison when the Black Panther Party was founded in 1966. He explains that he was inculcated with self-hatred and disrespect for black people, like most other blacks of the era. It was the Black Power movement and its influence on popular culture that particularly affected him, raising his political, cultural, and social consciousness. "There was," he notes "a feeling of change in the air. Jimi Hendrix, the best jazz musicians and various other artists were singing about change."[78] The black consciousness in music, he remarks, helped inspire his lifelong commitment to social justice. In 1969, two years after his release from prison, Zinzun gravitated to the Black Panther Party in Los Angeles as a community activist.

In some cases people criticized artists for not being connected to the larger political discourse of Black Power. After scathing comments that

Motown Records was insensitive to the black freedom struggle, the label's founder, Berry Gordy, started Black Forum, which released speeches from black leaders like Martin Luther King Jr., Stokely Carmichael, Amiri Baraka, and Elaine Brown. Brown was also a singer, and Motown even released an album of her songs. After eight LPs with dismal sales, Gordy closed Black Forum, but the label's mainstream releases had begun to reflect the impulse of the era's politics. From Edwin Starr's hit "War" to the Temptations' "Ball of Confusion (That's What the World Is Today)," social criticism on the Motown label softened the resistance that Gordy made to Marvin Gaye's seminal album of social commentary, *What's Going On* (1971).

Many groups reflected the type of evolution at Motown. The Isley Brothers, who had released *This Heart of Mine* (1966) with a white couple on the cover, delved into the new celebration of soul by 1969. All members replaced processed hair with natural and sang "Soul on the Rocks" to enthusiastic black crowds nationwide. Soul music was not alone in the celebration of the black aesthetic and black power iconography. Tenor sax jazz composer Rusty Bryant's *Soul Liberation* was released with a green, black, and red cover in 1970. In 1973 jazz performer Donald Byrd's *Black Byrd* similarly used the nationalist tri-color for an album cover. James Mtume, an early member of the Us organization, worked with the Herbie Hancock Sextet; and the jazz group offered artistic homage to the spiritual doctrine of Us with *Kawaida* in 1969. In 1971 The East Records released *Alkebulan,* an LP developed by the Mtume Umoja Ensemble.[79] Members of the Art Ensemble of Chicago often performed jazz in African attire. Famous jazz composer Archie Shepp wrote songs inspired by the assassinations of Medgar Evers and Malcolm X. Jazz artists, like their counterparts in soul, celebrated the new "black mood." They donned Afros and were generally photographed with serious and stoic visages—a clear departure from the grinning, happy minstrel stereotype many black artists felt was their antithesis.

Viewing art as a function of politics, musicians increasingly politicized their songs as extensions of black power. The Impressions typified general sentiment when Curtis Mayfield explained that "we couldn't get out and march, but we could inspire [black people]."[80] Black musicians made their point that they did not create music for the entertainment of whites. Their art was black art for, by, and about black people. If whites liked it, it was on black terms. It was, in effect, Black Power in music. In 1970 the Chi-Lites, a Chicago-based group, echoed the Black Panther Party when it released "(For God's Sake) Give More Power to the People." Many Panthers recognized their influence on popular music.

Despite these racially affirming songs and their influence on raising the political and cultural consciousness of the people, many in the Black Panther Party found such pro-black rhetoric fundamentally weak. Linda Harrison, a Black Panther in Oakland, warned readers of the threat of cultural nationalism that can be "summed up in James Brown's words—"I'm Black and I'm Proud." Harrison wrote that, "those who believe in the 'I'm Black and Proud' theory believe that there is a dignity inherent in wearing naturals; that a *buba* makes a slave a man; and that a common language— Swahili—makes all of us brothers." In reality, the oppressive "power structure . . . condones and even worships this new pride which it uses to sell every product under the sun. It worships and condones anything that is harmless and presents no challenge to the existing order."[81] Yet the Panthers were not absolute in their critique of black popular music. In 1969 the party had begun promoting the Lumpen, the Freedom Messengers, and the Vanguard, groups of Panther musicians and singers who produced soul and R&B. The *Black Panther* newspaper offered prominent advertisements for the groups' LPs. They performed at rallies and various functions to the delight of many who were ardent fans of black popular music. In-house groups were not the only ones to get favorable coverage in the *Black Panther.*

Minister of Education George Murray extolled the Impressions and their song "We're a Winner." The pro-black qualities of "We're a Winner" were appreciated by large segments of the Black Power movement and feared by some in the white media, many of whom refused to play the song on radio stations in fear that it would foment rebellion among blacks.[82] The song's call for resistance and its optimistic look at the black struggle was a positive part of revolutionary culture, Murray explained.[83] In his assessment of black popular music published in the *Black Panther* in February 1969, Murray declared that black music must be beholden to the welfare of the people. It should reflect the desire of the people to be free. In doing so, it will provide a necessary element for cultivating the "revolutionary culture" the struggle against oppression demanded. "Our music, rhythm and blues, jazz, spiritual music, must burst the eardrums of the whites who dare to listen to it. Eddie Harris plays a side called 'Listen Here,' where you hear actual screams, coming from a Black Saxophone. Those are the battle cries of mad, crazy black men, and the screams are coming from the honkey's throat as he and his wife are strangled to death, and robbed, looted, then set afire, for a change."[84]

Murray was departing from the class-based rhetoric of Newton, Cleaver, and Seale. A revolutionary culture, according to him, is "by definition antiwhite, anti-capitalist [and] anti-imperialist."[85] The official party line, however, was centered on a class-based struggle that considered racism secondary to the struggle against capitalist oppression. Cleaver wrote that the struggle against oppression in the United States must be seen as a struggle that transcends race.[86] A multiracial struggle, by nature, is stronger than one that is not, he argued. Race, he declared, was a subterfuge created by the ruling class to divide and oppress the people—whites and people of color. Despite the rhetoric of many cultural nationalists and others in the Black Power movement, the drama of revolutionary struggle among whites and blacks is played out on the same stage: "Because at the top opposed to both black people and white revolutionaries is a single ruling class; there's not a ruling class for blacks and a ruling class for whites, but there's one single class that rules all, that has a different set of tactics for each group, depending upon the tactics used by the groups, in the struggle for liberation."[87]

Most Panthers agreed that race was a tool the ruling class used to foster division among the oppressed masses of all races. The emphasis on cultural nationalism, they noted, was a distraction from the more serious problems with the fundamental political and economic order of the United States. Linda Harrison explained that "in all cases cultural nationalism—in the midst of struggle, seeks to create a racist ideology. To be racist in America is certainly justified, but it is a handicapped position to take as a revolutionary."[88] This position fundamentally agreed with the opinion of the largest segments of black America, although, of course, most were not revolutionaries. Still, there remained a vocal minority in black America who did not trust whites and had little faith in the ability of whites to transcend the racist culture in which they were reared. Some of these, like Murray, were party members.

Murray's article on music, culture, and revolution was published a month after members of the Us organization killed Panthers Bunchy Carter and John Huggins in January 1969. The January 25 and February 2, 1969, editions of the *Black Panther* were full of anti–cultural nationalist writings, which accused these nationalists, Us in particular, of being "black racists" for their rhetoric against whites and "pork chop nationalists"—extensions of the pig.[89] The newspaper even reproduced a *Wall Street Journal* article on Ron Karenga, Us leader, which discussed Karenga's "secret" meetings (not actually secret) with California governor Ronald Reagan, Los Angeles police chief Thomas Reddin, and other city officials. With evidence of this kind of collaboration, the party declared, cultural nationalism could not be a threat to the power structure. Murray's writing on black popular music, however, ran contrary to the party line.

Murray's advocating of race-based struggle reflects a particular loose-
ness in the party's ideological framework or, at least, the lack of a clearly
stated ideological framework to which all members adhered. This less-
than-strict adherence to ideological unity characterized the early and
rapid growth of the party during its second stage of revolutionary nationalism, 1968–70. Throughout its existence, however, the language of the
party leadership consistently projected certain staple beliefs, including its
disdain for cultural nationalism and its affinity to the people.

The ideological variations among Panthers are most apparent in the
national discourse regarding cultural nationalism. The national Party
leadership ridiculed and derided African names, clothes, and "race first"
rhetoric. Ironically, these cultural phenomena were becoming increasing
popular in black popular culture. As the burgeoning cultural nationalist
movement swept black America, the "People's Party" increasingly found
itself justifying its anti–cultural nationalist positions. Music was but one
facet of this cultural nationalist movement. Fashion was unequivocally its
most visible manifestation.

Fashion

In the late 1960s, when the Black Power movement was in full swing, its
influence was widespread in black popular culture, particularly among the
young. Fashion was significantly affected by the spread of black consciousness during this period. "Black is beautiful" became a ubiquitous
slogan. To the Panthers, the words represented an attempt to undermine
the more threatening revolutionary nationalism that tried to mobilize the
oppressed to challenge the political, social, and economic order of the
United States. While party members admired and saw value in the promotion and popularity of black culture, they believed that the new cultural
awareness was problematic.

The popularity of African bubas or dashikis did not reflect the radicalism the Black Panthers thought should characterize the movement against
oppression. Panthers across the nation derided the African attire worn by
many black people. Fred Hampton criticized the cultural nationalist who
"runs around here tellin' you that when your hair's long and you got a
dashiki on, and you got bubas and all these sandals, and all this type of
action, then you're a revolutionary, and anybody that doesn't look like
you, he's not; that man has to be out of his mind."[90] The real threat to the
power structure, explained Hampton, comes not from African attire but
from careful mobilization, political education, and revolutionary action of

the armed masses. This, he insisted, was the party's agenda. The cultural nationalists' attempt to forge a cultural revolution dedicated to "the creation, recreation and the circulation of black culture" was the act of people who were not seriously dedicated to the difficult struggle of liberation.[91] The proof was in the level of state repression experienced by the Panthers in comparison to the cultural nationalists. Hampton implored his listeners to "Check the people [who] are wearing dashikis and bubas and think that that's going to free them. Check all of these people, find out where they are located, find out the addresses of their office, write them a letter and ask them in the last year how many times has their office been attacked. And then write the Black Panther Party, anywhere in the United States of America . . . and ask them how many times the pigs have attacked them. That's when you figure out what the pigs don't like."[92]

As the Black Power movement crested in the early 1970s, African attire had transcended the community of organized black nationalists and become mainstream in black America. Cultural nationalists were not the only ones adorning dashikis. Between 1970 and 1974 *Ebony,* the leading African American magazine, ran several articles on African-inspired clothing.[93] This was a major departure from the traditional Western styles Fashion Fair had featured since the early 1960s. Some ads even depicted women on the floor near men's legs, in a stark visual affirmation of female subordination.[94]

Clothiers were not alone in utilizing African fashions in advertisement. Many advertisements capitalized on cultural nationalism to sell products, including cigarettes and liquor. It was this type of marketing savvy that evoked the Black Panthers' vitriol. This co-optation of the black consciousness movement by big businesses, often white-owned, countered the Black Power movement's fundamental thrust, reflecting what philosopher Herbert Marcuse described as the system's ability to reinvent, reorder, and morph itself by absorbing and co-opting tools of dissent.[95] The Panthers, however, often viewed this capitalist manipulation as a reflection of cultural nationalism's inherent frailties. "National black consciousness spread like an epidemic," noted an article in the *Black Panther,* "with it appeared the avaricious kook profiteer, the cultural nigger nationalist draped in a dashiki, sandals and other cultural paraphernalia and speaking ooga booga." While this movement may have helped beautify black America, "certain practitioners have brought ugliness to its very existence." These buba-wearers were little more than "opportunistic cultural practitioners [operating] as front men" to "further exploit" black people and impede real "revolutionary struggle." These "nigger pseudo-intellectual fools misled black people because they base black legitimacy around appearance and heavy lip-service."[96]

Despite condemnation of African clothing in the *Black Panther* newspaper and in speeches made by national leaders, local Panthers, particularly those in New York, were known for wearing dashikis and adopting African names. Many in New York were influenced by the long tradition of black nationalism in the city. The speeches of Malcolm X, who was critical of blacks with European names, as well as the nationalist efforts of the Yoruba Temple, Carlos Cook, and the African Nationalist Pioneer Movement, influenced local Panthers. Cultural nationalism was so popular among New York Panthers that West Coast Panthers complained of not being able to pronounce their African names.[97]

African-inspired clothes gained great popularity in the late 1960s and early 1970s, but the Panther Party was itself responsible for a significant feature of revolutionary chic. The Panther uniform included a black leather jacket, powder blue shirt, black pants and shoes, and a black beret. Except for the beret, militants already wore much of the uniform. Inspired by a film on the French resistance during World War II, Newton and Seale adopted the beret soon after the party's founding in 1966. The beret signified paramilitary action and serious militancy. By 1968 the Black Panther Party had national and international name recognition. The Free Huey movement, initiated in the fall of 1967 by Eldridge and Kathleen Cleaver, produced thousands of hotly demanded posters of the imprisoned minister of defense sitting in a wicker chair, wearing a leather jacket and black beret, and holding a rifle in one hand and spear in the other. The image was one of the era's most enduring.

From ghettoes to colleges, militant black youth donned black berets. At Luther College, a small liberal arts school in Decorah, Iowa, students formed the Black Student Union in 1968 and a governing "Cabinet of Five." In its group photo, the three women and two men reflected the sartorial influence of Black Power. The women wore dashikis and the men black berets. Though not Panthers or self-described revolutionary nationalists, the group photo reflects what was common in the era. The beret was a powerful icon of Black Power in general, and for many it represented an implicit association with the Panthers.[98]

The Summer Olympic Games in Mexico City gave the black beret global exposure in 1968. After winning the gold and bronze medals in the 200-meter race, Tommie Smith and John Carlos gave clenched fist salutes on the award stand. A declaration of their solidarity with the black liberation struggle, the gesture infuriated many white Americans. *Time* magazine said the action supplanted the games' theme of "Faster, Higher, Stronger" with "angrier, nastier, uglier." The Black Power gesture was "absurd" and a petty "public display of petulance." Brent Musburger in the *Chicago American* called Smith and Carlos "black-skinned storm troopers."[99] Avery Brundage, president of the International Olympic Organizing Committee immediately ordered the athletes' dismissal. Fellow black teammates were conflicted over the controversy. Some Black Power advocates argued against black athletes "running in Mexico and crawling at home." Later when three African Americans swept the 400-meter race, they donned black berets on the award stand. The gold medallist for the heat, Lee Evans, explained that the berets were an affirmation of their commitment and solidarity with the struggle of black people worldwide: "Black berets then were worn by the Black Panthers. I wanted to show black pride." Though they removed the berets during the national anthem, the image of the berets already had been broadcast to hundreds of millions worldwide. Ultimately, it was good press for the Panthers. After their return home Lee Evans, John Carlos, and Tommie Smith spoke to crowds of fans who cheered their militant defiance at the Olympic games.[100]

Often unorganized street youth imitated Panther dress. Regina Jennings, a party member, explains that local youth admired the Panthers so much that they appropriated the uniform. "Although this imitation made us feel rather proud, one had difficulty discerning Oakland youth from Panthers." Indeed, the Panther uniform could invite vicious aggression from police.[101] The party never took an official position on the popularity of its beret among black militants. If anything, the beret's popularity supported the party's argument that it was the vanguard party for the black masses. The Panthers were highly critical of the popular African styles, generally associating them with cultural nationalism. The Panthers failed to acknowledge, however, that they had also cultivated a cultural nationalist style. The beret became a major icon of revolutionary nationalism and black power. Eventually, Latinos, whites, and Asian militants would similarly adopt the beret, albeit in different colors. The nearly universal display of Afros among Panthers, as well as their celebration of soul music and other segments of African American culture in food, fashion, and language, reflects the party's intuitive appreciation for the role of culture in political struggle. However, the Panthers' inability to meld cultural nationalism more effectively with their revolutionary politics may have caused unnecessary animosity between them and the larger Black Power movement, which included the arts, academia, and various cultural phenomena.[102]

The Black Panther Party leadership was, in many regards, insightful and accurate in its critique of cultural nationalism. Wearing an Afro or dashiki or speaking Swahili would not effect fundamental systemic change. Poor whites who had European names, clothes, and worldviews remained poor, despite their belief that whiteness was the standard by which all else was judged. A white Santa Claus, white Jesus, white angels, and even a white God did not erase white poverty or stop Uncle Sam from sending poor whites to Vietnam. Moreover, the good that black cultural nationalism offered was often undermined by businesses that used the symbols of black consciousness to push tobacco and liquor and promote problematic gender roles in the black community. The zealous commercialization of Black Power helped sanitize and co-opt the potentially radical movement.

Yet the party leadership was also myopic in its approach to cultural nationalism. The party's reaction to cultural nationalism reflected the regional difficulties faced by an organization trying to be national. The West Coast Panthers were particularly hostile to cultural nationalism because of their antagonism toward the Us organization. The promotion of cultural nationalism by Us seemed entirely impotent and misdirected to the Panthers, who had had comrades die at the hands of Us members. Instead of separating the cultural nationalists' culturally affirming philosophy from its acrimonious relationship with Us, the Panther leadership rejected most of the cultural nationalist ideals.

The rank and file of some branches like New York, however, demonstrated that it was possible to be both culturally affirming and revolutionary. African names and dashikis did not separate members from the party's Marxist-Leninist or Intercommunalist politics. The degree of alienation from black people caused by its anti-cultural-nationalist position is unclear. Most black people did not know the details of Panther ideology.[103] The Panthers did, however, win considerable support from a wide cross-section within black communities across the country, as well as among many white, Latino, and Asian American radicals.

In Chicago, the local Panther chapter, under the leadership of Fred Hampton, made arduous attempts to politicize the largest street gang in the United States, the Black Stone Rangers, led by Jeff Fort. Fort and Hampton met personally and, despite attempts by the FBI's Counterintelligence Program to have Fort kill Hampton, the party maintained amicable ties and even recruited a few Rangers.[104] The Rangers, while remaining a street gang and involved in criminal activities such as extortion and murder, eventually changed their name to the Black P-Stone Nation, perhaps in tune with the "nation time" theme of the era. When Chicago police assassinated Hampton in his sleep on December 4, 1969, the Black P-Stone Nation sent at least one thousand members to show last respects to the slain revolutionary.[105] The appeal and respect for the Panthers extended beyond the confines of the lumpen, however.

The Chicago branch had supporters from all segments of the black community. Through Hampton's organizing, students were successful in changing the name of Crane College to Malcolm X College, securing its first black president, and expanding resources and academic programs at other city colleges. Many middle-class blacks admired and supported the efforts of the local Panthers. Some celebrities covertly funded Panther survival programs such as the free medical clinic and free breakfast program. When several Panthers were arrested in 1969, on charges that would later be dismissed, famed comedian and actor Richard Pryor posted bail for them. Even white actors Jane Fonda, Donald Sutherland, and Marlon Brando extended support to the party.[106]

An ABC-TV poll in April 1970 revealed widespread support for the Black Panther Party in black communities. When asked what organization had done the most for black people in the last two years, the Black Panther Party came in third, following the NAACP and SCLC. Furthermore, the Black Panther Party was the *only* black organization respondents thought would increase its effectiveness in the future. Most thought that the NAACP and SCLC would lose influence and eventually diminish. Finally, 62 percent of those polled admired the Black Panther Party.[107] Also, the Panthers boasted the second most widely circulated black newspaper in the country. The *Black Panther* had a weekly circulation of 100,000, second only to the Nation of Islam's *Muhammad Speaks,* with a daunting circulation of 500,000.[108]

Clearly, the Black Panther Party's affinity with black people and popular/folk culture was a strength. Its language was not paternalistic, condescending, or contemptuous. The party wanted to convey a love and affinity for the people, and did so uniquely. As the people's party, the Panthers developed strong ties in black communities across the country. The Panthers avoided ideas that reduced the people to mere sheep following the herd toward barbarism or civilization. The party rejected the civilizing mission that was the ideological backdrop to every major black nationalist organization of the era. While the Panthers were not typical nationalists, they adopted significant elements of nationalist discourse, eventually creating a radical ethnic nationalism that would inspire non–African Americans.

The party's attempt to attract and focus on the lumpen, however, proved problematic. The glorification of drinking, tolerance of drugs, physical intimidation, and widespread public use of profanity ultimately isolated the Panthers from many black people. Moreover, it encouraged antagonistic relationships between those of different classes within and outside the party.

With the daunting responsibility of leading the fight, the Black Panther Party offered revolutionary guidance and direction to the people while simultaneously affirming its affection for them. The party wanted to "swim with the masses" in order to demonstrate its sincerity toward and identification with them. Uncritically, however, the Panthers would allow themselves to fall victim to myopic and simplistic notions of ghetto authenticity. Despite the class diversity within the Panther rank and file, Panther leadership embraced incredibly limited perspectives of class. The valorization of lumpenism was problematic on various levels. It opened the way for rogue and criminal behavior, destabilizing the party and inviting police aggression. Furthermore, it reduced impoverished black people into a cliché of hard-living, rough-and-tumble "field slaves," ready at a moment's notice to destroy the master's house. Conversely, middle-class black people were lumped into a group of pampered, timid, self-interested Negroes unwilling to confront seriously the exigencies of oppression. The truth was much more complicated, as the Panthers would learn.

CHAPTER 5

"Move Over or We'll Move Over on You"
Black Power and the Decline of the Civil Rights Movement

By 1966 civil rights leaders had reorganized their activities to address the conditions that gave rise to Black Power and its nationalist exponents. Moderates attempted to thwart the spread of Black Power militancy in northern cities where black nationalists were blamed for fueling civil unrest and undermining the efforts of the civil rights movement. Despite these efforts, the spirit of black nationalism could not be placated with Gandhian rhetoric or speeches extolling integration. It was clear that a new consciousness had emerged among African Americans and that moderates ran the risk of losing influence and respect in black communities.

The fissure between militant advocates of Black Power and the liberal and moderate proponents of integration was apparent by 1966. The Student Nonviolent Coordinating Committee (SNCC) and Congress on Racial Equality (CORE) altered their earlier positions on integration and nonviolence. The leading moderate organizations, the National Association for the Advancement of Colored People (NAACP) and the Urban League steadfastly continued their policies that aimed to integrate black people into the fabric of the United States, chiefly by legal means. They also virulently denounced Black Power. The Black Power slogan seriously disturbed most whites and moderate blacks, who considered it divisive, violent, and pregnant with antiwhite hate.[1] Moderates feared the slogan would destroy the progress the civil rights movement had made since the 1950s. For them, the fear of "white backlash" was very real. The Southern Christian Leadership Conference (SCLC) denounced Black Power in 1966, although its leader, Dr. Martin Luther King Jr., was not as eager to isolate the proponents of Black Power as were the leaders of the NAACP and the Urban League. King hoped to maintain a level of cohesion and professional tolerance within the leading civil rights organizations. It was increasingly evident, however, that the movement had become more polarized, ultimately giving birth to another, more radical and militant movement with sundry manifestations in the political, educational and cultural mainstream of African American life.

The controversies over Black Power were fueled largely by the general ignorance surrounding the slogan's meaning. While it meant different things to different people, there were some general constants. Black Power celebrated black pride and directed new attention to the historical accomplishments of black people in the United States and elsewhere. It also stressed the importance of black self-determination. This self-determination generally fell short of territorial separatism and strict black nationalism, although black nationalist groups were also Black Power adherents. The language Stokely Carmichael used immediately following the Meredith March Against Fear was much less vitriolic than Black Power rhetoric became within a few years. The earlier definition did, however, address core concerns among Black Power advocates:

> Too often the goal "integration" has been based on a complete acceptance of the fact that *in order to have* a decent house or education, Negroes must move into a *white* neighborhood or go to a *white* school. What does this mean? First of all, it reinforces among both Negroes and whites the idea that "white" is automatically better and that "black" is by definition inferior. Secondly, it allows the nation to focus, for example, on a handful of Negro children who finally get by Southern racist mobs and into white schools, and to ignore the 94% who are left behind in unimproved, all-black schools. Such situations will not change until Negroes have political power—to control their own school boards, for example.[2]

Fundamentally, Black Power, as an amorphous and popular idea, affirmed black people in ways that the civil rights movement did not. For the NAACP and others, separation from white people did psychological harm, as litigants stressed in the *Brown v. Board of Education* case. There was no argument that white children suffered from racial segregation. The implied message was that separation from white people could be deleterious. Black Power rejected this assumption. For Black Power advocates, integration did not make black students learn better, buses ride smoother, or water fountain water taste better. The ubiquitous practice of de jure and de facto racial segregation that dated to the early nineteenth century forced black people to cultivate and rely on black-controlled churches, professional societies, schools, and social groups. These institutions, black people came to realize, were not by nature inferior to white ones or integrated ones. Instead of closing the social gap that separated whites and blacks, the gap widened in some respects in the late 1960s. The social segregation long enforced by whites was reinforced by blacks, despite the growing tolerance for social integration among whites. By the close of the decade Black Power's appeal eclipsed the integrationist drive. The ramifications of Black Power were felt from prisons to Ivy League schools, creating lasting impressions and altering the way race and racial etiquette were understood in America.

The Black Power movement had many adherents. Clearly, SNCC and CORE were its early organizational representatives, but the Nation of Islam (NOI) was the movement's benefactor. It provided the nationalist backdrop for Black Power. The axiological framework of Black Power rhetoric was formed around the rhetoric of the Nation of Islam. Malcolm X was the most popular conduit through which NOI cosmology passed to larger sections of black America. Millions of black people heard the national spokesman on radio, television, and on college campuses. Others visited local temples or mosques where they heard ministers speak about the plight of the "so-called Negro." They listened to Muslims explain why people of African descent were "black" people, not "Negroes"—a term used by whites to facilitate their domination over people of African descent. Black, the Nation taught, was the label that reflected "knowledge of self" and a rejection of white supremacy. The Nation also boasted the largest black newspaper in the country, *Muhammad Speaks*. By no means was the NOI a marginal force in black America.

Burn Baby Burn

While Black Power had its origins in different political, cultural, and social phenomena in various parts of the country, Los Angeles offers a revealing study of Black Power and the emergence of the Black Panther Party. It was in Los Angeles that one of the decade's first major urban rebellions helped change the scope of the black liberation struggle. The city was also home of perhaps the most tumultuous black nationalist community in the country, where deadly armed conflict took place between police and black nationalists and between black nationalist organizations.

The 1965 Watts rebellion was an ominous sign for political observers and civil rights activists who had focused much of their activity against racial injustice in the South.[3] Large segments of black communities outside the South seethed with resentment, frustration, and a growing black militancy by the middle part of the 1960s. Some members of these communities gravitated to the Nation of Islam's brand of black nationalism or that of the smaller, local organizations such as the Yoruba Temple or African Nationalist Pioneer Movement in New York.[4] For many others, no organization spoke to their fundamental needs. The Muslims' strict moral and religious code and ostensibly conservative character dissuaded many from joining the NOI. The middle-class orientation of the NAACP, CORE, and the National Urban League made many poor blacks feel overlooked, and the southern-based efforts of the SCLC and SNCC isolated many poor blacks in cities like Chicago, Philadelphia, Detroit, and Oakland who did not typically experience a de jure form of white supremacy.

L.A. militants emerged with a vociferous call for radical black nationalism in the wake of the rebellion. Unlike New York, the black nationalist community in Los Angeles was not particularly large in 1965. Two organizations dominated the southern California scene, the Nation of Islam and the Afro-American Association (AAA). The AAA emerged out of a reading group founded by several graduate and professional school students at the University of California at Berkeley in 1961. Members met in law school student Donald Hopkins's apartment and read works by and about Marcus Garvey and E. Franklin Frazier and listened to recordings of Malcolm X. Although many were impressed with Malcolm's formidable debating skills, none was willing to become a Muslim. Within several months the group expanded beyond the Berkeley campus community and included several students at Merritt College in Oakland and other noncollege people. By the beginning of 1962 the reading group had begun to meet at Downs Memorial Methodist Church and sponsored Monday night lectures that brought up to 200 people each week. The meetings attracted many from the Oakland area who were growing disenchanted with the largely slapdash local black organizations. Local young people like Bobby Seale, Huey Newton, Ernest Allen, Willie Brown, and Ron Dellums attended lectures and readings hosted by the Afro-American Association, as it was called by March 1962. By early 1962, Donald Warden, a Howard University graduate and law student, assumed leadership, and the association continued to grow rapidly.

AAA members read books and articles and heard lectures on the histories and cultures of African people on the continent and in the Diaspora. The association aimed to satisfy community and social group needs, and not all activities were nationalist oriented. For example, some older women members formed sewing clubs. The organization promoted the cultivation of a "black consciousness" and advocated "buy black" campaigns to support black businesses. The AAA identified with Africa in an era when Africa, for most Americans, was reduced to racist images derived from Tarzan books and movies. The AAA's emphasis on African history and culture undermined much of the misinformation members had learned about Africa and moved many in the direction of cultural nationalism. As early as 1962, some members began wearing African-styled garb. A few members adopted African names, and some women began wearing their hair natural.[5] By 1963, the organization had expanded its membership to over 200 people. Although the AAA was a local organization, Warden had contacts across the state and in 1963 expanded its mission to southern California.

Los Angeles and Black Power

The Afro-American Association established a branch in Los Angeles in 1963, and Ron Everett, a twenty-two-year-old graduate student at UCLA, became its first chairman. L.A. association members formed reading clubs at Aquarian Books on Santa Barbara Boulevard in South Central. Aquarian, owned by Al and Beatrice Ligon, was a meeting place for many who were gravitating to the nascent black nationalist community. Through Everett's contacts at UCLA, many students were drawn to the AAA. Everett, who visited the local Muslim temple, admired the AAA's intellectual curiosity, affinity with the larger community, and exploration of African history and culture. An erudite student, Everett was in the process of learning Swahili and developing new ideas about nationalist organization. He met Malcolm X on several occasions through the Nation of Islam and even enjoyed private conversations with him. Malcolm X and the AAA shaped Everett's developing worldview, but the Watts rebellion pushed him into new arenas of activism.[6]

Despite the veneer of tolerance and opportunity in Los Angeles, the city was not unlike any other U.S. city in the 1960s. Eighty-eight percent of blacks in L.A. lived in segregated communities. Blacks were concentrated in the area of Watts and its surrounding communities of South Central Los Angeles. In these areas, citizens lived in a population density nearly twice that of Los Angeles County.[7] The poverty rate was more than two times that of the city average; unemployment in Watts was 34 percent.[8] Police brutality was a very serious concern for black residents of Los Angeles, whose numbers had been historically low among police officers. In 1965 the police force remained over 90 percent white, although people of color represented nearly a third of the city's population.[9]

On a hot August 11 afternoon, a traffic stop in the Avalon district of South Central resulted in the arrest of motorist Marquette Frye for drunk driving. A crowd gathered to watch the activities of the officers. After a scuffle erupted between Frye's mother and the officers, a woman, believed to be pregnant by some witnesses, was arrested for interfering with the duties of an officer. As the police manhandled the woman, the growing crowd grew hostile; bottles were thrown at the police car as it pulled off. The following six days were the most destructive period of urban unrest in the United States since the 1920s. Thirty-four people were killed, and the city suffered nearly $200 million in property damages.[10] The shock of Watts reverberated throughout the country. Although there were seven incidents of urban unrest in 1964, none compared to the level of destruction seen in Los Angeles.[11]

Following the rebellion, Everett left the AAA and formed the Us organization. The name of the organization was not an acronym. It implied an in-group affinity and oppositional relationship with *the other*—"them" or whites. Pulling from his experiences in the AAA and his association with the Nation of Islam, Everett created a group that was highly disciplined, black nationalist, and on a civilizing mission. Members shed their European names and adopted African ones. Us formed a quasi-military wing, the Simba Wachanga (Swahili for "Young Lions"). Like the Fruit of Islam (FOI), the Simba were highly trained in martial arts. Unlike the FOI, however, they also trained with firearms.[12]

Through his contacts in various community projects, Everett, now known as Maulana Karenga (Swahili for "keeper of tradition"), quickly attracted members to his new organization. Speaking on local television shows, he discussed the difficulties black people faced in the rebellion's aftermath. Karenga was also central in forming Community Alert Patrol (CAP), which monitored police activity with law books, cameras, and tape recorders. CAP had a major appeal among many who were radicalized by the rebellion. Hoping to galvanize the energy of the unrest, Us found recruits among some who had been participants in the unrest, including gang members. The Gladiators, a gang from the western middle- and lower-middle-class parts of South Central, provided several members for the Us organization.[13]

While Los Angeles's new militant organizations attracted new recruits, the NOI remained the largest black nationalist group in the city, despite its insular nature. It provided the community with a vehicle for institution-building that the newer organizations such as the AAA, CAP, or Us did not. The Muslims were not known for their activism in the black community, however. Largely self-contained, they did not challenge police brutality in any direct fashion. The Nation's racialist, quasi-Islamic theology was also difficult for many Christians to accept. Moreover, many had grown intolerant of the Nation's militant talk and tepid action.

For many, the Watts rebellion had been a politicization process. Street gangs such as the Outlaws, Avenues, Hat Gang, Rabble Rousers, and Park Boys made up the scores of gangs that predated the notorious Crips and Bloods that emerged in the early 1970s. After the rebellion, black gangs such as the Slausons, Businessmen, and Gladiators became less known for attacking other black people and increasingly active in joining black radical organizations. A general truce emerged in the wake of the unrest, and many gang members joined the black nationalist organizations that sprouted up in South Central. It appeared that the black gang scene in Los Angeles was in rapid decline between 1965 and 1969.[14] Some older gangsters remember virtually no fighting between gangs during that period.[15] The violence that characterized the gang culture did not disappear, however. In some ways, gang violence mutated into the tumultuous world of the black nationalist scene of the city.

Ron "Crook" Wilkins, a member of the Slausons who joined CAP, found a new and more effective outlet for his political enthusiasm. Although he joined the Nation of Islam in 1965, Crook quickly became disaffected with it. Its anti-Malcolm sentiment disturbed him during a period in which his appreciation for Malcolm's militancy and political and cultural consciousness was increasing. The Muslims' rigid moral code also was trying for the nineteen-year-old. Young male members were not allowed to look at women in the eyes or be alone with them. There were not many younger sisters in the Nation at the time, and they were not allowed to fraternize with nonbelievers. Perhaps the most important factor that pushed him out of the Nation, however, was the Muslims' unwillingness to confront the police who incessantly brutalized and harassed them in particular and black people in general. Crook was told to "pray to the east" when an officer attempted harassment. The local mosque was no stranger to police aggression. Three years before the Watts rebellion, a deadly police assault had left one Muslim dead and several others wounded.

Around midnight on April 27, 1962, two white police officers stopped two black men who were carrying clothes from a car to the mosque, less than a block away. Ronald Stokes, one of the Muslims, gestured with his hands as he argued with the officers. A scuffle began when a policeman attempted to grab Stokes's hand. Stokes gave resistance. The officers opened fire. Muslims nearby, heeding the belief that they had a right to self-defense, ran to the aid of the two. The *Los Angeles Times* initially reported that several other Muslims engaged the officers in a "blazing gunfight," leaving seven Muslims and an officer shot. Stokes was handcuffed and lying in a pool of blood from a gunshot wound to the head when the ambulance arrived. Another Muslim, William Rogers, was bleeding from the abdomen, paralyzed. One Muslim's lower jaw was broken in half from police kicks. Paramedics treated the officers first. It was later confirmed that all the Muslims were unarmed. The officer was most likely shot by another officer.[16] Fourteen Muslims in total, including those shot, were charged with assaulting an officer. The police were found not guilty of killing Stokes. The shooting of the other unarmed men was also ruled justifiable. Muslims were livid, as many in the larger black community had been.[17]

Some Muslims went against the order to eschew guns. Others obtained knives and prepared to attack whites. Malcolm X flew to Los Angeles and, immediately recognizing the tense atmosphere, instructed followers: "We are going into the streets not to begin war with the devil. We are going to sell newspapers."[18] Not satisfied with the cautious approach, a small group of Muslims calling themselves "a band of angels" assaulted white drunkards in downtown Los Angeles. Malcolm X condemned the angels. The attacks stopped, and many Muslims departed from the Nation in disgust at its inability to respond to the police terror.[19]

L.A. Muslims came from criminal backgrounds similar to those of Muslims in other cities. Many had been former gang members and other street toughs who were familiar with a culture of violence and intimidation. While "Negroes," they directed their violence against other black people, but as reborn black people, many Muslims viewed their prior behavior as indicative of their slavish adherence to white supremacy. They had been mere tools of the devil. As Muslims they were cleansed of their fear of white people. Whites were not only fallible and vulnerable, but they were inferior in mind, body, and spirit to black people. That Muslims should tolerate police terror seemed opposite of everything they had been taught as Fruit of Islam. The Nation's inability to obtain justice in the 1962 case was an early example of the limitations of its program. The NOI leadership was loath to admit its powerlessness in protecting the mosque from attack. Unarmed defenses against police proved disastrous. Elijah Muhammad attempted to reassure followers that Allah would protect and defend his chosen ones. When an airplane crash resulted in the death of over 120 white Georgians shortly after the acquittal of the L.A. officers,

Elijah Muhammad proclaimed that Allah had rendered justice on the devil.[20] Despite the obvious irony in the fatalistic positions of the NOI leadership and its traditional criticism of fatalistic "spookism" in the black church, many NOI members remained as steadfast to the faith as they had always been. Some others, however, would be shaken by continued police harassment of the L.A. mosque.

In a 1965 raid on Mosque Number 27 police joked that they made the building look like "Swiss-cheese" after firing scores of rounds into its Central Avenue edifice. Several Muslims were willing to retaliate against the offending officers, but Minister John Shabazz directed them to refrain from violence and sell *Muhammad Speaks* with more fervor. "Each *Muhammad Speaks* will be like a bullet against the devil," Muslims were told. Crook, young and militant, thought the Nation ineffective and left, later to join CAP and SNCC.[21]

The Muslims: Conservative Militants

In many regards, the stories of Crook and Karenga's political evolution represent a microcosm of many who directly participated in the Black Power movement. The Nation of Islam generated a respectable level of support and admiration in black communities nationwide. The popularity of Malcolm X and Muhammad Ali, as well as negative attacks in the white media, helped make the Nation the largest and most resilient black nationalist organization since Marcus Garvey's Universal Negro Improvement Association (UNIA). For many, however, the era's political, cultural, and economic challenges demanded much more than religious attention. It is in this context that Black Power flourished during the late 1960s and early 1970s.

The intensification of civil rights activity put more attention on the tepid politics of the NOI by the early 1960s. Many civil rights activists believed that while the Nation had the more militant rhetoric, the activists had more militant action. A number of Muslims left the Nation to form their own organizations before the Black Power movement emerged. In some cases, the Nation expelled members for being too militant. In the early 1960s Shaykh Muhammad was put out of the Philadelphia temple after his behavior was considered a liability for the organization. Muhammad's plans included violent confrontation with racist police. These intentions were unacceptable to NOI hierarchy.

After his dismissal, Shaykh Muhammad formed the African Asian Culture Center in North Philadelphia, fusing NOI theology with other teachings, and immediately recruited new members. Many of them, including Shaykh, deviated from the NOI uniform by wearing a fez and facial hair. In late August 1964 civil unrest erupted in a black section of North Philadelphia, resulting in 348 injuries and more than 600 arrests. Shaykh Muhammad was among those arrested. His $10,000 bond was so exorbitant that Cecil Moore, NAACP lawyer and head of the local NAACP chapter, called it a "ransom." Police raided Muhammad's Culture Center and found various weapons, including a loaded .22-calibre automatic pistol and several bottles with rags stuffed in the necks. The notoriously racist deputy police commissioner Frank Rizzo called Muhammad the leader of a "black supremacy group" and argued that Muhammad, more than any single figure, had instigated the violence. Shaykh Muhammad's organization was, according to Rizzo, fit with "a few hundred followers . . . more than enough to stir up trouble."[22] Shaykh Muhammad was not alone in engaging in nationalist activity outside the Nation of Islam. Across the country, an audacious black nationalist organization was formed in 1962, becoming one of the first organizations to extend the NOI's philosophy into a broader scope of cultural nationalism.

In 1962, before Ron Everett became Maulana Karenga and heralded a new appreciation for African culture, Minister Charles CX De Blew broke from the Nation of Islam and became the first major cultural nationalist on the West Coast. In June 1962, De Blew, who helped establish temples in Seattle and Portland, left the NOI because of what he considered an "internal power struggle." Renaming himself Al Sultan Nasser A. Shabazz, he co-founded the African Descendants Nationalist Independence Partition Party (AD NIP) and became its first prime minister and national party chairman on October 14, 1962.

Also known as the Black Guards, AD NIP grew out of a conference on slavery reparations held in Philadelphia. Bringing together various nationalists, including "Queen Mother" Audrey Moore and Oserjeman Adefumi, the new organization paid homage to Marcus Garvey as "the First Black Revolutionary, Father of Black Nationalism." Much like the UNIA, the San Francisco–based organization celebrated pomp and used military uniforms for its membership. The Black Nurse Corps was reminiscent of the UNIA's Black Cross Nurses. The structure of AD NIP also reflected its demand for a black nation-state. It established the United African Peoples Republic Provisional Government and national holidays for the birth and death of Malcolm X, Patrice Lumumba, and Medgar Evers, as well as the four girls murdered by white terrorists in a Birmingham church in 1963. Former Garveyite Audrey Moore was elected the minister of foreign relations and Adefumi became deputy prime minister. With its members' African names and African garb, AD NIP deviated from the UNIA and NOI in celebrating cultural nationalism.

Despite its adoration of Africa, however, AD NIP had no plans for a mass exodus there. Instead, it demanded all land south of Delaware to the southwest corner of New Mexico. There, the new government would establish a "concrete wall along its borderline. It will also be fortified with troops to guard the Republic." Though its membership included many former NOI Muslims, AD NIP made clear that it was a secular movement with a strong emphasis on ethics and morality. Much like the NOI, AD NIP accused black people of self-destructive behavior and irresponsibility. "We are robbing and stealing from each other day and night." "Negroes," Shabazz noted, were guilty of "committing indecent acts with each others wives and girlfriends." The organization also embraced the NOI's doctrine that all people of color are "black" and vilified interracial marriages with whites. Unlike the NOI, AD NIP publicly supported arming black people and direct action self-defense against racist attack. Calling themselves the "vanguard and defender" of the black community, AD NIP advocated an all-black police force in black communities.[23]

Though it tapped into the general themes of the Black Power era, AD NIP never gained considerable attention. It remained relegated to the fringes of mainstream media attention and declined in significance in the 1970s. AD NIP's inability to grow was most likely a result of the chasm in age between its leadership and the average member of a black power organization, which was under thirty. Queen Mother Moore, for example, had been active in the UNIA during the 1920s and was sixty-three years old in 1963. Prime Minister Al Sultan Nasser A. Shabazz had been a minister in the NOI in the 1950s, when most Panthers were still in grade school. In an era of baby boomer radicalism, a charismatic leader over forty did not attract many followers. Even the NOI experienced its most precipitous growth between 1952 and 1964, during Malcolm X's role as a prominent minister and national spokesman. Though AD NIP never captured the national imagination, it was one of several organizations, however, that found its earliest inspiration in the Nation of Islam.

That so many black nationalists once had been members of the Nation, or were influenced directly by it, had a profound impact on how nationalists interacted with and reacted to the Muslims. In Los Angeles, a hotbed of violence and antagonism within the black nationalist community, the Nation was a stabilizing force for many. Members of the Los Angeles Black Congress, an umbrella organization, were often relieved to see Muslims at the more acrimonious gatherings.[24] On many occasions, Muslims provided a level of restraint and discipline at the Black Congress when animosities between black militants boiled over.

Karenga, who was very prominent in the congress, was a threatening character to some participants. In late 1967, Ron "Crook" Wilkins and Panther Elaine Brown initiated a vote that Karenga no longer be addressed as "Maulana"—an esteemed title of "Great Leader" in Swahili. "Call him Brother or nigger," Wilkins insisted. At the next meeting, Karenga led more than forty Us members into the Congress—many brandishing guns. "I understand some people want to criticize Us brothers," Brown remembers Karenga saying. "If you cannot deal with me politically, perhaps you might want to deal with me militarily. Can you dig that, Brother Crook?" Although Crook held his ground, the threats clearly intimidated most congress members. "Karenga," Brown recalled, "had solidified his position as head of what would come to be considered the most militant black organization in Southern California."[25] Others note that the Muslims, who were represented at the congress, were not moved by the militaristic posturing of Us or by subsequent attempts at bullying by Panthers.[26] When others were intimidated, Muslims stood their ground, undeterred and firm in their stance. "The Muslims," stated a former congress member, "never cowered during any gun pulling situations. They simply remarked that such chaos would never happen if black people followed the teachings of the Honorable Elijah Muhammad. And nobody messed with them."[27]

Though the Nation's lack of activism, insular community, and somewhat aloof nature disturbed other organizations, most had a peculiar respect for the Muslims. Us members threatened and bullied some organizations and people, as did the Panthers, but the Nation remained unbothered. Many ranked the Nation of Islam's martial-arts-trained Fruit of Islam as the most disciplined, well-trained, and formidable body of black people in the community. Clyde Halisi, a former Us member, recounts that the Nation was "the only organization that could go around denouncing Malcolm X and not be attacked. Muslims were well known for their ability to defend themselves and provide disciplined, highly skilled Fruit of Islam to neutralize threats in the black community. They had the most respected military unit of any black organization in the city."[28] According to Skip Johnson, "The Muslims had the best image, if not the best press, in terms of being able to deal. But the reputation was to respond to threats to themselves."[29] This reputation was not confined to Los Angeles. Lee Lew-Lee, a former member of the Harlem branch of the Black Panther Party, recalled that in New York the "FOI was possibly the best trained and most feared by the [black] populace. No one could mess with the Muslims."[30]

Perhaps the FOI's reputation dissuaded militants from attempting to intimidate Muslims. Numerous nationalists had belonged to the NOI, which may have contributed to a level of deference and respect. Former members knew firsthand the capabilities of the FOI. A list of former Muslims in Los Angeles reads like a list of who's who among black nationalists: Bunchy Carter, deputy minister of defense for the L.A. Panthers; Crook Wilkins; Eldridge Cleaver; and Melvin X, a leader in the local student movement, as well as many others, like Karenga, who attended the temple on occasion. The Nation clearly played a major role in germinating the political consciousness of all major black nationalist organizations. For many, the Nation's influence was so profound because in the late 1950s and early 1960s it was alone in advocating its message. John Shabazz, the local minister of Mosque Number 27, was similar to Malcolm X in his oratory and attracted hundreds to the mosque.[31] In addition, the Muslims were sharp dressers, and their unmatched discipline was impressive. The Shabazz restaurant at Fifty-first and Main Streets, with its great food, music, and atmosphere made the Muslims popular among many. In the era of Black Power, however, many found the Nation out of step with the spirit of political and cultural consciousness.

A new and profound appreciation for blackness characterized Black Power. Although it was an extension of the Nation of Islam's praise of black people and their historical achievements, for the new black militants, Black Power meant more than an inversion of the declaration of white supremacy. The militant slogan was also an attempt at creating psychic connections to Africa, something the Nation had not substantively done. Black Power also endorsed activism in ways the Muslims did not. Furthermore, Black Power, in most forms, extolled political participation, which made a clear break from the classical types of black nationalism (UNIA, NOI) that relinquished the American political apparatus to whites. Black Power melded the axiology of black nationalism with the activism of the civil rights movement and forged a new identity among the mass of African Americans.

Academia, Black Youth, and Black Power

For generations, black students at traditionally white colleges in the North and West (they were barred from white colleges in the South) were ostracized and faced ridicule and outright violence. At Indiana University, black students in the 1940s were only allowed to swim in the university pool the day before it was drained and cleaned. They were also barred from eating at local restaurants in town. At dozens of schools, black athletes faced humiliation when opposing teams refused to play against integrated teams. For the small number of black students on white college campuses up to the mid-1960s, the environment was typically unwelcoming. Arthur Miller, who entered the University of Illinois at Urbana as a freshman in the fall of 1964, recalls the pervasive antiblack sentiment he experienced. While the university boasted nearly thirty thousand students, African Americans numbered around a hundred in the 1964–65 academic year, accounting for less than one-half of 1 percent of the student body. Miller recalls that he was never invited to any social functions by white students and was greeted with "nigger go home" scrawled on his dormitory room door. His experience was not unique, but although most experienced white hostility, black students had no organized community besides small fraternity and sorority chapters. "Black students," Miller explains, "were still trying to be 'white.'" Integration was the aim of the civil rights movement, and despite insults and discrimination from their white peers, black students were loath to create any black organizations. "We resolved to seek white acceptance by being like [white students]."[32] As young activists in the movement grew weary of seeking white acceptance, Black Power emerged with a profound appeal.

Spawned from the student-led militancy of SNCC, Black Power advocates had an early base of support on college campuses. Many young people were exposed to the rhetoric of Malcolm X and the Nation of Islam. Rejecting the general impulse to assimilate and seek inclusion into the larger mainstream of white universities, groups of black students began demanding resources for race-based student organizations in the fall of 1966. At San Francisco State College, James Garrett helped form the country's first Black Student Union (BSU). A year later, the school established the first black studies program. Black students across the state formed similar organizations the following semester. In 1969 the National Association of Black Students broke from the mostly white National Student Association (NSA) and demanded $50,000 in "reparations" from the NSA.[33]

By the close of 1969, most major universities and colleges with any sizable number of black students had formed BSUs or Black Student Associations. On most white campuses, BSUs demanded a physical building and full-time staff to direct black-related programs. These institutions generally became known as Black Cultural Centers (BCCs). BCCs functioned as the umbrella entity for black organizational activity on white campuses. Through the BSUs and BCCs, black students extended demands for rigorous recruitment of black faculty and staff as well as black studies programs. In scores of cases, black students made lists of demands, occupied buildings, and rallied for greater resources. At the University of California at Los Angeles, BSU president Floyd Hayes III and other students walked into the chancellor's office without notice and demanded meetings. Without concerns of formality and deference to authority, black students typically saw their efforts in the broader context of resistance to racist domination in an era of Black Power. Hayes was not unlike his counterparts around the country in style and strategy. In stark contrast to the actions of the first black students at white universities in the South a few years earlier, black students by 1968 were developing defiant methods that represented the new black mood. The demands paid off. By 1970, around two-thirds of U.S. four-year colleges offered courses related to black studies. By 1973, over 1,200 college and universities in the country offered over 5,611 courses in black studies.[34]

The climate of Black Power even affected high schools. In 1968, a study by the California Teachers Association found that black students at Berkeley High School felt "profoundly alienated" from the school. In the fall of 1968, students, who had organized a BSU, issued demands, including hiring more black faculty, soul food in the cafeteria, and a black studies department. All demands were met, and Berkeley became the first high school in the country with a black studies department. Similar demands for curricula changes were made at high schools across the country.[35] Though formal negotiations took place between black students and white administrators, informal negotiations were also significant. While black students demanded scholarly considerations of black contributions to society, they also insisted on new respect from whites. In many cases, the new spirit of resistance to white supremacy manifested itself in violent confrontations on high school campuses, as black and white students engaged in renegotiations of racial etiquette.

White Americans had enjoyed servile and comical representations of black people since the late nineteenth century in various entertainment media. From the "Supercoon" minstrels, through characters such as Man Tan and Stephan Fetchit, Negroes were fearful, childlike, and passive. Black stereotypes served very precise functions. The juvenile and intellectually challenged black mass was unfit for responsible citizenship, but blacks' joyful disposition clearly demonstrated that second-class citizenship was of little concern for them, the logic went. The coon and happy

Negro were the most enduring images that whites had of blacks. A 1963 *Newsweek* poll revealed that the most popular stereotype that whites held about black people was that "Negroes laugh a lot." At 85 percent, the stereotype was the most common among all categories and the most popular among whites from every region.[36] By the era of Black Power, many young blacks that had been reared on images of servile and joyous blacks in movies and on television constructed new standards for interracial interactions. They rejected these images in an effort to affirm their humanity in ways that laws could not. Across the country, black youth developed new standards of racial etiquette, forcing changes and shifts that could not be realized by legislation. Gone was the passive and happy Negro.

In the late 1960s, white flight drastically altered the demographic landscape of communities across the country, and black youth played important roles in the process of informal racial negotiations. Chicago's South Shore community was one such area in flux. The neighborhood, a white pocket in an increasingly black south side, had long been populated by Irish, Poles, Jews, and various other European groups that became less ethnically identified and more racially (white) identified.[37] By 1967, South Shore was experiencing violent clashes as white and black people vied for control of public space. Hot points were public parks and beaches and schools. At South Shore High School the black student population jumped from 1.5 percent in 1963 to 54 percent in 1967 and to 73 percent in 1968. The dramatic change reflected the rapid flight of whites from the South Shore community. White students who had engaged in humiliating attacks against black students for years were on the defensive as black militancy swept the student body. A black student union, Nommo, was formed in 1967 and led protests for various school reforms. There were several cases of racial clashes in hallways, and during a football game one white student was chased by a mob of black males. "I don't know what the white boy said or did," recalls Deborah Reynolds, who was a student at the school, "but there was a lot of angry black students after him."[38]

In Chicago's Oak Park, an area known for its virulently racist opposition to open housing, Austin High School similarly changed. In 1963 the school was over 99 percent white. By 1968 black students made up roughly half of the student body. Clashes between black and white students were common, causing alarm for those who envisioned a much more peaceful integration. Unlike the racial taunts black students experienced in Little Rock in 1957, students in these Chicago schools were rarely seen fleeing white attackers but boldly challenged racist behavior. In

California, black students even developed a racial fight chant at schools where busing brought black students into greater contact with whites: "A fight, a fight, a black and a white! If the brother don't win, we're gonna all jump in!"[39]

These informal ways in which black youth rebelled against white supremacy were an essential part of the psychological process of resistance. The fights, short tempers, and intolerance for any perceived infraction against black humanity were pervasive among young blacks. They represented a clear rejection of the general ethos of peace from the civil rights movement, yet they affirmed black people in ways that the movement did not. They unequivocally rejected the stereotypes of the perennially happy and slow-to-anger Negro. This process of informal negotiation was not confined to high schools. In the military, young blacks challenged racists incessantly. Arthur Miller, who had left the University of Illinois after a year of racist "torment," joined the army where he was socially grounded among other black soldiers but still exposed to racism. Unlike his reticence when called "nigger" in college, he struck a follow soldier when he was called one in 1968. The white soldier was stunned, falling to the ground in pain. Standing over the man, Miller dared him: "say it again!" Instead, the man apologized for the remark. For Miller, the new standards of black militancy would not tolerate racist remarks without challenge. When he returned home to Chicago, he was amazed at the cultural shifts that altered racial etiquette.[40]

Many of the shifts in social intercourse between blacks and whites occurred in the streets. Though from Chicago, these youths were familiar with the most virulent forms of white supremacy. As one young man explained, "In a sense . . . Mississippi was right across the street . . . Down south they have white sheets on but in Lawndale [an all-white Chicago enclave] they have on blue sheets." The reference to the police officer uniform reflects the level of acrimony between black youth and white officers of the law; however, white civilians were also agents of white power throughout Chicago and other cities. Blacks were routinely chased, beaten, and called racial epithets in white neighborhoods. Some areas were more notorious than others.[41]

Ironically named Rainbow Beach at 77th and South Shore Drive in Chicago was ground zero for several mini-riots between whites who vowed to "keep the niggers out" and black would-be beachgoers. Black youth emerged as central to the drama over public space. Through the early 1960s blacks were largely limited to 63rd Street Beach and would have been routinely insulted and forced out of other ones. The area was one of many that blacks purposely avoided out of fear of whites. Even some black gangs were reluctant to venture into white areas, despite the fact that they regularly engaged in violent clashes with other black gangs. By 1968, however, black street youth purposely visited the Rainbow Beach and dared whites to call them niggers, clashing with white gangs on occasion. In no uncertain terms did the Black Power movement affect the general notions of deference to whiteness and respect for white space. Black nationalists like the Revolutionary Action Movement (RAM), the NOI, and others systematically courted black gangs. One gangster explained, "The militants came in and say [sic] why be a gangbanger and kill each other when you can kill the honkey and we began to see that the enemy was not black." The new militancy inherently rejected fear of white power. Elzy, a twenty-year-old Vice Lord, states, "we were scared of the honkies but this awareness thing has kicked all that bullshit aside."[42] Various clashes erupted into the early 1970s, by which time the beach had become virtually all black.

This renegotiation of racial etiquette, as crude as it appears, was a direct response to the crude and violent nature of white supremacy. Students who recalled their silent reaction to being called "nigger," returned such epithets with "honkey," "peckerwood," "cracker," "ofay," or any other similarly offensive pejorative for whites. Others modified in-group references to whites such as "Mr. Charlie." The new preference became "Chucks." Similar stories resonate from prisons and at the workplace. While a black person's violent reaction to a racist slur did not necessarily cause the racist to denounce racism, it caused many to reconsider employing the term to a black person's face, thereby altering traditional modes of racial decorum.[43]

Black students' activism and attitudinal positions were inextricably connected to the sociopolitical environment around them. By extension, black student activities were not only concerned with the conditions on campuses but were also directed toward off-campus events. As explained earlier, Black Power did not usually mean black nationalism. It was an affirmation of black people's rights to self-determination, as well as full citizenship and access to resources enjoyed by whites. From Ivy League schools like Cornell, Yale, and Columbia to small state colleges, black students increased their militancy on college campuses in the late 1960s.[44] In many cases the Black Panthers were central to campus activities.

Despite the Panthers' emphasis on organizing the lumpen, the party was incredibly active on college and high school campuses. In several cities, like Chicago and Indianapolis, the Panther chapters emerged out of SNCC contacts. At UCLA, Yale, and Morgan State University, Panthers were active in student protests and demands. In Chicago, Panthers in the BSU initiated the renaming of Crane Community College to Malcolm X Community College in 1969. Though the Nation of Islam was less than pleased at the recognition students gave its heretical former member, the black community was impressed with the change. Not only did Panther participation in college activities garner more members, it also generated more sympathy. In December following the assassinations of Panthers in Chicago, the University of California at Berkeley's BSU rallied against "genocide, murder and repression of the Black Panther Party!!" Many students held vigils for slain Panthers Fred Hampton and Mark Clark. In the spring of 1970, Tennyson High School students in Haywood, California, joined California State College students to picket "pig raids on the Panthers." The Berkeley BSU similarly demanded the freedom of "Huey, Bobby, Erika and over 400 other political prisoners" in America. Slogans and terms coined by the Panthers such as "all power to the people" and "pigs"—a derisive term for police— became ubiquitous in student protest literature and speeches.[45] The party's influence on the black student movement was palpable. Moreover, the systematic efforts to broaden its appeal paid off. While students were often adversarial in their relations with college administrators, black students on white campuses had a very different relation with black professors, who were significantly affected by this new militancy.

By the late 1960s there was a very visible and pervasive level of black consciousness among black academics across the country. Black intellectuals, historically more zealous about racial integration than pursuing black nationalism, were some of the most outspoken proponents of Black Power and black consciousness. Some like political scientist James Turner considered themselves "Malcolmists" and adherents to black nationalism. Others like Angela Y. Davis, a young philosophy instructor at UCLA, joined radical organizations such as SNCC and the Black Panther Party.[46] Robert Allen, Robert Chrisman, Harry Edwards, and other young scholars procured speaking engagements nationwide, and black colleges increasingly lost faculty to white institutions. Only twenty years earlier, white colleges had refused to hire black scholars. By 1969, however, they were in great demand on white campuses. While black intellectuals as a group shifted from political leaning toward the impulse of quasi-nationalist Black Power, it is clear that they were positioned to benefit from the efforts of Black Power advocates on campus. The shift was not confined to those who could significantly boost their own income and prestige, however. Black students and intellectuals were affected by the thrust of Black

Power, as other segments of black America had been. This shift did not occur without challenges. Roy Wilkins, head of the NAACP, for example, denounced the "reverse racism" of Black Student Unions and warned that black studies programs would leave black students ill prepared for life.[47]

To the chagrin of black moderates and some disillusioned and confused white liberals, the sympathy for Black Power continued to expand after 1966. Even some white professors embraced Black Power rhetoric, as had some white students. William Domboff, a white professor at the University of California at Santa Cruz argued that whites should "leave Blacks alone." In the gendered language typical of the era, Domboff notes that "I suggest that you do what the Black man has told you to do: let him do his own thing and you get to work building a party that can unite with him some day far off down the road after you've overcome your own racism and he's made up his mind about where he's going and with whom . . . he's got to do it on his own in order to win his manhood."[48] The sympathy of white academics like Domboff considerably expanded opportunities for people of color in the academy. There was also the pressure from black militants that forced the hand of white college administrators to meet demands of black students. In an era in which racial and ethnic diversity were frowned on by most white Americans, academia became the first major institution to tolerate, if not laud, multiculturalism. Though black intellectuals in academia were often zealous supporters of Black Power by the close of the decade, black professionals from various fields also embraced the axiology of Black Power.

Between 1968 and 1970 dozens of organizations were formed, including the Association of Black Psychologists (ABPsi), National Conference of Black Political Scientists, Association of Black Sociologists, Association of Black Anthropologists, National Association of Black Social Workers (NABSW), and National Society of Afro-American Policemen, Inc. The mission statement of ABPsi reflects the influence of Black Power as a guiding force behind the founding of black professional associations during this era: "Guided by the principle of self determination, these psychologists set about building an institution through which they could address the long neglected needs of Black professionals."[49] A period of unprecedented access to white professional associations gave raise to black ones. Several of the organizations were formed during the national conventions of the larger, white-controlled associations like the American Psychological Association and the American Political Science Association.

In all cases, black professionals eschewed the idea that they work within the larger professional societies to direct resources and attention to black communities, despite the presence of white sympathy. Instead, themes such as autonomy and self-determination dominated organizational focus. Various groups attempted to address issues they felt were peculiar to black people. NABSW, for example, "was formed in response to issues related to providing human services in the Black community, educating social workers for effective service in the Black community, and providing opportunities for participation of Black social workers in the social welfare arena."[50]

These organizations differed from their predecessors such as the National Medical Association (NMA) or the National Bar Association, founded in 1895 and 1925 respectively, in more than rhetoric. (Note the absence of a racial designation in their names.) Older black professional organizations were generally products of exclusion from white societies. Since the American Medical Association barred black membership, African American medical professionals were forced to form their own association. The explanation of NMA's founding sounds almost apologetic in a 1908 issue of the *Journal of the National Medical Association*. "Conceived in no spirit of racial exclusiveness," writes editor C. V. Roman, M.D., "fostering no ethnic antagonism, but born of the exigencies of the American environment, the National Medical Association has for its object the banding together . . . the men and women of African descent who are honorably engaged in the practice of the cognate professions of medicine, surgery, pharmacy and dentistry."[51] This language stood in direct contrast to those organizations that broke from larger white ones in the late 1960s. Black professional organizations born of Black Power were unapologetic in their quest for independence and self-determination.

Without doubt, the impulse of Black Power reoriented the thrust of popular African American politics, which originally sought inclusion into the ostensibly white American mainstream. This change occurred despite public protests from more moderate black leaders still wedded to integration. Many black professionals also maintained membership in the larger associations, however. They also increasingly taught at traditionally white institutions. Black Power granted African Americans a level of autonomy and space that, in some ways, fostered essentialist notions of race but simultaneously allowed them to challenge racism, cultivate black racial awareness and devote resources to the expansion of black opportunity and uplift. They were often reformist rather than revolutionary. They fundamentally challenged traditional notions of race while exploiting the apparatus of various professions. These societies developed scores of scholarship funds, mentoring and internship programs, and awards for professional work heretofore ignored.[52]

The cultural nationalist and militant sentiment of the era was clear. Black professionals not only developed new black space, they celebrated a new "black aesthetic." Students engaged in "head dunking" of women who still wore straighten hair. A perm on a black coed in 1970 was as uncommon a sight as an Afro had been in 1965. UCLA professor Angela Davis's Afro became iconic as an affirmation of blackness and identification with Africa, though her politics transcended cultural displays of consciousness. Throughout the era, the organization most responsible for this new racial consciousness uneasily observed its fruit. The Nation of Islam had never positively identified with most of Africa and was uncomfortable with the new cultural nationalism.

Cultural Nationalism and the NOI

In the tradition of classical black nationalists, Elijah Muhammad identified more overtly with North Africa and Arabia than he did with sub-Saharan Africa. Black people, he taught, originated in Asia. While blackness was praised, the broad features and kinky hair of African people were not characteristics of Allah's blueprint for humanity. The Original People, Muhammad explained, had black skin with fine features and straight hair. The modern physiognomy of black people was the result of Shabazz, an ancient scientist from Mecca who attempted to lead his tribe into Africa to conquer the rough environment. Instead, the Tribe of Shabazz was "toughened" by the harsh climate, resulting in kinky hair and broad facial features. Not only had the Tribe of Shabazz lost its original phenotype, it experienced a declension into barbarism. The tribe lost its knowledge of Islam and high sciences, instead becoming part and parcel of "a jungle life," allowing "the weaker of [themselves] to rule," ultimately facilitating the efforts of Yacub's evil progeny.[53] For Elijah Muhammad, many of the ahistorical and polemical lessons of African history white racists taught were virtual truths. While dismissing whites as devils, the Nation's theology was fundamentally affected and influenced by myopic European views of Africa, and the Nation's rigid conservatism did not make room for the militant aspirations of millions of Black Power advocates who attempted to bridge a cultural chasm between themselves and Africa and further remove themselves from the cultural clutches of white supremacy.

While it is true that Elijah Muhammad was a stalwart of blackness when it was not popular, his brand of racial pride was circumscribed by his conservatism. Muhammad had considerable praise for the efforts of the new African nationalists and their emerging countries. He admired the industrial aspirations of these African nations, but his praise for Africa's new independence was couched in a traditional Western concept of modernism and progress. Black people universally admired new hospitals, highways, urban construction, and schools in Africa. Muhammad wanted as much for black people in the United States. Technical skills, therefore, were very important to the Muslim leader, but serious appreciation for traditional African culture was not in the Nation's scheme. Africa, in his view, was in need of "civilization." In 1972, the NOI leader declared that the Nation "must go to Africa . . . I am already civilized and I am ready to civilize Africa." He attacked African Americans who sought to secure liberation via cultural affinities with Africa. Those who celebrated traditional African culture would only "be degrading themselves." Africans, Muhammad explained, are truly dedicated to their liberation by "giv[ing] the benefit of their knowledge, skill and wealth to their own people. Those who do not are called traitors, defectors, spies, tools and Toms."[54] Still, his praise for African hard work and integrity did not translate into a promotion of "traditional" African culture.

According to virtually all classical black nationalists, African people on the continent had been uncivilized and backward; Elijah Muhammad agreed with this analysis.[55] For these nationalists, the West provided a standard of civilization. Finely tailored suits were symbols of high status for whites, not kente cloth robes and cowrie shells. Muslims embraced these symbols of civility in the early stages of the Nation of Islam's development and did not changed their positions. In fact, the Nation had not significantly altered its ideological positions since its founding in 1930.[56] What may have appeared radical in earlier periods seemed dated in 1968.

The Growth of Black Power

There were scores of urban rebellions in the summers of 1966 and 1967. Despite the rhetoric of civil rights leaders, the rebellions grew more frequent with each passing summer. Many black and white moderates feared a "white backlash." Others, including Martin Luther King Jr., however, discounted the term. White backlash, according to King, was little more than a convenient way for apathetic or antipathetic whites to justify their lack of support for or active hostility to the efforts of civil rights activists.[57] King recognized that many white northerners were fond of paying lip service for the civil rights movement, but the North was clearly no bastion of liberty and equal opportunity. Of the nearly one hundred cases of urban rebellion in 1966 and 1967 only a small minority took place in the South.[58] King knew that there was a growing militancy, anger, and spirit of radicalism in the urban ghettoes of the North and West. If moderate black leaders failed, Black Power could very well win over the efforts of peaceful integrationists, many thought. By 1966 the race was on to galvanize and harness the anger, frustration, and energy of the black ghettoes outside the South. Civil rights moderates hoped to circumscribe the activities of the Black Panther Party and advocates of Black Power. Veterans in SNCC, likewise, aimed to achieve success by tapping into northern militancy. King, disturbed by Watts, immediately set out to cut off similar conflagrations in other cities. In 1966 he moved to Chicago in an attempt to bring attention to the more insidious types of institutionalized racist oppression in the North. He and others realized, however, that Black Power was more formidable than they had imagined. Indeed, it was for many an idea whose time had come.

In January 1966, King announced his plans to move to Chicago to wage a "nonviolent war" on slumlords, segregated schools, City Hall, moneylenders, job discrimination, and real estate interest. "Our work," King explained, "will be aimed at Washington." While King claimed that his activities were directed toward the white power structure, they ostensibly represented an attempt to thwart the spread of Black Power and militant black nationalism by providing a more constructive and effective alternative to what he considered "a revolution [that has] degenerated into an undiscriminating catchall for evanescent and futile gestures." For King, black nationalism and Black Power were "a philosophy nourished solely on despair [and] a slogan that cannot be implemented into a program."[59] King's activities would draw attention to the injustices faced by black northerners, whose needs the civil rights movement had not seriously considered. In addition, the new focus of the SCLC was intended to demonstrate to whites the pervasive nature of racial oppression, show northern blacks that King was dedicated to eradicate injustice everywhere, and make clear that violent civil unrest was an ineffective way to effect positive change. Because of its record of overt institutionalized racism, Chicago, many in the SCLC thought, was an ideal place to launch the northern campaign.[60]

King and the SCLC leadership recognized the threat black nationalist rhetoric posed to their plans and the increasing likelihood of violence. As David Garrow writes, "The Watts riots had left the black movement in an unhappy state," and Chicago granted movement leaders the opportunity to affirm the efficacy of love and nonviolence. "I have faith . . . that Chicago . . . could well become the metropolis where a meaningful non-violent movement could arouse the conscience of this nation to deal real-istically with the northern ghetto," King claimed.[61]

With profound faith, King ventured into the city that some considered the "new capital of black nationalism."[62] It was not only a bastion of white racism and antipathy, it was the national headquarters for the country's largest black nationalist organization. The Nation of Islam had a formidable presence in the Windy City, especially during the age of Black Power.

King, well aware of the new, more militant, spirit of black people, did something he had never been willing to do before: he publicly met with the country's leading black nationalist leader. On February 23, 1966, King and Elijah Muhammad met and discussed the black freedom struggle. King, long a proponent of universal humanism, was forced to ask Muhammad about the Yacub story. Whites, King argued, could not all be dismissed as devils. Muhammad retorted, "Dr. King, you and me grew up in Georgia and we know different kinds of snakes. The rattlesnake was poisonous; the king snake was friendly. But they are both snakes."[63] They reportedly had a hearty laugh, but King was not any closer to being a black nationalist or believing in universal white deviltry.

King's meeting with Muhammad was part of an attempt to make an appeal to the militant youth who considered him an "Uncle Tom." Black militant youth pelted him with eggs in Harlem, ridiculed him in Watts, and booed him in Chicago. As a leading SNCC advocate of Black Power, Willie Ricks, explained, "the people began to consider King out of touch with the struggle. Many viewed him as an Uncle Tom by 1966."[64] King was very much aware of the growth of militancy and nationalism. He was more aware of the antiwhite sentiments among many blacks who had grown pessimistic about what they saw as inveterate white racism. He still found it necessary to remind people that "there are some white people in the United States just as determined to see us free as we are to free our-selves."[65] Despite his constant urging for racial reconciliation, King was faced with trying times and vicious racism. White Chicagoans would soon reveal a degree of racial hatred that he had never witnessed in his life, ulti-mately pushing King toward a quasi-black nationalist position.

In July 1966, SCLC protestors staged demonstrations against Chicago's racially restrictive housing policies. Protestors were met by mobs of whites taunting marchers and attacking them with rocks and debris. King, who was out of town, returned to Chicago and promised to lead a nonviolent march into the all-white Gage Park and Chicago Lawn areas. Six hundred marchers attempted to walk from Marquette Park to realty firms several blocks away, under the protection of one thousand police officers. Seconds after King stepped from his car he was felled by a rock, which struck his right temple. Dazed, King remained on his knees for a few moments, then stood to see thousands of hostile and jeering whites. The crowd of five thousand whites significantly outnumbered the police and marchers. Many waved Confederate flags and placards reading "Nigger Go Home!" "White Power," and "Go Back to the Zoo." Racists gleefully chanted, "HATE! HATE! HATE!" as marchers walked under a barrage of bottles and stones. One section of the mob proudly sang their ode to white supremacy:

I wish I were an Alabama trooper
That is what I would truly like to be;
I wish I were an Alabama trooper
'Cause then I could kill the niggers legally.[66]

One civil rights marcher from Mississippi declared that in all of her days of experience with racists, she had never seen a Nazi swastika until the Chicago mobs. Even for King, Chicago's white supremacist mobs—complete with entire families and children yelling racist epithets and vulgar language—were a new and sobering experience. "I have never seen as much hate and hostility before, and I have been on a lot of marches."[67] While King never abandoned his positions on nonviolence and racial reconciliation, he was changing with the times. In 1967 King began questioning the efficacy of seeking integration with whites in neighborhoods when whites incessantly fled to new, all-white areas or mounted violent resistance, resulting even in death for black people. Blacks were always playing "follow the whites" in order to integrate. Dismayed, King remarked that "I don't believe in black separatism. I'm against it . . . But I do say this. It seems that our white brothers and sisters don't want to live next door to us . . . So . . . they're pinning us in central cities . . . We're hemmed in. We can't get out . . . what we're going to have to do is just control the central city. We got to be the mayors of these big cities. And the minute we get elected mayor, we've got to begin taxing everybody who works in the city who lives in the suburbs. I know this sounds mean, but I just want to be realistic."[68]

Moved by the evolving militancy, King was also careful to tap into the new cultural nationalism. He increasingly recognized the growing level of racial consciousness among African Americans and often spoke the language of Black Power and more frequently spoke to the militants' frustrations. In 1967 he wrote that Black Power was not completely futile or destructive, a modification of his initial rebuke of the slogan. As James Cone explains, "King tried to invest [Black Power] with positive meaning [when he saw its growing popularity]. He lauded its emphasis on black self-esteem. 'The Negro is in dire need of a sense of dignity and a sense of pride, and I think Black Power is an attempt to develop pride. And there's no doubt about the need for power—he can't get into the mainstream of society without it.'" King went further to declare that "Black Power means instilling within the Negro a sense of belonging and appreciation of heritage, a racial pride . . . We must never be ashamed of being black." Even the SCLC by 1967 recognized the power of cultural nationalism, when several placards at its annual convention read "Black is beautiful and it's so beautiful to be black."[69]

In 1967 King revealed a more radical analysis of oppression in America, calling for "democratic socialism" and increasingly criticizing capitalism's shortcomings. While addressing the American Psychological Association, he castigated white America as "poisoned to its soul by racism." His indictment of white America was much stronger than in his previous speeches, which specifically targeted white racists. Speaking about white Americans in nearly monolithic terms, he explained that "white America is seeking to keep the walls of segregation substantially intact while the evolution of society and the Negro's desperation is causing them to crumble. The white majority, unprepared and unwilling to accept radical structural change, is resisting and producing chaos while complaining that if there were no chaos orderly change would come." King denounced the hypocritical nature of white Americans and insisted that if one "calculated and compared . . . the law breaking of a few days of riots [with the violations of the white man], the hardened criminal would be the white man." The largely white group listened quietly as King celebrated the "inner transformation that is liberating [black people] from ideological dependence on the white majority." He continued to explain that black people were not troubled by the so-called white backlash to black militancy. White backlash "awakened [black people] and revealed the nature of the oppressor. To lose illusion is to gain truth. Negroes have grown wiser and more mature and they are hearing more closely those who are raising fundamental questions about our society whether the critics be Negro or white. When this process of awareness and independence crystallizes, every rebuke, every evasion, becomes hammer blows on the wedge that splits the Negro from the larger society."

Though King's vituperative language sounded more akin to post–Nation of Islam Malcolm X than his 1963 "I Have A Dream" speech, King had not abandoned his vision of a society no longer beholden to the social construct of race and its inherent limitations on humanity. King clearly grew weary of the assiduous pursuit of white acceptance and appeals to integrate into the largely hostile white society. He also textured his speech with staples of Black Power, including the celebration of black independence from Eurocentric paradigms of thought and analysis. Like the Panthers, he avoided essentialist rhetoric that argued for strict black nationalism. Though the new black consciousness was good, "black people still have faith in a dream that we will all live together as brothers."[70] King's newly modified vision was much more in line with Black Power than it had ever been. It was critical of the idealistic demand for integration, though desegregation was essential to expanding black opportunities for uplift. It also placed great value on the psychological importance of being black in a virulently antiblack society. The power of cultural nationalism was not lost on King. He was not alone among the leading civil rights leaders who were warming to Black Power. For some, however, the "warming" appeared to be driven more by expediency, the need to respond to the pervasive political and cultural ramifications of Black Power than by a genuine embrace of its principles.

Increasingly, King and other more moderate black leaders, found themselves vilified by black militants and even challenged by rank and file members of their own organizations. Moderates like Whitney M. Young Jr., executive director of the Urban League, and Roy Wilkins of the NAACP were called "enemies of the people."[71] The NAACP experienced upheavals in all of its national conventions between 1967 and 1971, led by Young Turks who attempted to make the organization more progressive and "in tune" with the Black Power movement.[72] More often than not, the NAACP leader became the focal point of militant animus. In 1969, after Wilkins denounced black students' efforts to form black studies programs, the NAACP head was derided in the *Black Panther* as "Uncle Roy," who had "stooped to kiss the boots of the power elite." The "Negro moderate," the article explained, must learn that "Black People in this country are no longer interested in tokenism and compromise." The black students were "to be commended for the courage they have shown in seeking their right of self-determination," and the writer encouraged black parents to support the efforts of their children in their fight for "self-determination" and rebuke the efforts of "Negroes such as 'Uncle Roy' Wilkins" who were detached from the masses of blacks, living instead in a "bygone era" while attempting "to maintain their social and economic status by siding with the power structure."[73] The widespread criticism of Wilkins, like that leveled by the Panthers was not, of course, isolated to people outside of the NAACP.

Shortly after the Panther diatribes, Celes King of the Los Angeles branch of the NAACP denounced the executive director as the "greatest Uncle Tom in America." Philadelphia's chapter head, Cecil Moore, was suspended for calling Wilkins and other moderates "the white man's errand boys." Others considered Wilkins a "white man who somehow came out the wrong color." Whitney Young of the Urban League was also routinely criticized by black militants, some of whom believed that "a black man today . . . is either a radical or an Uncle Tom."[74] The rate of criticism that moderates received in black communities was growing steadily by 1967, as black people donned Afros and African names and intellectuals threw their full support behind black studies programs, despite discouragement from moderates.

Whitney Young and other moderates had to modify their positions on Black Power if they hoped to maintain a following in black communities. Once a vehement opponent of Black Power, by mid-1968 Young recognized the popularity of the slogan. In July he remarked that "the words . . . have caught the imagination, and they come to convey above all pride and community solidarity—and this is a positive, constructive concept." Cheers erupted from the crowd, where people gleefully announced that "the brother's come home!" One young social worker declared to Young, "You have made the decision to walk among your people without fear and to be a true leader rather than being a tool of the establishment." In a further affirmation of his new fondness of Black Power, he greeted the Urban League's fifty-eighth annual convention with declarations that Black Power "is the power of Negroes to choose: to live in harmony with whites, to live among themselves amid decent surroundings—even to exclude whites if they wish." The white officials of the Urban League also voiced support for Young's speech. James A. Linen, president of Time, Inc., and national president of the Urban League, declared that he was an advocate of Black Power. "Of course I'm for Black Power," he stated, "but not for black terrorist power."[75]

Even Richard Nixon, who ran a presidential campaign on restoring "law and order" and "patriotism," capitalized on Black Power by encouraging capitalist enterprises in black communities that will result in "black pride, black jobs and . . . black power."[76] Perhaps his rhetoric paid off. In 1972 the National Council of Afro-Americans, a group of black Republicans, held a dinner to benefit Nixon's reelection campaign. The group even praised Strom Thurmond, the notoriously racist senator from South Carolina who denounced expanding democracy to black people and broke from the Democratic Party after it endorsed civil rights for all Americans. Another group of black Republicans attracted two thousand blacks, including football star Jim Brown and Betty Shabazz, Malcolm X's widow. Some complained that they did not know that the event was partisan and were shocked to hear speakers laud Nixon's efforts to benefit the "black struggle." One member even compared the president to Jesus Christ.[77] These black GOP organizations were formed specifically to exercise the same "self-determination" that advocates of Black Power believed essential for black people. Like the Afro-American Patrolmen's League, the Association of Black Social Workers, and the other organizations born during the Black Power era, they found race important enough to operate separate from their larger white associations. Indeed, Black Power had an appeal across ideological lines, largely because the exigencies of race operated across ideological lines. Furthermore, these organizations reveal that being an advocate of Black Power did not necessarily mean that one supported radical politics or even substantive change for black uplift or equality.

While it is possible that King and other moderates came to believe in the genuine efficacy of Black Power, they were probably just catching up with the mood of the black masses, which had grown increasingly warm to nationalistic rhetoric since 1964. There was also an attempt by the more moderate elements to co-opt Black Power by "sanitizing" it and making it palatable to powerful whites and white liberals who supported the civil rights effort. Whitney Young clearly was not a militant or fan of black nationalism, yet he embraced Black Power in an effort to bridge the growing chasm that separated him from the political mood of the black masses without fundamentally modifying his political platform.

By adopting Black Power he helped suffuse the slogan with a more innocuous meaning for many whites. Black Power, he explained, did not have to be antiwhite or violent. That Stokely Carmichael and Floyd McKissick had made the same insistence meant little for the white media. Young was, after all, often considered the most "responsible" of black leadership in the white press.[78] He spoke to the wealthy and powerful business elite and procured millions of dollars for the Urban League by the late 1960s. It was unlikely that he was becoming an antiwhite violent black nationalist, and, in response to those who were concerned that he might be abandoning his moderate politics, Young assured them that he had not changed his position at all.[79] Young was simply helping to lead a process of deradicalizing Black Power by ascribing moderate principles to a fundamentally nebulous slogan. Black Power often meant little more than an affirmation of the American tradition of ethnic politics; however, its defiant style evoked a particular militancy that was hard to deny. This militant tone attracted millions to the slogan as the decade progressed. Anti–Black Power moderates soon realized that they could embrace Black Power and imbue the slogan with moderation without fundamentally changing its essence. This tactic, along with the commercialization of Black Power, was an effective attempt to defang the homegrown menace to white America.

Black Power and the Church

The political and social thrusts of the 1960s affected all major African American institutions. The decade brought substantive change in the ways in which race and power were understood in America. Generational, regional, and class shifts were felt nationwide in black America, and its churches, long the cornerstones of the black community, necessarily adapted to the times.

Leading black theologians became promoters of Black Power after 1966, despite the anti–Black Power resolution made by the largest black religious body, the National Baptist Convention (NBC), in 1966. The NBC rejected the militant slogan because of its nationalist overtones. Black Power ran contrary to the organization's Christian goal of reconciliation. Other leading Christians, however, disagreed with the NBC resolution.

Soon after the NBC anti–Black Power resolution, an ad hoc group of ministers formed the National Committee of Negro Churchmen (NCNC) to "speak a word of clear analysis" in an arena of confusion surrounding Black Power. On July 31, 1966, the NCNC published a full-page advertisement in the *New York Times* to proclaim its support for Black Power. In November 1967 the growing NCNC, then comprised of twelve protestant denominations, announced its decision to work with Black Power advocates. Led by Rev. Benjamin F. Payton, the NCNC declared its "effort to relate to the Black Power movement without adopting a philosophy of separation or black superiority. Our definition of Black Power is the power to participate." This move signified a major shift in religious politics in black America. Other Christian churches across the country made similar declarations of support for Black Power, if not full-fledged endorsement of black nationalism.[80]

In February 1968 the group Black Methodists for Church Renewal delivered its "Black Paper" to the United Methodist Church and affirmed its unabashed support for Black Power. "Black Power," the paper reads, "provides the means by which black people do for themselves that which no other group can do for them." It also "means the development and utilization of the gifts of black men for the good of black men and the whole nation." As historian Vincent Harding notes, Black Power fit comfortably into the religious ethos of the black struggle: "The qualified universalism of Black Power is also streaked with vivid suggestions of Messianism at many points."[81] Marcus Garvey, Malcolm X, Elijah Muhammad, and others represented strong Messianic figures who have been considered harbingers of liberation for black people. Moreover, these leaders have also created a language of black liberation with rich, religiously discursive qualities. Infused into Christianity, Black Power, by necessity, undermines the white supremacist religion promoted by the Christian enslavers of African people. In the case of the Nation of Islam, Black Power offered a new affirmation of black identity. As the Nation struck a cord with many who were disaffected with worshiping a white-looking savior in the age of Black Power, black churches increasingly jettisoned their paintings of a white Jesus. During the rise of African-centered Christianity, the Nation's influence was not ignored.

In 1968 theologian Joseph R. Washington Jr. recognized that the black church must respond effectively to the new black militancy or face challenges from the burgeoning Nation of Islam. "The widespread repudiation by many black Americans of a white Christ has added to the attractiveness of the Black Muslim movement," he wrote. He also complained that the black church "has failed miserably" to relate to the oppression of black people, as well as to the urban rebellions that had swept the country.[82] In reaction to the influence of the Nation of Islam and Black Power expressed by some black churches, religious leaders developed a more rigorous and militant interpretation of Christianity and its role in the black freedom struggle.

Bishop Joseph A. Johnson Jr. of the Christian Methodist Episcopal Church taught of Jesus "The Liberator" who was the power, love and wisdom of God. Johnson instructed black Christians to reject the white-looking image of Jesus, which represented "the image of the oppressor." In order for black people to utilize Christianity effectively as a vehicle of resistance to oppression, he argued, they must renounce the bastardized interpretations of a timid, weak, otherworldly Jesus, which is grounded in a "severely limited" white theology. In many ways, the language of the new Black Power Christians appears to be an answer to the criticisms leveled by the Nation of Islam, which argued that Christianity was "one of the most perfect black-slave-making religions on our planet." Mark Chapman writes that "the relentless critique of the Nation of Islam and the emergence of Black Power caused the creditability of the Christian faith to be severely tested in black ghettoes across the nation."[83] By 1968 the idea of a black Madonna and child was not as absurd among blacks as it had been in the 1950s. All types of black churches commissioned paintings of a dark-skinned Jesus, as more people referenced Revelation 1:14–15 to affirm their belief that the historical Jesus shared the "bronze" complexion and wooly hair of black people.[84] While churches gravitated toward Black Power and nationalism, they also found themselves serving the political aspirations of the leading revolutionary organization of the era—the Black Panther Party.

Early in the development of the Black Panther Party, it had established amicable ties with black churches. The first free breakfast programs were held mostly in black churches across the country. By 1969, the Panthers were feeding an estimated ten thousand children each morning, mostly in black churches. Cities like Chicago, Indianapolis, San Francisco, and Oakland were fortunate to have churches that eagerly opened their doors to the party's survival programs. Father Earl Neil of Oakland even likened the party to Jesus the Liberator when he told reporters that "the only difference between Jesus and the Black Panther Party is that Jesus fed 5,000 and the Black Panther Party feeds 10,000."[85]

For the Panthers, the church was an important connection with the masses of black people whom they sought to lead. Intent on being the vanguard party of the revolution, they were well aware of the central role that the church played in black communities. Because of ideological problems with many black churches, however, some Panther chapters severed ties with the church and even offered harsh condemnation of religious leaders. In 1970, Chief of Staff David Hilliard spoke to the National Committee of Black Churchmen in Berkeley, California, and denounced the ministers in attendance as "a bunch of bootlicking pimps and motherfuckers."[86] Although Hilliard was later chastised for his remarks, many Panthers believed that the ministers of black churches generally offered otherworldly solutions to worldly problems. Many Panthers agreed with Karl Marx's assertion that religion is the opiate of the masses.[87]

The Black Panther Party was the result of Black Power and the stubborn practice of racial oppression. It was a reflection of the political shifts occurring among black people, and it revealed the shortcomings of the civil rights movement. The focus of civil rights leaders on southern white supremacy often overlooked the oppression black people faced in other parts of the country. Moreover, the civil rights movement failed to address substantively the deeply ingrained and profound psychological consequences of being black in a virulently antiblack society. The frustration of urban blacks in the North and West was manifested in scores of urban rebellions between 1964 and 1969. After landmark civil rights bills were passed in 1964 and 1965, civil rights leaders were forced to redirect their activities to stave off the spread of militancy and nationalism, which pervaded black communities nationwide.

Out of the contest for control of the somewhat nebulous slogan developed a new movement. The proponents of this movement helped meld the cynical nationalism of the Nation of Islam and the hopeful activism of integrationist civil rights proponents. The Black Power movement emerged from this fusion of tactics and axiology. It was not wedded to the territorial separatism of black nationalism. It did not forfeit American citizenship. It did not abandon activism out of a distrust of white institutions. Nor did Black Power advocate for white acceptance. It did not appeal to white America's moral conscience through passive resistance. It affirmed black people, their history, their beauty, and set them at the center of their own worldview. It approved black anger at the vicious cycle of white supremacy. It also declared black people's right to autonomous space within white-controlled domains. Whether in professional associations or prisons, black people carved out autonomous spaces to exercise self-determination.

As black anger boiled over in city after city, it became apparent that the language of nonviolence was not as popular among blacks as many would have liked to believe. The language of integration, too, lost its appeal among many blacks who increasingly established and cultivated separate black institutions, such as academic theme houses, churches, professional societies, and other organizations that nurtured black consciousness, independent of white people. Moderate black leaders and organizations that once claimed that integration was inextricably linked with black liberation were forced to modify their language in order to maintain legitimacy among the black masses. Black moderates abandoned the vitriolic language they initially had used to denounce Black Power, as a large cross-section of black people gravitated to Black Power as the decade came to a close. By the early 1970s moderate African Americans who once refused to use the word *black* as a term of racial designation had not only abandoned the word *Negro* and embraced the Black Power slogan but were increasingly defending the most bombastic and visible revolutionary black group in U.S. history—the Black Panther Party. It was clear that the Panthers reflected the militancy and political evolution of the times. While most blacks were not advocates of revolution, the Old Guard of black leadership knew it had to catch up with the militant and quasi-nationalist spirit of the times or lose influence and power in the black community.

In many respects, the civil rights leadership became victims of its own success. Between 1955 and 1965, almost 70 percent of all civil rights activity occurred in the South. As sociologist Doug McAdam notes, "Broadly defined, it was racial integration, in a variety of settings, that served as the fundamental goal of the movement until the mid-1960s." Moreover, the movement experienced a decline after it was unable to "mount or sustain . . . united efforts" as it had during its early stage, when its activities were concentrated around very visible and naked forms of racial oppression.[88] The laws that sanctioned white supremacy had been dismantled in every state by 1970.[89] It was the absence of racist laws, however, that seemed to push many oppressed blacks closer toward radical positions. Legal reforms in and of themselves did not ensure justice. A fundamental overhaul of the system seemed necessary. While most moderates would never openly endorse the revolutionary program of organizations like the BPP, they had discovered, by the close of the decade, a cause: defense of the constitutional rights of black radicals like the Panthers, who increasingly found themselves victims of state repression. Black communities voiced outrage at police aggression, and moderate leaders were sure to keep in step with the concerns of their constituency. Moderates were undoubtedly aware of and influenced by the polls that revealed the esteem in which people held the Panthers. Had moderates ignored the naked police aggression against black people, they would have risked losing their base of support in black communities nationwide.

At the same time, the Nation of Islam, once considered the boldest and most audacious black organization, rejected the new cultural nationalism and its identification with sub-Saharan African names, customs, and fashions. It also rejected direct confrontations with the state, embracing instead a tenacious self-help program that sought to provide basic necessities such as food, shelter, and clothing, all independent of whites. Despite its conservative nature, the Nation continued to grow in wealth and membership. It fully embraced a quiet program of nation-building, emerging as the richest black organization in North America, experiencing relatively little violent state repression and a decrease in vilification by white mainstream media.[90] The Nation had been for many a springboard for increased radicalism and political consciousness; it also served as a stabilizing force in some nationalist communities, such as in Los Angeles. In the late 1960s Los Angeles reflected the tumultuous nature of its recent conflagration. Competing factions there attempted to be soldiers in the struggle against oppression, but they sometimes fell into the schemes of their oppressors. Yet the Watts rebellion was more than a local phenomenon. It was a microcosm of the general political landscape and the emergence of new and radicalized members of the black urban poor—those to whom the Black Panthers appealed and those who caused angst among moderates nationwide. Ultimately, these radicalized elements helped forge a new identity for black people via the Black Power movement, with its far-reaching influence in political, cultural, religious, and educational arenas.

Black Power, despite the vitriol with which civil rights leaders attacked it, was not diametrically opposed to the civil rights movement. It complimented the movement in interesting and unique ways. It humanized whites as civil rights did not. It provided new cultural challenges to the vestiges of white supremacy that legal campaigns could not. It encouraged black people to boldly resist daily and constant encounters that challenged black humanity. Across the country, blacks and whites began a process of stark informal negotiations of a new racial etiquette. It was never a smooth or easy process, and it was often not pretty, but it helped bring black people closer to the liberation they sought and for which they struggled.

CHAPTER 6

Rainbow Radicalism
The Rise of Radical Ethnic Nationalism

The Black Power movement had a profound affect on the symbolism, rhetoric, and tactics of radical activism outside the African American community during the era of tumultuous political and social change in the late 1960s. Scholars have long credited the civil rights movement with fomenting the emerging liberation movements of women, gays, and others in the late 1960s and early 1970s. While the black struggle for civil rights undoubtedly affected the growing efforts of other marginalized and oppressed groups in the United States, it was the Black Power movement that had some of the most visible influences on the radical activist struggles of Latinos, Asians, and Native Americans, giving rise to a visible movement of radical ethnic nationalism and new constructions of ethnic identity. Young activists of all backgrounds had been impressed and inspired by the militancy, political analysis, organization, and symbolism of black nationalists and Black Power advocates. No organization influenced these burgeoning militants more than the Black Panther Party (BPP).

The Nation of Islam (NOI), chief benefactor of the Black Power movement and largest black nationalist organization in the country, had long embraced all people of color as members of the family of black humanity. Still, the Nation's language, symbolism, and general cosmology were geared toward African Americans. There were Latinos, Asians, and others who joined the NOI, but for non–African Americans, the Black Power movement demonstrated that ethnic nationalism had incredible potential for political mobilization and resistance to the oppression and marginalization they experienced. For many, the BPP, in particular, represented the model for revolutionary struggle, resistance, and radical chic.

The party experienced precipitous growth in 1968, with more than thirty chapters emerging across the country. While thousands of African American militants were willing to embrace the party as a vanguard organization to lead the national struggle against oppression, non–African

Americans took notice. Conditions that gave rise to the radicalism that characterized Black Power similarly catapulted other minorities and even poor whites into militant activism in the late 1960s. Other people of color had languished under the domination of white supremacy in the United States for more than a hundred years. The militant call for Black Power reverberated in the barrios and ghettoes, engendering such organizations as the Brown Berets, Young Lords, Red Guard, American Indian Movement, and others that joined the chorus for liberation and radical political activism. By 1967 the Brown Berets had become the first major organization to model itself after the Black Panthers, emerging as the self-described "shock troops" for a burgeoning Chicano civil rights movement.

Throughout the West, communities with high concentrations of Mexican Americans passed laws barring Chicanos from attending schools with white children, obtaining municipal jobs, and even owning land.[1] Hundreds of thousands of acres of land were procured from Mexicans by Anglos between 1848 and 1960. Chicanos in the West became a source of cheap agricultural labor for Anglo landlords, much like blacks in the South. In the mid-1960s a movement to organize Mexican farmworkers, led by Cesar Chavez in California, gave birth to the Chicano civil rights movement.

The Chavez-led strike helped generate activism in barrios across the state. East Los Angeles, home to one of the largest Spanish-speaking communities in the nation, became a center of increasing political activism. Chicanos in the city suffered from police brutality and widespread discrimination in housing, education, and employment, as they had throughout the Southwest. Although Chicanos were California's second-largest ethnic group, they had only one state assemblyman and no state senators. In Los Angeles, there were no Chicano city councilmen or representatives on the county board of directors. By 1970 a full 80 percent of Chicanos were high school dropouts, a rate higher than any ethnic group in the city.[2]

In 1967 high school student David Sanchez organized the Young Citizens for Community Action (YCCA) in East Los Angeles. Attempting to meet the needs of the surrounding community, the YCCA surveyed the dilemmas of Latino students and sought Chicano representation on the L.A. board of education, campaigning for Julian Nava. Initially, a liberal, youth-oriented reformist organization, the YCCA quickly became affected by the wave of radicalism that swept the country. With the help of Father John Luce, YCCA opened a coffee shop, La Piranya, in September 1967, which provided a meeting place for Chicano youth and others who read poetry, held meetings, and took part in informal political discussion groups. There, young Chicanos talked about the tumultuous political and social climate that had given rise to Black Power, student radicalism, and a generally militant mood among many young people. Police brutality, poverty, and pervasive discrimination against Chicanos were issues of frequent debate. La Piranya also served a meeting place for many of the leaders of the Black Power movement, including H. Rap Brown, Stokely Carmichael from the Student Nonviolent Coordinating Committee (SNCC) (who also served as officials of the Black Panther Party), and Maulana Karenga, from the Us organization. Books and tapes by and about Malcolm X were exchanged, and, like black people, many Mexican Americans gravitated to a more salient racial and cultural affirmation that was not dependent on whites.[3]

On November 24, 1967, police officers who had been called to a civil disturbance in East Los Angeles beat one man unconscious. According to eyewitnesses, the man's wife and daughter were also beaten, pulled by the hair to a squad car where they were arrested and taken to jail. Similar stories of police brutality had been long known in black and Chicano communities in Los Angeles. It was the new militant climate, however, that moved Sanchez and other members of YCCA to seek redress, by placing police brutality central to the agenda of Chicano activism.[4]

On December 3, David Sanchez formed the first unit of the Brown Berets, which demonstrated in front of the East Los Angeles Sheriff Station and the Hollenbeck Division of the Los Angeles Police Department. In addition to creating a formal organization to protest police brutality and the general oppression of Chicanos, Sanchez developed a uniform for its membership. Each of the twelve members wore a brown beret as his new uniform, demonstrating to spectators that the group was unified and militant.[5] Many observers knew that the beret had been derived from the uniform of the Black Panther Party for Self-Defense.

The BPP adopted the black beret as part of its uniform in 1966, along with the black leather jacket, black slacks and powder blue shirt, and black shoes.[6] While black militants before the party had worn sunglasses and leather jackets, the beret was the Panthers' unique symbol, and it soon became an icon of militancy and radicalism across the country. For Sanchez, the beret symbolized "the dignity and pride in the color of my skin and my race."[7] It also represented his identification with the Panthers' revolutionary program.

While Sanchez spearheaded a new revolutionary nationalist group, Denver-based Rodolfo "Corky" Gonzales cultivated a Mexican-American brand of cultural nationalism and helped popularize the term *Chicano*,

which supplanted *Mexican-American*. While there are different explana-
tions of the word's origin, according to Gonzales, Chicano was a name
with deep historical meaning, rooted in a rich and proud tradition.[8] Like
the term *Negro*, Mexican-American, to Gonzalez and others, reflected a
confused, culturally ignorant assimilationist, wedded to the system of
oppression and exploitation that trampled on the rights of the brown
masses. These "Anglo-prones" eagerly defended white supremacy, even
to the extent that they accepted their own inferiority. The acceptance of
their inferiority was indicative in their eagerness to jettison any cultural
trappings of their Chicano heritage and their willingness to idealize whiteness. Speaking Spanish was discouraged, as were holidays, rituals, and
other aspects of Mexican culture. Chicano, by contrast, proudly affirmed
self-determination.[9]

Like the newly popularized word *black*, Chicano came from the people,
not the oppressors. It was a word the people chose to identify and define
themselves. It also spoke to the myths that characterize cultural nationalist
traditions, an essential part of nationality formation, as political scientist
Karl Deutsch has explained.[10] Like black nationalism, Chicano nationalism
celebrated a past envisioned as an almost Edenic pre-European-contact
world. That past served a source of pride and fundamentally undermined
the history lessons taught in schools, in which non-Europeans were perennially marginalized and relegated to secondary roles as backdrops to the
stage of European history and civilization.

People of Mexican descent in the United States, had, like other people
of color, sought to approximate the cultural standards of white Americans,
despite whites' overt hostility toward them. From the European standard
of beauty to the pride that people took in claiming European ancestry (or
denying Indian and African ancestry), Mexican people experienced the
psychological effects of racism. In a culture where Spanish ancestry and
white skin had benefits, Chicano cultural nationalists insisted that they
were a "bronze" people, whose native ancestors built great monuments
and civilizations, such as Aztlan. They revered the Aztecs for their cultural
and material achievements. Some nationalists even dropped their Spanish
names, considered symbols of European imperialism and conquest of the
Aztec empire. Like the black nationalist adoration for the empires of
ancient Egypt, the Swahili, or West Africa, Chicano nationalists conveniently overlooked the fact that the Aztecs had built their massive empire
on the backs of subjugated, exploited, and oppressed victims.

In a political climate that saw black nationalists bicker over the role of
cultural and revolutionary nationalism, many Chicano nationalists easily

merged the two types. The Panthers, self-described enemies of cultural "pork chop" nationalism, were able to influence the Berets significantly in their rhetoric and symbolism without substantively affecting the Berets' position on cultural nationalism. The Berets created titles for their leadership that mirrored the party's: minister of information, minister of defense, minister of education, and prime minister, among others. They also adopted eight points of attention, which listed the BPP's eight points verbatim.[11] In their "13 Point Program" the Brown Berets made eight of the ten demands in Panthers' Ten-Point Platform and Program, including "an end to the robbery of our community by the capitalist businessmen," exemption for all Chicanos from military service, the release of all Chicanos from jails, and the immediate end to police brutality.[12] Though supportive of Chicano cultural nationalism, the Berets were not tolerant of conservative economic programs couched in the seemingly radical rhetoric of "Chicano Power."

In language reflective of the BPP's leftist politics, the Berets were highly critical of the Chicano pride that sought community development through capitalism. "Many so-called Chicanos leach off the people, just because they are Chicanos. Many times the sign that says *'se habla espanol'* [Spanish spoken here] really means, 'come in we'll speak in Spanish and I'll charge you 30% credit charge.'"[13] Still, the Berets and other militant Chicanos celebrated cultural nationalism extensively: "Before we could move the system that oppressed us, we first had to realize our own identity. Because of the cultural and psychological genocide suffered by Chicanos, many of us did not realize our own identity. We called ourselves everything from Spanish to American of Mexican ancestry. Many Chicanos were ashamed of being Mexican or Chicano, because the racist system only showed us as bandits or lazy dumb winos. By bringing the true history of Chicanos to light all of *La Raza* can be proud of a great culture and history."[14]

Control of the public schools was central to the Berets' effort to realize a more appropriate study of Chicano history and culture. Suffering from high drop-out rates and a school board that appeared indifferent, if not hostile, the Berets worked closely with the "Eastside Blowouts" of March 1968. During these blowouts, nearly ten thousand students in five East Los Angeles high schools walked out of classes, demanding better education and Chicano control of schools. The result was an upsurge in Chicano student and youth militancy across the Southwest. Thousands of high school students walked out in cities in California, Texas, Arizona, and Colorado demanding similar reforms.[15] With the increased activism came new police attention. On June 9, 1968, three months after the initial blowouts, police raided the homes and offices of thirteen Chicano activists, who were arrested on charges of "conspiracy to disrupt the schools." Los Angeles County district attorney Evelle J. Younger charged the activists with a felony that could have resulted in prison sentences of 66 years for each person convicted. Seven of the thirteen who were arrested were Brown Berets, including founder David Sanchez, who was preparing for his high school prom when police took him to jail.[16] Although all were acquitted of these charges after two years of appeals, police harassment continued as the Berets became more militant in their organization of Chicano youth. Despite the violent gang epidemic of East Los Angeles, police devoted more attention, including arrests, surveillance, and man hours used to disrupt the Berets than any gang in the city.[17]

In May 1969, the Berets opened the East Los Angeles Free Clinic on Whittier Boulevard to serve poor Chicanos in the area. An expansion of their activities also included the Chicano Moratorium rally held in December at Obregon Park, which brought together two thousand people to protest the Vietnam War and the exorbitant death rate of Chicano soldiers. The Second Chicano Moratorium rally at Laguna Park produced five thousand marchers, but it was the Third Chicano Moratorium that would make history as perhaps the largest Chicano rally ever, when between twenty and thirty thousand people marched on August 29, 1970.[18]

Despite arrests of their leadership, the bombing of their headquarters, and factionalism, the Brown Berets continued for two more years until they disbanded in the fall of 1972. At a press conference that October, David Sanchez announced that the organization of ninety chapters and five thousand members would dissolve so as to avoid further disruption of the Chicano Power movement by repressive agents of the state. Subsequent U.S. congressional hearings on the FBI and COINTELPRO confirmed that the Brown Berets had been targeted for neutralization. As the hearings revealed, neutralization included, at times, extralegal activities such as break-ins, false correspondence, wiretaps, beatings, and even murder.[19]

For many Chicano activists, the Berets' revolutionary program invited police attention. Much like activists in the black community, some nationalists found a more subtle celebration of ethnic nationalism more effective in mobilizing militants. While they were not afraid of confrontational language, the cultural nationalist elements of Chicano Power flowered in the late 1960s and early 1970s, without significant cases of violent police repression.

Corky Gonzales helped spearhead a cultural renaissance through the Chicano Arts movement, which provided a scathing critique of white

America and paralleled the Black Arts movement. Gonzalez's 1967 epic poem "I Am Joaquin" became a staple of Chicano reading. Luiz Valdez's Teatro Campesino showcased Chicano talent on stage, while skilled Latino artists painted murals depicting romantic and politicized scenes of Aztlan, the Aztecs, and Mexican and Chicano history. In the realm of music, *corrido,* Chicano soul music, grew popular in barrios throughout the southwest and California.

Like their black counterparts, Chicano nationalists celebrated a new and dynamic language, replete with political meaning. Writer Jose Montoya produced some of the first Chicano literary pieces that used *calo,* or street slang. This use of calo further rejected the white American cultural standard, as had been the case with black poets who freely bastardized standard English with proud and pervasive usage of black vernacular. Relying heavily on Spanish as a language of Chicano nationalism, militants borrowed from the Black Power movement to create terms such as *Tio Taco* (literally, "Uncle Taco"), "Uncle Tom"; *carnales,* "brothers"; and *vendidos,* "sell-outs."

In April 1969 Gonzalez spoke at the Youth Liberation Conference in Denver and implored *La Raza* (the race/people) to remove themselves from the clutches of the *gabacho* (honky/whitey) and ground themselves in a world where they are in power. In a strong call for nationalism, the conference adopted a declaration, the "Plan Espiritual de Aztlan (Spiritual Plan of Aztlan)" in which people dedicated their efforts to "reclaiming the land of [our ancestors'] birth and consecrating the determination of our people of the sun." They continued to state that "Aztlan belongs to these who plant the seeds, water the fields and gather the crops and not to the foreign Europeans. We are a bronze people with a bronze culture. We are a nation."[20]

Chicano nationalism adopted its own symbols and ideals that embodied the ethos of self-determination and radicalism. Aztlan, as homeland to Chicanos, affirmed their right to the land where they lived—superceding and rejecting the white nativist exhortation to "go back to where you came from" and dismissing any notion that America was a white man's country. Some activists held placards that read "Aztlan: Love it or Leave it."[21] Chicano cultural nationalism simultaneously undermined the traditional Mexican racial and social hierarchy that made Spanish ancestry a source of pride and privilege. White skin had long symbolized prestige in Mexico, as it had in the United States. Chicano nationalists, however, departed from this paradigm and conspicuously celebrated a "bronze" nation, deriding European foreigners. White Americans had been put into the position of explaining their right to the land in North America. Despite this overt nationalism, as the case with Black Power advocates, Chicano militants did not abandon their rights to public or private institutions controlled by white people. Instead, these nationalists sought to carve out their own space within white-dominated domains. No institutions demonstrated this contest for power more than colleges and universities.

Due to the successes of the civil rights movement, white colleges and universities that had long practiced discriminatory polices to curtail the attendance of students of color experienced a significant increase in minority students by the late 1960s. Black students, inextricably connected to the political climate of their communities, clamored for self-determination through Black Power on campus. The cry for Black Power realized black student unions and black studies programs, as well as more recruitment of black faculty and staff. Beginning in California, Chicano students, who were some of the closest allies of African Americans, also demanded changes in the college curriculum. By 1969, Chicano students had created a popular Chicano Power movement on campuses throughout California and the Southwest.

In 1968 black students at San Francisco State College protested and demonstrated in favor of black studies. Other students of color joined their efforts and formed the Third World Liberation Front (TWLF). The TWLF brought together black, Chicano, and Asian American students for the first time in any major student activism. The demands for black studies evolved to include Chicano/La Raza and Asian American studies as well. The TWLF moved across the bay to the University of California at Berkeley and inspired students there to launch a large, protracted, and militant struggle for curriculum and administration changes.[22]

At Berkeley, long a hotbed of student activism, the massive student strike led by the TWLF began on January 22, 1969, and included five demands: (1) a Third World College to teach the history and current events of "Third World" people; (2) the hiring of more people of color by the university at all levels of the administration, from faculty to workers; (3) the recommendations of a selection committee to be composed of people of color and decisions not based on academic achievement alone; (4) Third World people's control of all programs affecting Third World people; and (5) no disciplinary action to be taken against the strikers. The movement was supported by a clear majority of students of color, where protests often attracted more than 1,500 students, half of all students of color at the university. White students eager to assist TWLF efforts formed the White Student Support Committee.[23]

The strike lasted for weeks, until the National Guard, San Jose and San Francisco tactical squads, and more than seven hundred Oakland and

Berkeley police were mobilized to put it down. Beatings and mass arrests pushed many students into greater radicalism, while others were discouraged from further action. A state of emergency was declared on campus and on the last day of finals in March 1969, nine weeks of confrontation came to a close. Negotiations and a series of compromises produced the Ethnic Studies Program. This process was more or less duplicated across the country, although the rich mix of ethnic groups was generally a California phenomenon.[24]

Influenced by the political and cultural climate in their respective communities as well as their involvement in the TWLF, Chicano and Asian American students moved closer to radicalism by 1969. Many Chicano student organizations were born out of this growing political and cultural consciousness. Between 1968 and 1969, numerous organizations representing Chicano students emerged on college campuses in California and the Southwest: Mexican-American Students (MAS), Mexican-American Students Confederation (MASC), Mexican-American Youth Organization (MAYO), Mexican-American Youth Association (MAYA), and United Mexican-American Students (UMAS). The Movimiento Estudiantil Chicano de Aztlan (MECHA) was formed at a conference in October 1969 with a hundred students, scholars, and activists who envisioned a unified plan to work for the benefit of Chicano students on college campuses.[25] Throughout the region, MECHA organized—often in alliances with African and Asian Americans—for Chicano and ethnic studies programs.

Chicano students, as well as blacks and Asians, created student newspapers that brought attention to current events in their respective ethnic communities—college and otherwise. Such papers reported favorable coverage of the Chicano student movement while denouncing the "gabacho system" and the racism of their "gringo fellow students." Although the Black Power movement influenced them, Chicano student activists were not without conflict with Black Power advocates. In 1970, Stanford University's MECHA chapter submitted a budget of $20,395 for the 1970–71 academic year, but disgruntled Chicano students complained that, "a coalition between conservatives and blacks has offered MECHA a token $5,800 in an attempt to buy us out." The university's Chicano student paper, *Chicanismo,* denounced the "gringos and their lackeys on this campus."[26] The struggle for resources college administrations earmarked for minority students would cause similar spats on other campuses in the state. Still, the occasional friction was overshadowed by the alliances and unity black and Chicano students celebrated. In the same issue in which it condemned black "lackeys," *Chicanismo* found inspiration in the words of black nationalists. Quoting Stokely Carmichael, the paper declared that, "integration is a euphemism for white supremacy." The paper also quoted Black Panther Eldridge Cleaver and found power in the unifying term "Third World people," which included people whose ancestors were from Africa, Asia, and Latin America.[27]

The creation of the TWLF in the Bay area mobilized and inspired thousands of Asian American students, as it had other students of color and many whites. Berkeley's *Asian Student* newspaper provided a history of the Asian Student Movement and acknowledged the influence that black students brought to the college arena. "Our black brothers and sisters were the first to cry out in protest in the civil rights movement and were the first to make militant radical demands for the transformation of society. Out of this grew the Asian Student Movement."[28]

Like other people of color, Asians in the United States had long experienced virulent and legally sanctioned racism. Some groups even petitioned the courts for legal status as "whites" in order to avoid the systemic oppression they experienced. They were unsuccessful.[29]

Influenced by the cultural and political currents of black nationalism and Black Power, Asian American militants found themselves consciously transforming the public image of their pan-ethnic "nation." Rejecting the stereotype of the timid, obsequious, and quiet Oriental, young Asian American militants affirmed themselves as radical harbingers of progress who were no longer enamored of whiteness. In 1968 the Asian American Political Alliance was formed at Berkeley and for the first time brought together disparate ethnic groups of Asian students. Richard Aoki, a Japanese American raised in West Oakland, joined the Black Panther Party while at Merritt College with Huey Newton and Bobby Seale. He later joined the AAPA after transferring to Berkeley. Aoki, a field marshal for the Panthers, explains that he "went underground to look into the Asian Movement to see if we could develop an Asian version of the BPP." Aoki soon became the spokesperson for the AAPA. The AAPA developed close ties with the BPP and the Red Guard, an Asian American organization modeled after the Panthers.[30] They often co-sponsored demonstrations and panels calling for justice for the Panthers and an end to "the pig repression of the Vanguard Party." With some members donning berets and sunglasses, the AAPA organized students around issues related to both the university and nonuniversity communities. As Vicci Wong, founding member of AAPA notes, "It wasn't just a local thing or just for our little group in college. We identified with the struggles that were going on then. We fought harder because we didn't see it as just our own fight."[31]

Students demanded more faculty and students of color, as well as an end to the Vietnam War, police brutality and the exploitation of Asian farmworkers. The Berkeley AAPA worked with a growing number of visible Asian American student leaders in the state, such as Jack Wong, a student activist at the University of California at Santa Barbara. These student activists called for more Asian American representation in college administrations, but they also put the politics of these Asian Americans under heavy scrutiny. Asian ancestry was not enough for AAPA support. Wong called the Japanese American acting president of San Francisco State College a "tool of the white power establishment" for resisting demands of the TWLF. Not satisfied with simply calling President Hayakawa an Uncle Tom, Wong and others also called him an "Uncle Charlie," derived from the Charlie Chan detective series.[32] That a Japanese American was derided by using a term derived from a Chinese character also demonstrates that race transcended ethnicity among these student activists. It was clear that the younger generation of Asian Americans had made a break with their parents' popular image as tolerant, apologetic, and meek "permanent foreigners," unwilling to jeopardize their pursuit of white acceptance by complaining too much. As the AAPA declared: "We Asian Americans believe that heretofore we have been relating to white standards of acceptability, and affirm the right of self-definition and self-determination. We Asian Americans support all non-white liberation movements and believe that all minorities in order to be truly liberated must have complete control over the political, economical and educational institutions within their respective communities."[33]

Dedicated to the mission of strong community ties beyond academia, Berkeley students traveled to Agbayni Village, a poor rural California retirement community for farmworkers, half of whom were Filipino men. These elderly were typically without a family and alone. Students provided development work and petitioned for farmworker rights.[34] In 1973 the Asian Student Union formed a community committee responsible for developing student support for issues in Chinatown, Manilatown, and Japantown. Often considered less audacious with their radical politics than their white, black, or Latino counterparts, Asian student activists were visible in the political discourse of the era, particularly on the West Coast. They provided films and sponsored panels on socialism, the Chinese Revolution, and class struggle, as well as antiwar activities. The relations between campus militancy and community militancy were as inextricable in Asian American communities as they were in Chicano and black communities.[35]

Asian Americans were forming radical organizations outside of academia as well. The most visible organization was the Red Guard, which grew out of the Bay area's dynamic political and cultural climate. Named after Mao Tse-tung's unit of young revolutionaries who burned the property of capitalists and counterrevolutionaries during the Chinese Cultural Revolution, the Red Guard was founded in 1969 in San Francisco. Like the Berets, the Red Guard saw the Panthers as an example of radical resistance to racial and class oppression. Armed, the Red Guard openly declared itself a Communist organization, a bold move in Chinatown. Fully aware of the incredible taboo against radical leftist political activity in the Chinese American community, the group initiated a series of projects to meet the people's basic needs. It was able to prevent the closing of a tuberculosis-testing center in Chinatown, exposing the fact that the TB rate in the city's Chinatown was the one of the highest in the country. It also worked with the Asian Legal Services and had a thousand cases of people who resisted the draft, via the Asian American Draft Help Center. The Breakfast for Children program chiefly fed black children from public housing projects in or around Chinatown. The program was modified to feed poor elderly, which brought many Asian senior citizens to the program.[36]

While the Red Guard saw itself as a Chinese American version of the Black Panther Party, it was also very well aware that the dynamics of the black and Chinese American communities were different. Alex Hing, a Red Guard co-founder who assumed the title minister of information (one of several titles that mirrored those in the BPP) explains that "we tried the model ourselves after the Panthers. When it didn't work, we gave it our own characteristics." To that end, the Guard hoped to serve the people in the same manner the Panthers had, but it also had a strong political and cultural affinity to Asia and was particularly concerned about China's role in global affairs. Moreover, the Guard understood Chinese American anxiety over the tenuous status of Chinese as American citizens. Only in 1965 did the U.S. government lift its more than seventy-year immigration restriction on Chinese. By campaigning for U.S. recognition of Beijing, the Guard demonstrated its political and cultural identification with mainland China; it also invited repression by the FBI and CIA.

The Red Guard's activities, which included efforts to seat China at the United Nations, were firmly connected to the larger leftist community, which proved to be of serious concern for U.S. foreign policy during the cold war. Leftists, influenced by the rapidly changing geopolitical landscape, increasingly assumed the mantle of radicalism in the contextual framework of anti-imperialism. Anti-imperialism had a profound resonance among radicals who were self-described "Third World People." This term declared their affinity with the struggles of people in Africa, Asia, and Latin America. It also postulated that "internal colonialism" was the mechanism by which people of color were subjugated in the United States. This rhetoric invariably found considerable coverage in the press of both communist and capitalist countries.

International news coverage reported on the plight of black people in the United States to millions worldwide and even influenced radicals overseas. The urban rebellions, shoot-outs with police, assassinations, and student upheaval were reported in countries that the United States considered friendly as well as in those it considered hostile, which caused headaches for the State Department. For communist countries, the social and political unrest in the United States indicated the inherent contradictions of a capitalist and imperialist society. Following the assassination of Martin Luther King Jr. in 1968, Mao Tse-tung led hundreds of thousands of Chinese demonstrators to denounce white supremacy in America. Mao was certainly not alone. Fidel Castro, president of Cuba, and other leaders of socialist countries eagerly exploited the news of civil unrest to denounce the United States and its subjugation of black people. The militant struggle of black people received more international media attention as the collective efforts of Black Power advocates provided a subtext to the American cold war dichotomy of "democracy" versus "communism." This was, of course, a false dichotomy that assumed that the United States was pro-democracy when it was actually pro-capitalism. As it demonstrated in its friendly foreign relations with Zaire, Haiti, South Africa, Rhodesia, and dozens of other undemocratic states, capitalism was more favorable than democracy for U.S. foreign policy makers.

For many international observers, the intensification of violent clashes between Black Panthers and the police through 1969 made the party the rightful revolutionary vanguard of the country's bourgeoning left. Communist countries North Korea and China issued favorable statements regarding the Panthers by 1969. In 1970, the International Section of the Black Panther Party, led by Eldridge Cleaver, established an "embassy" in North Korea. David Hilliard, Panther chief of staff, requested representation from the Red Guard for the eleven-member trip to North Korea. Alex Hing joined Hilliard and others in visits to North Korea, Vietnam and Algeria. As the Red Guard enjoyed international press and greater visibility, police harassment led to a steady decline in members.[37]

Like other radical organizations of the era, the Red Guard attracted a youthful membership, peaking with about two hundred members before police repression reduced membership to a few dozen. Their uniforms, which included army field jackets and red berets, were instant targets for the police. Red Guard members complained about systematic police harassment, being unable to walk down the street without being put up against the wall, frisked, and asked for identification. Their offices were constantly raided, often without sufficient pretense. In a cold war climate of fierce anticommunism, the FBI and CIA were eager to undermine the Red Guard and the Panthers for their domestic and international political activism. With joint efforts between federal and local law enforcement agencies, the Red Guard experienced significant challenges from police and the intelligence community, leaving the organization moribund by 1971.[38]

Unlike the Panthers, the Red Guard avoided the Custer-like defenses of their office during police raids, despite one armed standoff that a member had with police. A March 1969 issue of the Red Guard paper states that four "pigs" arrested Tyrone Won who was leaving Red Guard headquarters with a disassembled rifle. Later, while released on parole, Won joined a Black Panther who was also fleeing police and escaped to Mexico where they hijacked a plane for Cuba. In 1971 members decided to disband the Red Guard. Most joined other Asian American leftist organizations, particularly, I Wor Kuen, a New York–based organization that had become national by the early 1970s.[39]

Founded in 1969, the I Wor Kuen (IWK) was named after a secret society of Chinese rebels who tried to expel Westerners from China and dispose the Qing dynasty beginning in 1895. Called "Boxers" in the West, the I Wor Kuen attacked Westerners and Western influence in China, evoking outrage from the West, which eventually repressed what became known as the Boxer rebellion. In the United States, Yu Han and Yu Man, two graduate students from mainland China, led the IWK. The IWK was an extension of the radical ethnic nationalist discourse of the era. It was a Maoist organization that was ideologically modified to adapt to the highly racialized climate of the United States, while simultaneously adhering to the class-centered language of Maoism and Marxism. As former member Lee Lew-Lee explains, "the IWK was like the Black Panther Party, the Young Lords and the Red Guards" and was "patterned after the Red Guards." Like other militant groups, the IWK hoped to form an essential vanguard in its ethnic community to mobilize its people for a class-based revolution that would destroy racial and class oppression. Synthesizing theories of class struggle from Frantz Fanon, Mao, Lenin, and Marx, as well as the ever-dynamic Panthers, the IWK considered U.S. Chinatowns to be internal colonies. Neocolonialism provided them with a sound explanation of the system of oppression that exploited Chinese Americans and other people of color in the United States.[40]

While attempting to organize the Asian American community, the IWK, like the Red Guard, was confronted by deep-seated hostility from Chinese Americans who rejected Communist China and thought that leftist activities would reflect negatively on the Asian American community at large. Hoping to protect the Asian American community against any police state repression or future attempts to relocate citizens into internment camps, the IWK maintained a largely marginal voice in Asian American political discourse, despite its growth, which allowed it to work closely with the Red Guard and eventually absorb many of its remaining members. In 1975 it merged with the predominately Chicano August 29th Movement to form the League of Revolutionary Struggle.[41]

While the Red Guard, AAPA, and IWK pulled heavily from the college-educated middle class, the Yellow Brotherhood (YB), a Los Angeles–based organization that emerged in 1969, like the Panthers attracted many "brothers off the block." Formed out of a nexus of political militancy, ethnic pride, and general social pathos, the YB was the first of any radical Asian organization of young militants in the city. It comprised former gang members, ex-convicts, and ex-servicemen. Many were Nisei and Sansei—second and third generation Japanese Americans—who were unnerved by the political reticence that seemed to characterize their communities, particularly in an age when other ethnic groups had galvanized around radical ethnic nationalism. Speaking about their parents, one former YB member states that "they're hypersensitive or hyperapologetic. We [younger generation] picked up some of that." According to another, "That is why the Yellow Brotherhood was so controversial. We weren't hyperapologetic." As many Japanese Americans were instructed to resist racism by seeking white approval through cultural assimilation, the YB joined the chorus of black cultural nationalists that vilified assimilation with whites. "We were told to outwhite the whites and groups like the YB . . . said 'Fuck the whites. Fuck that shit.'" The time had come for radical political organization in the Asian American community, but for Guy Kurose, it was initially an uphill battle he was not willing to wage.

Guy Kurose, a Japanese American, joined the Seattle branch of the Black Panther Party at age sixteen. Raised in the black community, he naturally gravitated to Black Power with his friends. "I . . . listened to [James Brown singing] 'Say it loud, I'm black and I'm proud.' I wanted to be there too." However, unable to fully extricate himself from socially dysfunctional behavior, Kurose, like many other Panthers, carried his lumpen life into the party. "I was a renegade Panther. We were what Bobby Seale called 'jackanapes,' kids that had good intentions but were relating strongly to hoodlumism." Deeply involved with the Black Power movement, Kurose was unaware of any community of young Asian revolutionaries until a visit from Mo Nishida, Victor Shibata, and Warren Furutani from California. His immediate reaction: "I don't need to talk to no Japanese motherfucker who thinks he's white, man." He stayed in the BPP until he entered college, where he joined the Asian Student Coalition and carried over the radicalism that he had learned in the Panthers, even fighting police on campus.[42]

Kuruse later moved to Los Angeles where he worked closely with other Asian radicals in leftist groups such as the Yellow Brotherhood, Joint Communications, and the Asian American Hardcore. While the Yellow Brotherhood pulled heavily from nonacademics, like the Panthers, it also struggled over jackanape activities. Los Angeles had a serious gang presence that extended into the Asian American community. Gangs such as the Ministers, Shokashus, and Constituents became politicized in the late 1960s, as had gangs in the black community, but as YB member Art Ishii noted, "Gangsters don't give a shit about Red Books." The YB challenged the pervasive notion of Asian meekness, yet simultaneously struggled with self-destructive tendencies. Former members take pride in being the "first ones talking shit and kicking ass" but admit that they were marginalized by the larger Asian American community in ways not experienced by black nationalists in their communities. However, this alienation did not stop other militant, street-based Asian organizations from developing.

The Asian American Hardcore, like the Yellow Brotherhood, attracted former junkies, gang members, and convicts. Mo Nishida, a former member, explains that the Hardcore grew out of the tumultuous political and cultural climate of the Black Power movement in general and the Black Panthers in particular. "I think that the idea was percolating around because of the notoriety of the Panthers . . . When the Panthers came forward, the idea of trying to get some of our people back from the other side of capitalism came up, so some of us talked about needing to form a group like that. With the Panthers as a model, we could serve the people."[43] The Hardcore established an office on 23rd and Vermont Avenue and began detoxification programs for drug addicts, as well as a political education class, Christmas programs for the poor and other programs for the elderly. The group, taking a sartorial cue from the Panthers, as others had, wore fatigues and red berets as part of their uniform. Clearly the Panthers loomed large for the small band of revolutionaries in Los Angeles.

Members of the Hardcore met with Panthers, including national leaders like Eldridge Cleaver and Bobby Seale. Yet, as Nishida says, "We were small potatoes compared to those guys . . . but we never felt that way." Like many self-described revolutionaries of the period, members of the Hardcore believed that the revolution was imminent and that the Panthers would be its vanguard party. "The Panther Party was the basic acknowledged leadership in the Revolutionary Nationalist Movement. They set the whole stage." When the FBI unleashed its unprecedented repression, in concert with local police, the Panthers were decimated as no organization in twentieth-century U.S. history had been. "After the Panthers got wasted by COINTELPRO . . . there was disillusionment about the political line of the Panthers." Nishida explains that despite the Panthers' revolutionary posture, "when they couldn't respond to the killings by the police, it [screwed] everybody's mind up."[44]

After the revolutionary, gun-toting posturing of the Panthers evoked the deadly wrath of the government, many members of the Asian American Hardcore moved into other arenas of political discourse, no longer desirous of following the Panther line, in toto. As community-based organizations with strong ties to the street, the Yellow Brotherhood and Asian American Hardcore turned stereotypes of Asian Americans on their ears. Asian-descended young people rejected the term *Oriental* in the late 1960s and embraced a Pan-Asian term for the first time: Asian American. Many organized around a simple Asian identity, unlike the typically nationality-based organizations prior to the late 1960s, such as the Japanese American Citizens League or the Chinese American Citizens Alliance. Affected by Black Power, they promoted the slogan "Yellow Power" and raised the clenched fist in union with other "Third World People" on college campuses and in streets across the country. While they avoided the type of deadly conflict with law enforcement agencies the Panthers experienced, they offered material and moral support to the Black Panther Party, as well as a scathing critique of the political, social, and economic systems that converged to undermine the Panthers and others.

Native American Ethnic Nationalism

The smallest minority group in the United States, Native Americans, like other people of color, found great inspiration in the examples of radical ethnic nationalism in the Black Power movement. Like Asian Americans, many Indian ethnic groups organized around narrow ethnic identities until the 1960s where a pan-Indian consciousness was forged in a new and militant effort, the Red Power movement. The general circumstances that led to radical ethnic nationalism were identical to that of other minority groups. Native Americans long suffered under blatant and brutal forms of white supremacy. Killed by wars and disease, displaced from their lands, forced into reservations, Native Americans had by 1970 become the ethnic group with the lowest standard of living in the United States. Rates of alcoholism, high school dropout, unemployment, and death were higher for them than for any other group in the country. Indian teenagers' suicide rate for was one hundred times that of whites.[45]

In the mid-1960s the Black Power movement had impressed Clyde Warrior, a Cherokee college student, who envisioned pan-Indian nationalism modeled after SNCC. Warrior helped form the National Indian Youth Council (NIYC) and pushed "red power" in its newspaper, *ABC: Americans before Columbus*.[46] Informed by the new militancy of young people, the NIYC helped spread the message of new activism on college campuses nationwide, providing suffuse radical analysis of Indian political, social and cultural concerns. The general mood of militancy continued to grow, and Dennis Banks and George Mitchell in Minneapolis founded the American Indian Movement (AIM) in 1968. As Ward Churchill and Jim Vander Wall explain, the Black Panther Party loomed large for Banks and Mitchell. "[AIM] was self-consciously patterned after the Black Panther Party's community self-defense model pioneered by Huey P. Newton and Bobby Seale two years previously in Oakland."[47] In fact, like the Panthers, AIM's first major project, the Minneapolis AIM Patrol, was designed to end police brutality. Like the Brown Berets and others, AIM formed a platform that was influenced by the Panthers, although AIM's twenty-point platform was less dependent on the Panther's platform and program.[48]

Other Native American activists had begun to rely on media-attracting protests such as the occupation of Alcatraz Island in San Francisco Bay. In November 1969 an ad hoc group, Indians of All Tribes, landed on Alcatraz, claiming it "by right of discovery." Two weeks later more people arrived. Reflecting the ubiquitous aim of ethnic nationalists, the protesters announced that "the Indians of Alcatraz want self-determination for all native Americans." Hoping to be "fair and honorable" in their relations with white inhabitants, the new arrivals announced that they planned to "purchase said Alcatraz for twenty-four (24) dollars in glass beads and red cloth, a precedent set by the white man's purchase of a similar island about 300 years ago."[49] The reference to the purchase of Manhattan by Europeans in the seventeenth century reflects the pan-Indian consciousness and new ethnic nationalism that relied on common historical myth and the promotion of a general historical experience that textured the collective consciousness of national identity. This process of pan-ethnic nationality formation was bolstered by the rhetoric of the late 1960s. The new occupants of Alcatraz also demanded "RED POWER to Red People!" Not to be out of step with the larger ethnic nationalist movement, they also insisted that along with red power, there must be "Black, Brown, Yellow and white [power] also." At bottom, they argued that they wanted "All power to the people."[50]

By 1970 AIM had become a national organization and generated considerable media and police attention. The FBI began a rigorous campaign to circumscribe its development, although AIM continued to find larger audiences and sympathy across racial lines, particularly on college campuses. In 1970 the Native American Student Association was founded at the University of California at Berkeley and worked in alliances with MECHA, the Students for a Democratic Society (SDS), and the Black Student Union. Vernon Bellcourt, executive director of AIM, spoke on campus in March 1973 and helped raise funds for Indian children and denounced police harassment of AIM.[51] That same month U.S. military units, as well as local authorities, interrupted an AIM occupation of Wounded Knee, South Dakota. After a standoff that lasted seventy-one days, two FBI agents and five Native Americans were killed; several more were wounded.[52]

Several AIM members were arrested as a result of the Wounded Knee conflict. Yet despite the violent conflict with law enforcement agencies, AIM alone remained one of a few radical ethnic nationalist organizations of the late 1960s that survived into the 1980s and beyond. Chapters expanded throughout the country and continued to sponsor community development programs aimed at satisfying the political, social, and cultural needs of Native Americans, engendering a more popular base of support as the militant rhetoric subsided.

Puerto Rican Nationalism

Jose "Cha Cha" Jimenez, a leader of the Puerto Rican Young Lords street gang in Chicago, grew more affected by the civil rights movement and the rhetoric of Black Power by 1968. Cha Cha brought new members into the organization and began developing community programs such as a community summer picnic, a drug education program, and a Christmas giveaway of food and toys for impoverished people in the Puerto Rican community. The Lords even began dialogue with the largest street gang in the country, the notorious Black Stone Rangers, and co-sponsored a "Month of Soul Dances" with them.[53] While these efforts impressed many liberals, Illinois deputy chairman Fred Hampton and the local Panthers hoped to make the Lords into revolutionaries.

In accordance with the party's theories of class, the Panthers viewed the politicization of the Young Lords as an essential process in the political transformation of the country's internal colonies. The urban rebellions that often included the poorest and most maligned elements in the community were the precursor to revolution. The lumpen had guns and were not afraid to use them. Unfortunately, they were not yet politically sophisticated enough to aim in the direction of the "pig power structure" more frequently. These rebellions, insisted Huey Newton, were "sporadic, short-lived, and costly in violence against the people." The task of the Panthers was clear: "The Vanguard Party must provide leadership for the people. It must teach correct strategic methods of prolonged resistance through literature and activities. If the activities of the Party are respected by the people, the people will follow the example."[54] The efforts of the Lords and the Rangers indicated a political transformation that could make them into agents of liberation and harbingers of freedom, justice, and power for the people.

As Hampton began negotiating with Jeff Fort, leader of the Black Stone Rangers, he also met with Jimenez, who was warmer to the idea of revolution than Fort had been. Impressed with the bold and brash militancy that characterized the Panthers, Jimenez envisioned a Puerto Rican revolutionary organization to realize liberation for Puerto Ricans on the island and in the mainland. The Young Lords began to realize that they had been acting more like social workers by only addressing the symptoms and not the cause of social illness. Like African American gangs, the Lords became critical of their street violence. They initiated a peace treaty with virtually all of their former enemies and advised them to cease the fighting against each other but address anger "against the capitalist institutions that are oppressing us." The Latin Kings, the city's largest Latino gang, began to organize as well, even opening a breakfast program for children. By 1969, the Young Lords had officially joined in a pact with the Panthers and the Young Patriots, a gang of white Appalachian youths from the city's Uptown section on the North Side.[55]

In this new "Rainbow Coalition," the Lords and Patriots dutifully modeled themselves after the Black Panther Party. In their respective communities, the Lords and Patriots held political education classes, sponsored free breakfast programs for poor children, and monitored police activities in an attempt to curb police brutality. They created an organizational structure that reflected Panther influence, which included ministers of information, defense, education and a central committee with field marshals. The Patriots developed an Eleven-Point Program and Platform that borrowed heavily from the Panthers, as did the Lords' Thirteen-Point Program and Platform.[56] All three organizations sponsored events together, providing joint speakers and joint security. It seemed odd for some black nationalists to see Fred Hampton give a typically awe-inspiring speech on revolutionary struggle, while white men wearing berets, sunglasses, and Confederate rebel flags sewn into their jackets helped provide security for him.

The Patriots, led by a seminary student named Preacherman, were quick to denounce racism, despite their proud display of Confederate flags. "We believe that to fight only for the interests of your close cultural brothers and sisters is not in the interest of all the people, and in fact perpetuates racism. We understand the struggle is a class struggle. All power to the poor and working people!"[57] While the Patriots followed the Panther line, which denounced cultural nationalism, they embraced subtle traces of it in their group symbolism (much like the Panthers themselves). The Patriots' tolerance of cultural nationalism was demonstrated in the celebration of their Appalachian and southern heritage. Poor white southern migrants had come to Chicago, as had thousands of poor blacks and Puerto Ricans, and despite their whiteness, experienced ridicule from other whites for their southern drawl and provincial proclivities. Their poor rural background was a source of shame for many who grew up in poor white areas in the city. Joining with the Panthers and Lords, the Patriots were able to bond with blacks and Latinos in class terms in ways that the Students for a Democratic Society or most other white radicals could not.[58]

Just as Chicanos and African and Asian Americans rejected the cultural orthodoxy that idealized the white American middle-class standard, the Patriots celebrated their poor white southern roots. The Confederate flag was a reminder and symbol of their incessant class struggle. The Patriots found pride in maintaining an affinity for their southern background and found no incongruence in identifying with anti-racism and the flag of the blatantly white supremacist Confederacy. The Patriots created a radicalism that found strength and cultural grounding in an odd mix of symbols and rhetoric. At bottom, the Patriots found their radical ethnic nationalism in the glorification of a poor southern white ethos that jettisoned the racism that typified the white South. This was done in the interest of a radical activist ideology that transcended race but did not ignore the centrality of race to political struggle. There were several other white groups that found the Panthers a model for radical struggle; however, the Patriots were the only ones who created a conspicuous radical ethnic nationalism.[59]

By 1969, the Young Patriots and Young Lords were becoming nationally known through their Rainbow Coalition, which was featured in articles in the *Black Panther* and other alternative newspapers. Also that year, the coalition sent representatives to the annual convention of the SDS, where Joe Martinez, an SDS member from Florida, met with Young Lord founders and was granted permission to start a branch in New York.

In New York, Puerto Rican nationalism was still growing. In the context of the militant student protests, some students at City College formed the Sociedad de Albizu Campos (SAC) in early 1969 to bring together the militancy of college radicals with that of the ghetto. In a struggle to bridge the chasm between unorganized street militancy and that of the college campus, community-based activists, Pablo "Yoruba" Guzman and David Perez joined SAC and became the links to the ghetto that the organization desired. Yoruba, with an Afro and dark skin, had a strong cultural nationalist affinity to both Africa and Puerto Rico. Perez, who was born in Puerto Rico and raised in Chicago, had involved himself in radical politics before moving to New York. SAC members were reading the *Black Panther* newspaper regularly and learned of Fred Hampton's Rainbow Coalition. After merging with other local Puerto Rican activist organizations, SAC met with Martinez and on July 26, 1969, a coalition was formed that became the New York State Chapter of the Young Lords Organization.[60]

The Young Lords from New York spread to several cities along the East Coast, including Philadelphia, Newark, and Bridgeport, Connecticut. Within weeks, the Lords captured headlines. In agreement with the Panther dictum to serve the people by meeting their basic needs, Lords asked local residents what they wanted. People informed the Lords that they wanted cleaner streets. The Lords swept streets in Spanish Harlem and put trash in piles in the middle of the street, demanding that the city pay more attention to the barrio. The images of radicals working for the people impressed many who eagerly joined the fledgling organization.[61] A hundred men and women took over Lincoln Hospital on July 17, 1970, to protest inadequate health care for the poor and neglect from the city government. Though the protesters were expelled by the police, the act brought attention to insufficient medical care in poor communities. The mayor of New York, John Lindsay, promised community activists that the city would build a new hospital on East 149th Street to replace the dilapidated Lincoln. The new hospital opened in 1976.[62]

Adherents of Puerto Rican independence, the Young Lords denounced the cardinal "three evils" of revolutionary nationalists: capitalism, racism, and imperialism. They sponsored free breakfast, drug detoxification, and garbage clean-up programs in several states. Their activities were numerous in every major Puerto Rican community. They brought attention to police brutality, worked closely with students on college and high school campuses, and even found success organizing in prisons. During the Attica Prison uprising in September 1971, insurgents issued a list of more than twenty demands to prison officials, including a request for the Young Lords and the Black Panthers to serve as observers and advisers. In many cities, Lords worked in alliances with Black Power advocates and helped realize more community control of police, political reform, and political mobilization for poor and working-class people. Like the Brown Berets, the Young Lords were able to work with organizations openly hostile to the Black Panthers, despite their official pact with the party. In the early 1970s the Young Lords in Newark, New Jersey, established an alliance with the Committee for a Unified Newark, led by Amiri Baraka, a leading cultural nationalist.[63]

The Young Lords and other revolutionary nationalist organizations saw how various communities of color in the United States provided cheap labor and resources for capitalists. Influenced by a theoretical rubric of racism, the capitalists found cheap, expendable labor that provided for improved quality of life for whites by expanding the white middle-class considerably. Increased numbers of people of color in urban areas allowed working-class whites to assume higher socioeconomic status. Because racism was very real, working-class whites, often beholden to white supremacy, refused out of ignorance and cultural tradition to consider the affinities they shared with working-class people of color. The Young Patriots hoped to demonstrate that working-class and poor whites could be mobilized and follow a revolutionary program led by a black organization, but while the Patriots, Rising Up Angry, and White Panthers of Michigan modeled themselves after the Black Panther Party, the party and Black Power had a special resonance for radicals of color.

Class exploitation was a major concern for leftists; however, the highly racialized climate of the United States made interracial political organization difficult, particularly with working-class whites, considered by many people of color to be a more overt and crude group of racists than the capitalist class. Moreover, the U.S. tradition of class exploitation was significantly bolstered by white supremacy, which had profound psychological and cultural ramifications.[64] People of color who were involved in the era's leftist liberation movements were committed to liberate themselves along class and cultural lines simultaneously.

There was a particular appeal that made the Panthers a model for many young people of color longing for an end to the racial oppression they had endured. Without doubt, the Black Panthers' machismo cool typified a revolutionary chic that prompted many to imitate the party. Like black people, other people of color had long languished under a system of racial domination that dehumanized, marginalized, and exploited nonwhites. For men of color, the dehumanization included emasculation, thereby fomenting a hypermasculinity in the age of radical ethnic nationalism.

For Chicanos, the situation was similar. Francisco Ramos, a Brown Beret, exclaimed that "there is a new breed of Mexican who is getting tired and angry and frustrated and will no longer ask for tomorrow; we want it now. We don't want to ride at the back of the bus; we want to drive it and own it if possible."[65] There was also a clear masculine emphasis that ran through Chicano power, similar to the language of Black Power proponents. Chicano students in California warned that they would vigorously resist the "emasculation" of Chicanos. Others wrote poetry to liberating Chicano manhood.

> Until yesterday you called me a good Chicano . . . I was meek, humble, god-damned ignorant.
> I was young, passive. I was a good american.
> I licked the hand that fed me crumbs.
>
> However, in transition, a new Chicano has emerged from the despair:
> A man-re-born a man, has learned to stand up, bear the burden of his people on his back.
> I—no longer dead. I—alive. See my people rising, my peasant blood sings with pride.
> See my people refuse to bend, prostitutes for an anglo dog.
> See a multitude of clenched fists, casting off shackles of death.
> See brothers join hand in hand, muscular and strong, march before the sun.[66]

With strong male-centered language, ethnic nationalists attempted to forge a new identity as "liberated" men. Despite the rhetoric that celebrated masculinity, largely rendering women invisible, challenges to this patriarchal discourse did not materialize during the earliest years of the ethnic nationalist movement. Women in the Brown Berets were active in all of the group's functions, which included military drills and protests; however, their role remained largely secondary. Women wrote for the organization's newspaper, *La Causa,* but rarely did their articles focus on sexism within society at large or within the Berets in particular. The liberation of La Raza was considered the primary focus, while women's liberation was often viewed as a white women's movement. In 1969–70 Grace Reyes, a writer for *La Causa,* wrote on subjects of particular concern to women. The birth control pill was an issue that had special significance for women, who could more effectively choose when to give birth. In general, feminists viewed the pill as favorable for women, but like many black nationalists, Reyes saw the pill as an insidious attempt to curb the birth rate of people of color, not as empowering to women.[67] By 1971 Chicano feminism emerged with demands to move women to the center of Beret activities. In a *La Causa* article, one writer complained that Chicanas had been active in all of the group's functions, but their roles in the organization's leadership were peripheral. Women were simply "working for the Beret guys" and not realizing their complete talents and skills.[68]

Women insisted that a successful revolution "must have full involvement from both Chicanos and Chicanas." Not to be confused with the growing Women's Liberation Movement, they declared that "we're not talking about women's liberation because, like that's not ours. That's a white thing. We're talking about our Raza's liberation." While Chicanas voiced their frustrations via the Berets' official organ, the recalcitrant male leadership made no substantive changes to the organization's relationship with women.[69] A similar movement to challenge patriarchy occurred within the Young Lords, resulting in very different reactions.

By 1970 the Young Lord Organization became the Young Lord Party and launched its bilingual paper *Palante!* in May 1970. Articles in *Palante!* expressed the revolutionary zeal that characterized the organization. Like the *Black Panther* and *La Causa, Palante!* reflected the hypermasculinity of the Puerto Rican nationalist movement. Moreover, the organization relegated women to peripheral roles in leadership, despite a general policy that granted all members access to all organizational activities. By 1970 a women's caucus was formed and began to meet weekly. Female members shared stories of confronting the sexism of their comrades on a regular basis. The women's caucus issued demands to the central committee for an end to sexual discrimination and full inclusion of women in the Lords' leadership. The all-male leadership reacted swiftly by promoting Denise Oliver and Gloria Fontanez to the central committee. The Lords also adopted a new slogan, "Abajo con Machismo!" (Down with Machismo!), which appeared in the newspaper and other official releases. They also made changes to the party's thirteen-point program to include denouncing sexism as point number five: "Puerto Rican women will be neither behind nor in front of their brothers but always alongside them in mutual respect and love."[70] For many members of the Young Lords, the effort to denounce sexism was an inevitable step in the movement toward liberation.

Some have argued that the Black Power movement was a particularly sexist phenomenon. It clearly lionized black men as macho leaders, fighters, and defenders of black people. The bravado, militant rhetoric and general character of Black Power were decidedly male-oriented. While Black Power advocates and Latino ethnic nationalists used hyperbolic language to articulate their politics, it must be acknowledged that it was the Black Panther Party that was the first major black organization to align itself with the women's liberation movement as well as the gay liberation movement. The Panthers also denounced sexism on several occasions and appointed women to key leadership positions. By 1973 the chairman of the party was a woman. The Young Lords similarly accepted the challenge to transcend the narrow confines of patriarchy and made substantive changes to their organization's rhetoric and style. Clearly, the liberation of a nation could not tolerate the oppression of its half.

There was no particular formula or model for ethnic nationalists to respond to sexism. Latino, white, and black Americans all lived in a patriarchal culture that openly advocated male domination. Mainstream black and Latino organizations reflected patriarchal traditions without considerable challenges and upheaval. It was the passion for total liberation that raised the expectations of struggle for many radical ethnic nationalists. Despite their criticism of the white-oriented women's movement, radical ethnic nationalists were aware that women's liberation was intrinsic to national liberation. Some, like the Brown Berets, were less successful than the Lords or Panthers in denouncing sexism.

Similar to the process of psychological oppression experienced by African Americans who lived in a virulently antiblack world, other people of color had to resist the culturally hegemonic forces of white supremacy as well as the de facto policies that discriminated against them. In this rejection of the cultural orthodox there emerged the opportunity to criticize and transform traditional gender roles. Not all ethnic nationalists organizations were as responsive to the challenges to patriarchy as the Panthers and Lords, who were not fully successful in realizing their goals to destroy sexism within their organizations. But the efforts to confront sexism in a very explicit way reflected the ability of the organizations to adapt, grow, and evolve in ways that many so-called mainstream organizations had not. It was their willingness to consider new challenges and ideas that made these ethnic nationalist organizations attractive to young people. In addition, the new militant ethnic pride drew many young people into the movement.

As they rejected terms such as *Negro, Oriental,* and *Spanish,* blacks, Asians, and Chicanos conspicuously celebrated their ethnicity in ways they never had. Part of the drive to adopt new terms for identification grew out of the common call for self-determination. The Nation of Islam had long derided black people for allowing whites to define them as Negroes. *Black* was the term the people chose, not outsiders. It was an inherently defiant term that rejected the negative associations with blackness that were pervasive in American culture. For Chicanos and Asians, the effort for self-identification was twofold. It also marked a departure from the manner in which people viewed these groups.

As one student newspaper stated, "Asian Americans took a turn and began to cast off the chains of complacency. To many Asian Americans there was a need to define ourselves, our history, culture and our roles in society."[71] The new term that affirmed self-definition symbolized a new age for those who resisted oppression. As with the term *Negro,* old terms represented obsequiousness and ignorance. Thus, to reject the old term meant to reject the old manner of politics and political mobilization. The Yellow Brotherhood and Asian American Hardcore created names that represented this transition into a new people. Self-described tough guys, the Brotherhood embraced the era's tendency to colorize races. "Black" and "white" provided an easy dichotomy in the discussion of race, while "brown," "red," and "yellow" conveniently seemed suitable for people seeking new definitions. Yellow, like black, carried negative connotations: weakness, fear, cowardice, and meekness—many of the stereotypes Asians fought. Just as black people had done with slogans such as "black is beautiful," the Yellow Brotherhood systematically created an image for themselves that was anything but meek and cowardly or dependent on conventional definitions. They were proud to come from the street and proved to be no "model minority" for white America. The Asian American Hardcore similarly adopted a name that dismissed the pervasive notion of weak, timid Orientals. They were, after all, hardcore, and certainly not Oriental.

Latino and Asian militants, following the modus operandi of Black Power advocates, made it obvious that they were no longer at the door of white America requesting acceptance. "Now the Chicano no longer relies on the good will of good intentions of the [white] liberal." Students demanded resources, no longer politely asking for them to stroke the ego of the gabacho or *gwai* (literally "demon/ghost"). These militants also made it very clear that white was not always right and that whites could no longer assume the cultural standard. Chicano students argued that the goal of Chicano studies was ultimately connected to the liberation of Chicano people. The programs must work "toward exposing to Brown students the evil machinery of the capitalist system and turning them on to revolutionary principles." Some programs were not progressive enough but simply "Coconut studies" (brown on the outside, white inside). A degree in that type of assimilationist program only enabled one to be a "true cocoanut" [*sic*] who "knows how to behave white, talk white, write white, paint white and draw white, in short, perform white tricks in exchange for fat checks acknowledged gratefully in the name of 'La Rahssa.' "[72]

The Chicano Power movement, the Yellow Power movement, and Puerto Rican nationalism were not solely dependent on Black Power for symbolism, political direction, or motivation. The movements necessarily influenced each other in alliances, networks, conferences, and general dialogue. Furthermore, the international dynamics that influenced Black Power similarly formed Latino and Asian struggle in the United States. Mao Tse-tung was an inspiration to Panthers, as well as to the Red Guard. Brown Berets and Young Lords had a particular affinity with Che Guevara, who was also an adored icon for the Panthers. Still, the Black Power movement helped form a period of social and cultural transformation that would have substantive effects on the cultural and political landscape of the country.

The Black Power movement articulated the anger of a generation created by the pervasive and insidious nature of racial subjugation. In no uncertain terms, it challenged the legitimacy of white supremacy—politically, culturally and socially. The visibility of Black Power meant that militants could not be ignored. They were featured on television shows, in newspapers, on college campuses, and on the radio. Popular culture paid great attention to the cultural transformation of the United States. The country was in a process of upheaval of its long-lasting traditions of racial hierarchy, and no organization caught the media spotlight as did the Black Panther Party.

Although there had been different social, cultural, and political exigencies in the various communities, the BPP proved to be a matrix for Latino, Asian, white, and Native American radicals. Imbued with a pro-

found sense of duty, obligation, resistance, and idealism, these revolutionaries were inspired, motivated, and influenced by the symbolism,
rhetoric and tactics of the Black Power movement in general and the Black
Panthers in particular. Black nationalists and Black Power advocates, by
example, demonstrated the humanity of white people in ways that Martin
Luther King Jr. and nonviolent integrationists did not. Integrationists on
a very basic and fundamental level acquiesced to white supremacy by
allowing whites to maintain an aura of power and prestige. Despite the
overt challenges to the authority of racist laws, there was a pervasive
assumption that moderate and liberal whites in the North could be persuaded to assist the southern-based freedom movement. Civil rights leaders constantly made appeals to white lawmakers, capitalist power brokers,
and white liberals for moral and material support.

Civil rights activists were certain to attend marches and sit-ins with
"respectable" attire. Men wore shirts and ties; women wore dresses. They
protested for desegregation and integration. While many clearly fought for
human rights, suffrage, and equal access to resources, the overall thrust to
the activities, as articulated by its national leadership, was integration. This
integration was contingent on white approval. Blacks were instructed to be
conscious of their speech, manners, dress, and general presentation in
front of whites. The NAACP argued that it was psychologically damaging
to a black child to be segregated in public school. No mention was ever
made of how psychologically damaging racial segregation was for white
children. The implicit belief was that a white presence made things better.
As Richard Newman, a professor at Boston University in the late 1960s,
said, "When civil rights leaders called for integration of higher education,
they were not hoping to send more whites to Howard University. They
wanted more blacks at ['white' colleges]."[73] Integration was a one-way
street that assumed that majority white was normative and desired.

Black Power rejected the idea that white people's acceptance was
desirable. Other people of color and even some poor whites, informed and
significantly affected by Black Power, also formed ethnic nationalist paradigms of resistance. As with their black counterparts, these ethnic nationalists organized in their communities, changing the social, political, and
cultural landscape. Furthermore, most of these ethnic nationalists copiously developed a theoretical construct of radical self-determination that
was not dependent on xenophobia. The radical ethnic nationalism of the
Black Panthers, Young Lords, Brown Berets, or Red Guard reflected a conscious effort to culturally affirm people who languished under a dehu-
manizing system of racial oppression, while it also refused to pander to

the convenient race-only discourse that attracted many. These proponents of radical ethnic nationalism glorified their ethnicity while they eagerly embraced a polysemic nationalist framework that pulled from Fanon, Marx, Lenin, and Mao. Too, they were significantly influenced by the BPP's political analysis and its thesis of revolutionary struggle.

Black Power's influence on non–African Americans altered the popular discourse and public discussion of identity and equality in the United States in significant ways. Outside and inside the radical leftist ethnic nationalist communities were militants who rebuked whiteness and the implications of whiteness, such as status dependent on the subjugation of nonwhites. In this contextual framework, many militants sought to "humanize" whites by stripping them of any trappings of cultural prestige or supremacy. The cornerstone to this reorientation was a rejection of integration. Radical ethnic nationalists struggled for a world where whiteness was no longer the standard by which all else was judged and for a class-free society. Yet rejecting the traditional class-based rhetoric of the left, the radical ethnic nationalists merged radical interpretations of race and class into their movements.

Radical ethnic nationalism attempted to overturn the white supremacy that had historically denigrated people of color in every arena of American life. To that end, whites were criticized in ways that they had never been. They were openly ridiculed for their smell, lack of rhythm, lack of hygiene, lack of morality, lack of beauty, and, at bottom, lack of humanity. While these criticisms may appear inconsistent with the ideals of Panther transracialism, some ethnic nationalists' ridicule of whites was an attempt to reconcile the new self-love with generations of self-hate. Whites were pushed off their pedestal of whiteness and all the implied honor, prestige, and respect that skin-privilege conveyed. Black Power and radical ethnic nationalism revealed the vulnerability of whiteness. Whiteness was not sacrosanct or without flaw. It was corrupt and inextricably bound to the frailties of humanity.

Beyond the cultural and psychological effects that radical ethnic nationalism introduced to the new left of the late 1960s and early 1970s, the movement was truly a unique phenomenon. There are no major examples of ethnic nationalist struggles that established alliances, as had young radicals of the Black Power era. African American, white, Puerto Rican, Chicano, Asian, and Native American radicals merged ethnic nationalist rhetoric with a struggle that emphasized class conflict and interracial coalitions. When the Black Panther Party coined the slogan "all power to the people," it was attempting to broaden the call for Black Power by transcending race. According to party chairman Bobby Seale, interracial coalitions are powerful examples of the people gaining strength in numbers in their efforts against the "power structure's oppression."[74] At the center of this movement was the Black Power movement, which provided the earliest examples of cultural nationalism and political organization around ethnic nationalist causes. The BPP served as a paradigm of radical ethnic nationalism and a vanguard party for the revolutionary nationalist movement. The Panthers provided an appeal that was unprecedented in the annals of radical struggle.

Though considered a black hate group by some whites; an irresponsible, careless, and disorganized band of immature radicals by some leftists; or too conciliatory to white radicals by some black nationalists, the Panthers' impact was indelible. A group that reached a peak membership of five thousand members, the party not only influenced radicals from every ethnic community in the United States, it inspired marginalized and oppressed people worldwide who created Black Panther Parties. Australian Aborigines, Sephardic Jews in Israel, blacks in Britain, and the Dalit in India all formed organizations that carried the name Black Panther Party, evoking the radical ethnic discourse of the organization. From the legacy of the Black Power movement are ethnic studies programs on college campuses, Kwanzaa, and a rich celebration of ethnic diversity and social activism in Latino, Asian American, and other communities throughout the United States.

Power and the People

The Black Power movement had profound effects on the development of America's collective racial and ethnic identity. From the rumblings of a small nationalist organization in the ghettoes of midwestern cities emerged an incredible transformation of the landscape of race. The civil rights movement played an essential role in undermining the legal structure of white supremacy. It did not, however, substantively engage the many psychological vestiges of racism. The cultural shifts that occurred in the Black Power era benefited blacks and other groups (whites included), forcing them to deconstruct widely held notions of race. The counterhegemonic thrust of Black Power ushered in new celebrations of blackness that had been absent from civil rights struggles. Additionally, Malcolm X, Martin Luther King Jr., and others were well aware that more militant actions placed the civil rights movement in a more favorable position to realize concessions from the white power establishment. In his "Letter from a Birmingham Jail," King appealed to government officials and other whites that "millions of Negroes, out of frustration and despair, will seek solace and security in black nationalist ideology, a development that will lead inevitably to a frightening racial nightmare."[1] Nonviolent demands for equality and racial reconciliation were much more favorable to whites than the radical alternatives of Black Power and black nationalism.

Ultimately, however, the modern black freedom movement must not be viewed necessarily as a contest of strategy and ideology between nationalists and integrationists. This is too simplistic. Black Power was an organic response to the limitations of rigid black nationalism and the civil rights movement. It embraced the notion that black people in the United States deserved access to resources, employment, housing, and equal protection under the law, just as whites did. It did not forfeit citizenship rights, as did black nationalists. In addition, Black Power endorsed an important idea: black self-love. Influenced by the Nation of Islam and other nationalists, black people sought to extricate themselves from the psychological entrapments of white supremacy. They enjoyed a popular celebration of black historical accomplishment, reclamation of Africa, and the importance of self-determination. In many respects, this emphasis on self-identity was contrary to the thrust of the civil rights movement, yet it became the dominant point of analysis and synthesis for African Americans.

While the efforts of civil rights activists destroyed the legal barriers that barred people of color from white colleges, Black Power's demands vastly widened access to these schools for black people and others. White colleges in the North and West did not welcome black students before 1966. The militant fervor of Black Power advocates, however, secured unprecedented resources for black faculty, staff, and students. Integrationist leaders like King, Whitney Young Jr. and Roy Wilkins did not equivocate on their positions that black student unions, black studies programs, and black cultural centers were wrong. They were a sad example of "resegregation," they lamented. They argued that black students would be ill prepared to compete with degrees in black studies. Moreover, black theme houses and black culture centers were contrary to the intentions of the civil rights struggle. They acquiesced to the prevailing racialist notions that suggested whites and blacks could not enjoy common space. It had become clear, however, that black people, particularly baby boomers, would not seek white approval and acceptance. Inasmuch as whites enjoyed their all-white domains, black people celebrated "self-determination" and control of black space. In the pursuit of a healthy, self-loving environment, black people carved out spaces for respite from what they considered a hostile world. They engaged in this process with the idealism and zeal becoming of their generation. The campus experience was a microcosm of black America. From social workers to firefighters, black people formed professional groups during the Black Power era. These organizations echoed the demand for self-expression and independence of black nationalists.

From the rejection of the term *Negro* to the popularity of the term *black,* the Nation of Islam was a formidable influence. Not only did the Nation provide the new militant movement with its patron saint— Malcolm X—but many other leaders of the movement such as Eldridge Cleaver, Huey Newton, Bobby Seale, and Maulana Karenga frequented local NOI mosques or were former members of the NOI. All major black nationalist organizations, save the Nation of Islam, admired and revered Malcolm in this period. Virtually all claimed to be ideological heirs of the former national spokesman of the Muslims, often picking and choosing aspects of and statements from Malcolm at different points of his ideological evolution.[2] One of Malcolm's "heirs," the Black Panther Party for Self-Defense, emerged with a bold type of militancy and bravado never before seen on that scale. However, the Black Panther Party was not completely unique among black militant organizations. In some respects, it was part of a pervasive and organic evolutionary reaction to the shortcomings of the southern-based civil rights movement and the inveterate nature of racist oppression.

The Panthers viewed their organization as the end result of an ideological transformation that was sweeping black America. This evolution began with nonviolent theories, tactics, and a commitment toward racial integration. While the modern civil rights movement had its roots in a long continuum of social and political protest against racial oppression, it is generally agreed to have begun with the grassroots mobilization and activism of the 1950s. The movement's failure to address the exigencies faced by black people outside the South (or in the post–Jim Crow South, for that matter) resulted in a more brash radicalism. This radicalism flowered in the late 1960s and early 1970s in the form of a popular racial consciousness among African Americans that was nuanced with black nationalism. In addition, the political consciousness of the era was significantly more militant than it had been during the early 1960s. Integration and nonviolence were reevaluated, and some considered a full overhaul of the political and economic order of the country. The Black Panther Party emerged as the foremost and most popular revolutionary organization of the period. Despite the ideological chasm that separated it from the masses of black people, who were not revolutionary or entirely leftist, the party had a significant following in black communities. It was, for many civil rights leaders, a clear sign of the shortcomings of the civil rights struggle.

The Nation of Islam emerged in the 1960s as the largest black nationalist organization since the heyday of Marcus Garvey's Universal Negro Improvement Association (UNIA) in the 1920s. The Nation, like the UNIA and other classical black nationalist organizations, in large measure, embraced Western standards of civilization and culture. The Muslims sought to civilize the uncivilized and awaken the "deaf, dumb and blind" Negro, fostering a spiritual rebirth of the Original People. Under the guidance of Elijah Muhammad, the Muslims expressed disdain for both non-Western traditional culture and an antipathy for black folk culture. The obvious difference between the Muslims and classical black nationalists was the Nation's rejection of Christianity, which it considered the religion made by devils for the express purpose of killing, enslaving, and oppressing black people around the world. While the Nation rejected white people and Christianity, it quoted from the Bible as much as it did the Qur'an. In spite of their rejection of white people, Muslims accepted the traditional European views of Africa and its indigenous cultures. In doing so, the Nation necessarily renounced the cultural nationalism that characterized black popular culture in the late 1960s and the early 1970s, though it still maintained a massive following, making it the wealthiest black organization in the United States—nationalist or otherwise.

The Nation of Islam directly influenced scores of nationalist and radical organizations, although it was not a particularly radical or even progressive organization. In most respects, the Nation was—to quote historian Claude A. Clegg III—a politically effete organization. While it offered a vituperative rebuke of white supremacy, it provided little in the way of a direct challenge to the white power structure. Yet large segments of the black community still held Muslims in high esteem for their upright, industrious, sober, and disciplined character. The Nation provided poor black people hope and salvation in ways that most organizations did not. Muslims rehabilitated the most hardened criminals, alcoholics, and drug addicts and provided goods and services, jobs, and quality schools to scores of thousands of black people nationwide. For many, these acts represented an earnest challenge to white supremacy. For others, the Nation's cautious and conservative policies fell short of making it a viable organization of black liberation. Viable or not, the Nation was clearly following the path of its nationalist predecessors.

The Nation applied conservative economic policies that originated with nineteenth-century nationalists like Martin R. Delany and Alexander Crummell, as well as twentieth century figures like the accomodationist Booker T. Washington and internationalist Marcus Garvey to the economic and political world of black people. Under the leadership of Elijah Muhammad, the Nation made considerable progress with few resources. It was this very conservatism, however, that pushed many members and potential members into more radical direct action political organizations such as the Panther Party. The pervasive political and cultural heterodoxy demanded more direct challenges to oppression than the Nation was willing to offer.

The Nation's legacy was apparent in the Black Panther Party's Ten-Point Program, military-style maneuvers, and marches, as well as other activities. The Panthers, however, took black nationalism to new levels. Among major black organizations, it alone glorified what it called lumpenproletariat culture, seeking to give voice to the voiceless masses of poor urban black people by adopting lumpen speech, culture, and politics—as they said (quoting Mao), "swimming with the masses." They spoke, fought, ate, partied, and lived like the lumpen. Though lumpenism gave the party so much of its character, unchecked lumpenism would help undermine it as well. The Panthers, in some ways, embodied the stereotypes of modern black nationalism. The national party leadership's penchant for drug use, drinking, and fast living represented many of the characteristics of modern black nationalism, as described by Wilson J. Moses and others, but these pathologies were not a universal feature of the party. While all chapters adopted the party uniform and conformed to other regulatory codes, not all chapters embraced patriarchy, drinking, drug use, or sexual promiscuity. Contrary to Moses's definition of modern black nationalism, the Panthers rejected the new exoticism and romantic notions and ideas of Africa and its cultures.

Both the Panthers and the Muslims were highly critical of cultural nationalism, but for very different reasons. The Panthers dismissed outright the classical black nationalist mission to impart Western civilization to the misled masses. Instead, they offered a critical look at the economic and political apparatus that oppressed people of color and poor whites. For the Panthers, culture did not bring freedom. Culture was learned human behavior that represented a group's traditions, mores, and folkways of a group. The culture of most Americans was influenced by the capitalist economic order, which, according to the Panthers, rested on the racial division of exploited peoples. Poor whites were oppressed because it was imperative to the capitalist agenda. That these poor whites were Eurocentric and often white supremacists was immaterial to their oppression—outside of the fact that it prevented them from forming alliances with poor people of color. Cultural nationalism was inefficacious because it failed to address effectively the fundamental causes of oppression, offering instead a romantic subterfuge of culture and race in place of class.

The Nation and the Panthers did have a mutual beef with one facet of cultural nationalism: its commercialization. Even in this context, however, they had different reasons for their criticism. Those in the Nation thought it ridiculous to buy "black power" underwear, watches, or other products from white businesses. That "devils" had co-opted a slogan and adopted symbols for black liberation indicated the slogan's profound frailties. For the Panthers, the commercialization of cultural nationalism reflected its largely inept and sterile nature. That corporate America could so easily adopt black cultural nationalist symbolism and sell goods to black people was a travesty. Advertisers of alcohol, tobacco, fashion, and even skin whitener quickly adopted this popular approach of resistance to oppression and black people's self-affirmation. Cultural nationalism's commercialization simply reflected the mainstreaming of Black Power. Like any popular idea, capitalist interests absorbed it.

Like the Muslims, the Panthers had significant levels of support in black communities nationwide. Black people attended rallies in defense of the party when it was under attack by the police. Black people of all economic classes supported its survival programs to feed, clothe, and provide medical care for poor people, particularly children. Moderates who had once virulently denounced Black Power found themselves defending the Panthers with bold and, at times, militant language. While the masses of black people were not revolutionaries or particularly leftist, they supported Panthers. Polls revealed that most African Americans admired the party, indicating that it was not a fringe organization. Indeed, more blacks admired the Black Panther Party than they did the National Urban League, which was universally considered "mainstream."[3] That level of support demonstrates black nationalism's impact and influence on the era. It significantly influenced mainstream black political, cultural, and intellectual discourse throughout the civil rights movement. Even when renounced and excoriated by "mainstream" black leaders and the white press, black nationalism gained popularity and eventually spawned the Black Power movement.

The movement for Black Power, steeped in the traditions of nationalism, celebrated black people and their self-determination as no mass movement had done before. Its far-reaching effects were manifested in religion, music, education, and politics. Faced with its saliency, moderate black leaders were forced to temper their opposition positions when African Americans embraced the militant slogan and idea of black self-determination. In addition, the rise of the Black Panther Party signified a growing threat to the political and economic status quo. Its popularity and revolutionary theories (an eclectic mixture of Marxism, Leninism, Maoism, Fanonism, and intercommunalism) evoked fear among the guardians of the established political and economic order. Federal, state, and local government agencies initiated a violent and often illegal campaign of unprecedented repression of the Panthers, resulting in outcries from all segments of the black community and among some whites as well. Eventually, the leading black moderates were forced to respond to the police action, denouncing it as "criminal."

With the Panthers, Black Power further mutated into radical ethnic nationalism and significantly affected non–African American members of the New Left as well. This unique form of nationalism influenced Latinos, Asians, Native Americans, and even whites. While the civil rights movement is credited for helping to dismantle white supremacy, Black Power's role cannot be overlooked. Although there were scores of radical black organizations in the 1960s, such as the Revolutionary Action Movement, Afro-American Association, Us, and Yoruba Temple, none had the daunting influence of the Nation of Islam. Ultimately, the Nation was responsible for retiring the word *Negro* in the Anglophone world. It provided the patron saint of black nationalism, Malcolm X, and helped provide the axiological foundation on which more radical organizations would build activities in college campuses, prisons, farming communities, urban centers, and even professional societies and popular politics.

The discourse of black politics cannot be limited to middle-class organizations but must be wide enough to include urban rebellion, student demonstrations, and other political phenomena. The radical and moderate politics of African Americans were inextricably linked in this period. It was the masses of black people, however, who determined the political direction of black America, and in the late 1960s and early 1970s the masses embraced black power, demonstrating that leadership often comes from the bottom up.

Black Nationalism after Jim Crow

The 1970s began with the same tumultuous spirit with which the 1960s had ended. Student protests, anti–Vietnam War demonstrations, and the Black Power movement spilled over into a decade that would eventually be remembered for its disco music, flamboyant fashions, and hedonistic and apolitical activities. By 1970 the frequency of urban rebellions had declined, and the radical spirit of black nationalism had slowly given way to an increased optimism that there was an expansion of democracy, justice, and access to power in the United States. Affirmative action, black studies programs, and the precipitous increase in black publicly elected officials proved effective in mitigating black radicalism. In addition, Black Power enjoyed a widespread commercial appeal that found its way into various arenas of popular culture. The nebulous term had been sanitized and repackaged by various forces, including liberal to conservative black and white leaders, as well as corporate America. From selling underwear to malt liquor, Black Power had marketing power. The subversive and subaltern had been embraced by the mainstream in zealous and profitable endeavors.

Also, a daunting and complex web of government repression undermined radical black organizations, often illegally and violently. The Black Panther Party, the most popular revolutionary organization, was the victim of an unprecedented assault from the Federal Bureau of Investigation and local police agencies. By 1971, the party had lost over twenty comrades to police gunfire and had expelled hundreds of others during its purge of suspected police agents. It was attacked in every city where it established offices, although larger cities like Los Angeles and Chicago, New York, and Philadelphia experienced more frequent and brutal police harassment than did smaller cities such as Baltimore and Portland.

The degree of government repression, loss of life, and siege mentality under which members lived produced an understandable paranoia, especially in its leader, Huey Newton, who was released from prison in July

1970 when his 1968 conviction for killing an Oakland police officer was overturned. Newton grew increasingly autocratic, undermining the governing body of the Central Committee and expelling numerous Panthers including Eldridge and Kathleen Cleaver for disagreeing with his new vision for the party. His "intercommunalism" was based on the Marxist-Leninist notion of class struggle and the international nature of capitalism. Newton argued that the party needed to reattach itself to the black masses after its emphasis on the gun had alienated it from the people. The party put more energy in its survival programs such as free breakfasts, liberation schools, free medical centers, and free clothing and bus shuttles for the elderly. Aloft in an expensive penthouse apartment, Newton enjoyed a celebrity's prestige and visibility. He was embraced by many white leftists in Hollywood, became a drug addict, and, according to some, attempted to take over the drug trade in Oakland.[1] Internal schisms resulted in expulsion and beatings. By 1973 the party had closed its local chapters and branches and directed remaining Panthers to relocate to Oakland where it was engaged in local politics and community organization. Oakland, according to Newton, would be the launching pad for the revolution. After Bobby Seale lost his bid to become Oakland's mayor in 1973, he, too, left the party and drifted out of public view.[2]

In 1972 and 1973 Newton had several run-ins with the police and was accused of pistol-whipping a tailor and beating a prostitute, who later died. Instead of facing the murder charge, Newton fled to Cuba in 1974, handing leadership of the organization to Elaine Brown, editor of the *Black Panther*.[3] Although Brown maintained the Panthers' remaining programs with relative efficiency, the party, in the words of Bobby Seale, was over. Decimated by police and government agents, plagued with militaristic bravado and paranoia and internal conflict, it had been reduced to a local organization with a small newsletter and a community school by 1977 when Newton returned to the United States to face charges later to be dismissed. In 1982 the doors of its community school were closed and Newton faced new charges of embezzling federal money from the school. An internal memo from party administrator JoNina Abron to Newton dated April 17, 1981, explains her departure from the moribund organization. The party's banking account, Abron wrote, "as of March 17, 1981 is $11.87." The amount in the account for its "Committee for Justice" had only $8.96.[4] Newton was convicted and served time for illegal gun possession in 1987. Despite his incessant legal problems, Newton managed to continue his education, eventually earning his Ph.D. from the University of California at Santa Cruz with a degree in the "history of consciousness." His dissertation examined the history of government repression of the Black Panther Party. Newton's drug addictions included the very addictive crack cocaine by the late 1980s, and in 1989 he was murdered by a drug dealer in the streets of West Oakland, within two miles of the party's first office.[5]

The story of the death and rebirth of the Nation of Islam is much less tragic. It was not only the richest black organization in the United States by the late 1960s, it was, according to the FBI, one of the most efficiently run and most difficult to disrupt.[6] Despite its antiwhite rhetoric, the Nation's mosques did not suffer from the type of police harassment that plagued the Panthers. This was largely due to the relatively nonthreatening nature of the Nation. This does not mean, however, that governmental authorities did not invest considerable time, money, and resources in trying to undermine the organization. Through wiretaps, break-ins, and extensive efforts of infiltrators, informants, and agents provocateurs, the FBI amassed thousands of pages of surveillance on the Nation. FBI agents were directed to develop creative ideas to destabilize the organization and exploit internal schisms. Still, the Nation did not evoke the level of alarm that the Black Panthers, Revolutionary Action Movement, American Indian Movement, or self-described revolutionary leftist organizations generated. Much of the hostility directed at the Nation demonstrated the racism pervasive in law enforcement. Inasmuch as whites in general were hostile to black people, whites in the FBI reflected the larger racial sensibilities of their time. As explicit racism became less virulent and less acceptable among whites, law enforcement likewise reflected this impulse. By the early 1970s the Nation and Elijah Muhammad were receiving accolades from white lawmakers across the country.

In many regards, the Nation's vision of the United States did not differ appreciably from that of the defenders of the status quo. The Nation was an ideal black organization for those conservatives who wanted to point to what can be done if blacks pulled themselves up by their bootstraps. A significant number, if not a majority, of men in the Nation had criminal backgrounds, yet recidivism was almost nil. The leader of one of the most efficiently run black organizations had never graduated from grammar school; however, the Nation had farms in five states and scores of lucrative businesses. The obvious signs of racial progress, the expansion of the black middle class, and black publicly elected officials reshaped the Nation's black nationalism. The praise Elijah Muhammad received from many segments of white America and the fundamental shifts in racial etiquette he witnessed in his lifetime forced him to loosen his rigid positions and begin to move away from the notion of universal white deviltry. A year before he died,

Muhammad announced to thousands of Muslims on Savior's Day 1974 that "It's time for us to stop calling white folks the devil because there's some black devils too . . . Give justice to him when it is due." When wealthy whites were willing to sell an elite country club on Chicago's South Side to the Nation, he implored followers to "not disrespect people that are trying to respect you." FBI agents even reported to President Nixon that Muhammad had considered attending the Republican National Convention in San Diego and endorsing the president. Nixon, without doubt, was excited to learn of a potential new base of support and may have been happy to see that his decision to laud "Black Power" years earlier was paying off.[7]

Praise for the Nation in the early 1970s must also be viewed in the context of radical ethnic nationalist unrest. The FBI and other forces had much bigger fish to fry. Armed revolutionaries with ties to countries like China and Cuba roamed America. Much as civil rights activists had appeared attractive in contrast to the vituperative Malcolm X and the anti-white Muslims in 1963, the Nation of Islam of 1970 was considerably more attractive than the Republic of New Africa, the Black Panthers, the American Indian Movement, and others who openly endorsed armed struggle and anticapitalist politics. With a veneer of black nationalist radicalism, the Nation was perfectly positioned to receive praise from government agencies.

Muhammad's son and heir, Wallace Deen Muhammad, was appointed leader of the Nation after his father's death on February 25, 1975, the day before the annual Savior's Day convention. Wallace assumed the daunting task of dismantling the racialist theology of the Nation. Within months, Wallace Muhammad declared that the Nation was no longer beholden to the Yacub myth, which he insisted was not to be taken literally, only metaphorically. Within a year, the younger Muhammad proudly declared the new orthodox Islamic nature of the Nation and invited whites to join the Muslim organization. Black nationalism was no longer to be a mission of the orthodox body that, according to its leader, should be more concerned with serving God than racial separation. Elijah Muhammad's plans to build a hospital to serve black people in Chicago were abandoned, as the new leader opened the organization's financial books to reveal the status of the Nation's massive empire. Some enterprises were in debt; others showed a profit. Unsuccessful ventures were sold and many other businesses were "privatized" and sold to members. Within a year of Muhammad's death, the Nation lost thousands of members and liquidated many of its business enterprises. The name was changed to the World Community of Islam in the West in October 1976 and it ceased to be a black nationalist organization.[8]

In August 1977, Silas Muhammad, former captain of distribution for *Muhammad Speaks* established the Lost-Found Nation of Islam to carry on Muhammad's original message of black nationalism. Despite speculation that he would do the same, national spokesman Louis Farrakhan insisted that he had no plans to break from Wallace Muhammad's orthodox organization, but in 1977 Farrakhan began to reorganize the Nation of Islam around the teachings of Elijah Muhammad.[9] Farrakhan met with members of the black nationalist community in Chicago, including Haki Madhubuti (formerly Don L. Lee). Despite ideological and religious disagreements, the former Muslim leader negotiated enough support from Madhubuti and others to expand his mission. With loaned space in basements, backrooms, and community centers, Farrakhan pursued the difficult task of rebuilding the organization run by Muhammad for forty years. Today, the Farrakhan-led Nation of Islam is one of a handful of organizations with similar names, all claiming to be heirs of Elijah Muhammad.

Farrakhan's Nation of Islam is popularly accepted as the continuation of Elijah Muhammad's legacy and has purchased many of the same properties Muhammad once owned, including a farm in Georgia and estates in Chicago and Phoenix. Farrakhan's organization has emerged as the largest black nationalist organization in America. Based in Chicago it remains very active in reforming criminals and drug addicts. It also has had considerable success providing unarmed security in housing projects across the country, reducing drug traffic and crime rates significantly in many cases.[10] Farrakhan successfully led the organization of the historic Million Man March, which attracted the largest number of black people ever assembled. Despite what appeared to some as its sexist and conservative overtones, mainstream black leaders who normally distance themselves from Farrakhan and the Nation were eager to speak at the October 16, 1995, gathering in Washington, D.C.

Due in part to the Nation of Islam's growth in the 1980s and 1990s is a greater appreciation for black nationalism in mainstream black political thought. Like his black nationalist predecessors, Farrakhan is disliked by most whites who know of him.[11] Similar to Marcus Garvey, Malcolm X, and Elijah Muhammad, Farrakhan remains a man of the people, able to attract sold-out crowds across the country, despite his vilification by many high-profile black intellectuals. In 1996 the National Association of Newspaper Publishers, the largest association of black newspapers, honored Farrakhan with its prestigious "News Maker of the Year" award for providing "moral guidance" and leadership in the African American community. Also the National Association of Black Journalists invited him to serve as a major speaker at its annual convention in Chicago that year. The broad-based acceptance of Farrakhan in the black community is clear, despite his demonization in the white-owned media. While his nationalist rhetoric is much less vituperative than the earlier stages of the Nation, he remains the country's leading black nationalist.

Throughout the 1990s Farrakhan increasingly distanced himself and the Nation of Islam from the caustic racialist rhetoric that has brought him notoriety. During the civil war in the former Yugoslavia in 1993, he spoke about the need to end the bloodshed and lend aid to Muslims who have been victimized by the conflict. Prior to that statement, the Nation had been loath to admit that white Muslims existed. He even made a trip in 1996 and danced with Muslims in Eastern Europe. In October 2000, Farrakhan, recuperating from prostate cancer, organized the Million Family March and welcomed whites as well as other people of color at the gathering of tens of thousands. His move away from rigid black nationalism may be a sign of the times; in the late 1990s, home ownership and educational levels in black America reached historic highs and unemployment and poverty rates reached new lows. Black nationalism tends to be more appealing in desperate times. The rise of Farrakhan's popularity in the 1980s coincided with declines in the quality of life for African Americans. The recessions of the 1980s and early 1990s hit African Americans hard. The deleterious effects of deindustrialization in cities like Gary, Detroit, Chicago, and others converged with the crack epidemic and devastated many communities. Scores of studies examined the "urban underclass" and the "endangered black male." The rise in crime had a vicious, two-pronged effect on many poor black communities, where a single murder often meant the loss of two young men: one to death, the other to prison. The Nation's "tough love" exhortations that blacks reject drugs, welfare, embrace the capitalist spirit of economic development, and denounce white supremacy found a captive audience.

The growing popularity of 1990s black nationalism was been manifested in popular culture. In the late 1980s and early 1990s hip-hop music had gone through a period of popular black consciousness. Platinum-selling rappers such as Public Enemy, Ice Cube, X-Clan, and Brand Nubian used excerpts from speeches made by Louis Farrakhan, Khalid Muhammad, and Malcolm X. Paris, an Oakland-based rapper, called himself the "Black Panther of hip-hop" and even included the party's Ten-Point Program on the jacket of his 1992 CD *Sleeping with the Enemy*. Of all black nationalist icons, none was as popular as Malcolm X: in the early 1990s there were X hats, t-shirts, shoes, and even potato chips, which generated millions of dollars in sales. In 1992 filmmaker Spike Lee produced and directed *Malcolm X,* an epic film based on the life of the nationalist leader. Three years later, Mario Van Peebles produced and directed *Panther,* based on Melvin Van Peebles's novel of the same name. There have also been political manifestations of the Panther legacy. In 1989, Milwaukee city councilman and former Black Panther Michael McGee formed the Black Panther Militia and threatened to engage in guerrilla warfare against the white power establishment if the city refused to effectively respond to the economic and material needs of the black community by 1995. The year passed without incident. There have been other groups that have claimed to be heirs of the Black Panther Party, including the New Black Panther Party in Dallas, which has been sued for "misuse" of the Black Panther Party name by former Panthers who are disturbed by the language, "bullying" tactics and gun brandishing of the new Panthers.[12]

Thirty years after the emergence of the Black Power movement, most leading universities in the United States have developed black studies programs; African Americans have embraced Kwanzaa, an African-based celebration created by Maulana Karenga; and black people in the Diaspora have made kente cloth one of Ghana's biggest exports. Black representations of Jesus are not uncommon in African American churches, and a black nationalist has emerged as one of the era's most influential leaders. The U.S. Postal Service has even issued stamps commemorating Malcolm X and Kwanzaa. Clearly black nationalism has continued to serve as a formidable body of thought with far-reaching influence and significance. Its contours remain complex, controversial, and multifarious.

African and Muslim names such as Jamal, Jamillah, Kenya, Kenyatta, and Malik are not particularly uncommon for younger African Americans. During the late 1960s, scores of thousands of young parents who were inspired by the tenets of Black Power named their children after kings, queens, and freedom fighters of the African world. Many more, who were not college-educated or without immediate access to books of African names, were likewise inspired by the impulse of self-definition, and Black Power became more creative. For many working-class and poor African Americans, self-definition took shape with the creation of African "sounding" names: Shaniqua, Lashronda, Sheleena, Sharonda, and others. These uniquely African American names are not found among those born before Black Power. They are fruits of the era. Though these neo-African names generally connote a particular class background and are sometimes derided, they reflect the fundamental thrust of Black Power: self-determination and a particular celebration of what it means to be a black person in America.

While most African Americans are not willing to pack up and relocate to Africa or establish their own state in North America, there remains a resilient search for affirmation of self-determination and identity. Racial consciousness, as amorphous as it can be, is a peculiar phenomenon in the United States. Despite the melting pot rhetoric, the country remains highly racialized. It is this racialized climate that will continue to make black nationalism appealing to many. Moreover, it is the incessant practice of racial discrimination and oppression that gives voice and audience to the ideology of race first.

Notes

Introduction

1. On the other hand, the racialized terms of black nationalism are only substitutes for the ethnic or religious differences that characterize nationalism elsewhere. Moreover, as late as the early twentieth century, some European nationalist organizations and movements used "race" to galvanize ethnic groups in nationalist struggles. The idea of race, as popularly used among such nationalist movements as the Basques and the Irish, was often little more than a synonym for ethnicity. Audrey Smedley, *Race in North America: Origin and Evolution of a Worldview* (Boulder, Colo., 1993), 10–15; see also David R. Roediger, *The Wages of Whiteness: Race and the Making of the American Working Class* (New York, 1991).

2. Theodore Draper, *The Rediscovery of Black Nationalism* (New York, 1970), 16.

3. Martin R. Delany, "A Project for an Expedition of Adventure to the Eastern Coast of Africa," reprinted in *Black Brotherhood: Afro-Americans and Africa,* ed. Okon Edet Uya (Lexington, Mass., 1971), 71, 75, 76.

4. Tony Martin, *Race First* (New York, 1976), 13–16.

5. V. P. Franklin, *Black Self-Determination* (New York, 1978), 198.

6. Marcus Garvey, *The Marcus Garvey and the Universal Negro Improvement Association Papers,* vol. 7: *November 1927–August 1940,* ed. Robert Hill (Berkeley, 1983), 108.

7. Marcus Garvey, *Philosophies and Opinions of Marcus Garvey,* ed. Amy Jacques-Garvey (New York, 1969), 104.

8. Ibid., 119.

9. Kenneth B. Clark, *Prejudice and Your Child* (Boston, 1963) and *Dark Ghetto: Dilemmas of Social Power* (New York, 1965).

10. St. Claire Drake, *Black Metropolis* (Chicago, 1945), 58; Elaine Brown, *A Taste of Power* (New York, 1992), 42.

11. There is some dispute over the exact circulation of the *Crusader* at its peak. According to Cyril Briggs, it was 36,000. Authorities in New York, however, estimated 4,000. Historian Winston James believes the number was closer to 20,000. See Winston James, "Being Red and Black in Jim Crow America: Notes on

the Ideology and Travails of Afro-America's Socialist Pioneers, 1877–1930," *Souls* 2, no. 4 (fall 1999): 54–55.

12. Winston James offers perhaps the most comprehensive analysis of the African Blood Brotherhood in *Holding Aloft the Banner of Ethiopia: Caribbean Radicalism in Early Twentieth-Century America* (New York, 1998), 155–84; see also Theodore G. Vincent, *Black Power and the Garvey Movement* (San Francisco, 1971), 75–85; Maxwell C. Stanford, "Revolutionary Action Movement: A Case Study of an Urban Revolutionary Movement in Western Capitalist Society" (M.A. thesis, Atlanta University, 1986), 77–79; and Wilson J. Moses, *The Wings of Ethiopia* (Ames, Iowa, 1990), 99.

Chapter 1. An Organization of the Living

1. Scholars such as C. Eric Lincoln, *Black Muslims in America* (New York, 1961); E. U. Essien-Udom, *Black Nationalism: A Search for an Identity in America* (New York, 1962); Mattias Gardell, *In the Name of Elijah Muhammad: Louis Farrakhan and the Nation of Islam* (Durham, N.C., 1996); Louis A. DeCaro Jr., *Malcolm and the Cross* (New York, 2000); and Claude A. Clegg III, *An Original Man* (New York, 1997), as well as Bruce Perry, *Malcolm: The Life of a Man Who Changed Black America* (New York, 1991) and Karl Evanzz, *The Judas Factor: The Plot to Kill Malcolm X* (New York, 1992) and *The Messenger: The Rise and Fall of Elijah Muhammad* (New York, 1999), have written extensively on the NOI, its theology and general history. Much of what follows is intended to place the Nation into the larger context of black nationalism. I examine the organization's theological framework to understand how the Muslims helped shape an era.

2. This era of modern black nationalism, as it is defined by Wilson J. Moses in *The Wings of Ethiopia* (Ames, Iowa, 1990), emerges after the decline of the Universal Negro Improvement Association in the 1930s and lasts through the present.

3. Muslim ministers always explained how the devil and his Negro agents had duped the "so-called Negro." Additionally, the NOI carefully noted that Muslims were persecuted because they were righteous in the land of the unrighteous. Muhammad preached a messianic message, imploring black people to "unite with me and with the help of Allah I will get you what you want. And I know what you want for I am your brother." Muhammad implies that he knows what black people want, even if they are not sure themselves. At the least, he knows *how* to get what they want. See Elijah Muhammad, *Message to the Blackman in America* (Newport News, Va., 1965), 217–19; see also Evanzz, *The Judas Factor,* 43.

4. Muhammad, *Message,* 9, 69, 111–22.

5. The ubiquity of antiblack sentiment and color division among blacks also influenced Allah's human form. Malcolm X, *The Autobiography of Malcolm X,* quoted in Kenneth C. Davis, *Don't Know Much about History: Everything You Need to Know about American History but Never Learned* (New York, 1990), 384; Malcolm X,

Harlem speech, ca. 1962, in *The True Malcolm X Speaks,* documentary by Debra D. Bass, Library Distributors of America, Inc., vol. 2 (Las Vegas, 1994).

6. Some rejected the term *Negro* in favor of other terms, such as *Nubian,* or *Moor.* In 1913 Timothy Drew founded the Moorish Science Temple of America (MSTA) in New Jersey and taught that Islam was the true religion of African Americans, whom he called "Moors." Renaming himself Noble Drew Ali, the self-described prophet of Allah insisted that Negro was an improper name for people of African descent. It meant "death," he warned. Furthermore, terms such as *colored, black,* and *Ethiopian* were also unsuitable for people who must be associated with a land mass, such as Morocco or even Asia. Ironically, however, he never argued that African was a suitable name. After a power struggle, Ali died in 1929 in Chicago under suspicious circumstances. The organization splintered and decreased in size, although it has survived. Although the Nation disavows any association with the Moors, historical evidence suggests otherwise. Moreover, Drew Ali's teachings are clearly echoed in the cosmology of the NOI. See Essien-Udom, *Black Nationalism,* 46–47, and Evanzz, *The Messenger,* 65–68.

7. Muhammad, *Message,* 18–20; Essien-Udom, *Black Nationalism,* 340–41. The FBI attempted to undermine the NOI by revealing that W. D. Fard was actually white. On July 29, 1963, the *Los Angeles Herald-Examiner* published an article, "Black Muslim Founder Exposed as a White," which included pictures of Wallace Dodd, arrested by Detroit police in 1933. The Nation denied the veracity of the story, insisting that the photo was not its founder. Although there is no definitive evidence on the origins of Fard Muhammad, theories abound. There is even evidence to suggest that Muhammad was of Pakistani origin. See Evanzz, *The Judas Factor* and *The Messenger,* and Monroe Berger, "The Black Muslims," *Horizon* 5 (winter 1964): 61.

8. Founded in 1889 by Mirza Ghulam Ahmad, the Ahmadiyya movement promoted Ahmad as the Mahdi, or messiah predicted by Islamic texts. Brought to the United States by immigrants from Pakistan, Ahmadiyya had begun to take root in black communities by the early 1920s. For an extensive discussion of the origins and identity of Fard, see Evanzz, *The Messenger,* 398–417 and 54–67 in the book. Other information on the Ahmadiyya movement can be found in Essien-Udom, *Black Nationalism,* 311, and Clegg, *Original Man,* 18–19.

9. For a discussion on the creation of "whiteness" and the benefits afforded white ethnics by racist policies in the United States, see David R. Roediger, *The Wages of Whiteness: Race and the Making of the American Working Class* (New York, 1991), and Alexander Saxton, *The Rise and Fall of the White Republic* (New York, 2003).

10. "Malcolm X Interview," *Playboy,* May 1963, 79.

11. Muhammad, *Message,* 216.

12. Ibid., 215–16.

13. Essien-Udom, *Black Nationalism,* 145, 153.

14. Evanzz, *The Messenger,* 398–417.

15. Perry, *Malcolm,* 205. In fact, when Wallace D. Muhammad took over the Nation in 1975, he instructed followers to view the Yacub myth as a "metaphor" instead of literal fact.

16. Ernest Allen Jr. "Satokata Takahashi and the Flowering of Black Messianic Nationalism," *Black Scholar* 24, no. 1 (winter 1994): 37; For further discussion of Japanese efforts to court African Americans and African American affection toward imperial Japan, see Gerald Horne, "Tokyo Bound: African Americans and Japan Confront White Supremacy," *Souls* 3, no. 3 (summer 2001): 20–24.

17. Clegg, *An Original Man,* 97–99; Gardell, *Elijah Muhammad,* 59–61; Essien-Udom, *Black Nationalism,* 80–85.

18. Muhammad, *Message,* 231.

19. "Malcolm X Interview," 79.

20. William Strickland, *Malcolm X: Make It Plain* (New York, 1994), 72; Evanzz, *The Judas Factor,* 71.

21. Strickland, *Malcolm X,* 84–85.

22. Evanzz, *The Judas Factor,* 131–132; Strickland, *Malcolm X,* 85.

23. *Sepia,* November 1959, 21.

24. Nicholas Lemann, *The Promised Land: The Great Migration and How It Changed Black America* (New York, 1991), 221–36.

25. Lawrence M. Friedman, *Crime and Punishment in American History* (New York, 1993), 173–75, 374–77; William Lee Brent, *A Long Time Gone* (New York, 1996), 101–3; August Meier and Elliot Rudwick, *CORE: A Study of the Civil Rights Movement, 1942–1968* (New York, 1973), 300; Akua Njeri, former Black Panther, interview with author, August 1995.

26. "The Nation of Islam," *Life,* May 31, 1963, 32.

27. Ibid.

28. Ramza Muhammad, member of the Nation of Islam, interview with author.

29. "The Nation of Islam," 32.

30. As explained in Claude Clegg's *An Original Man,* 98–99, Elijah Muhammad shifted the NOI's activities away from direct confrontations with white supremacy and the U.S. government, following his imprisonment for resisting the draft during World War II.

31. Harold Cruse, "An Afro-American's Cultural Views," in *Rebellion or Revolution?* (New York, 1968), 53, 56.

32. Ibid., 66.

33. Ibid., 60–61.

34. Quoted in Tujumoja Olaniyan, "African American Critical Discourse and the Invention of Cultural Identities," *African American Review* 26, no. 4 (spring 1994): 534.

35. E. Franklin Frazier, *The Negro Family in the United States* (Chicago, 1966); Melville J. Herskovitz, *The Myth of the Negro Past* (New York, 1941).

36. W. E. B. Du Bois, *The Souls of Black Folk: Essays and Sketches* (Greenwich, Conn. 1961), 16–18, and "The Conservation of Race," *The American Negro Academy, Occasional Papers*, no. 2 (1897): 10.

37. Robin D. G. Kelley, *Race Rebels: Culture, Politics, and the Black Working Class* (New York, 1994), 87, 88, 168–69.

38. "The Beast with the Eyes Before and Behind," *Muhammad Speaks*, May 18, 1973, 16–17.

39. Master W. Fard Muhammad and Elijah Muhammad, "Student Enrollment 1–10," in *The Book of Life* (New York, c.1964), available at: http://sunsite.unc.edu/nge/Book/StudentEnrollment.html (accessed September 28, 1996).

40. "Elijah Muhammad," *Muhammad Speaks*, January 16, 1970, 16–17.

41. Essien-Udom, *Black Nationalism*, 153–59.

42. C. Eric Lincoln, *The Black Muslims in America*, 3d ed. (Trenton, N.J., 1994), 28.

43. Essien-Udom, *Black Nationalism*, 155; Muhammad, *Message*, 72.

44. "Civil Rights Seekers, Unite with Muslims!" *Muhammad Speaks*, October 15, 1971, 16–17.

45. Quoted in Lincoln, *Black Muslims*, 65–66.

46. Sterling Stuckey, *The Ideological Origins of Black Nationalism* (Boston, 1972), 26.

47. Quoted in Essien-Udom, *Black Nationalism*, 154.

48. Stuckey, *Ideological Origins*, 26.

49. Malcolm X, "Message to the Grassroots," in *Malcolm X Speaks*, ed. George Breitman (New York, 1965), 6–8.

50. Elijah Muhammad, *Our Savior Has Arrived* (Hampton, Va., 1988), 211.

51. Elijah Muhammad, *The Fall of America* (Hampton, Va., 1988), 112.

52. Ibid., 116, 120; Ramza Muhammad, interview with author.

53. Muhammad, *Fall of America*, 199.

54. Muhammad, *Message*, 58.

55. Quoted in James H. Cone, *Martin and Malcolm and America: A Dream or a Nightmare* (Maryknoll, N.Y., 1991), 275.

56. Ibid., 277–79; Paula Giddings, *When and Where I Enter: The Impact of Black Women on Race and Sex in America* (New York, 1984), 261–75.

57. Muhammad, *Message*, 58.

58. Ibid., 60.

59. Ibid., 59.

60. Essien-Udom, *Black Nationalism*, 157–58.

61. William "Pete" Clark Jr., former member of the Nation of Islam, interview with author.

62. Cynthia S'thembile West, "Revisiting Female Activism in the 1960s: The Newark Branch Nation of Islam," *The Black Scholar* 26, no. 3–4 (1997): 41, 42, 45–47.

63. Muhammad, *Fall of America*, 105–6; Muhammad, *Message*, 273.

64. Essien-Udom, *Black Nationalism*, 246.

65. Ibid., 246.

66. Muhammad, *Fall of America*, 61–64.

Chapter 2. "There Go My People"

1. James H. Cone, *Martin and Malcolm and America: A Dream or a Nightmare* (New York, 1991), 91–92. Although the NOI generally avoided making official estimations of membership numbers, Elijah Muhammad declared that the organization was 300,000 strong during his annual Savior's Day speech, February 25, 1965. This figure is probably inflated. At the time, there were about fifty-four mosques in the country. The largest, in New York, had a membership of about 7,000. Many others had fewer than a hundred members. The most conservative estimate of around 20,000 is much too low. Considering the information available on the number of mosques, 100,000–150,000 is perhaps a more accurate number of active NOI membership at the time.

2. The struggle for civil rights is as old as the laws that denied them to black people in the United States. Though blacks had fought in various capacities for rights from the colonial era, the large, grassroots efforts of the modern civil rights period are unique. See the following for elaboration: Lerone Bennett Jr. *Before the Mayflower: A History of Black America* (New York, 1982), 377; Taylor Branch, *Parting the Waters: America in the King Years, 1954–1963* (New York, 1988); Charles Payne, *I've Got the Light of Freedom: The Organizing Tradition of the Mississippi Freedom Struggle* (Berkeley, 1995).

3. "Mother to Testify," *New York Times*, September 13, 1955; "Mississippi Jury Acquits Two Accused in Youth's Killing," *New York Times*, September 24, 1955; "The Accused," *Newsweek*, September 19, 1955, 38.

4. Since Milam and Bryant did not risk imprisonment due to double jeopardy, they sold their story to *Look* magazine. J. Edgar Hoover, director of the Federal Bureau of Investigation argued that the federal government had no authority to file charges against the men for killing Till, since no federal laws were broken. The Eisenhower administration did not view federal action necessary, despite public outcry. *The Nation*, September 17, 1955, 234–35; "The Shocking Story of Approved Killing in Mississippi," *Look*, January 24, 1956, 60; "No True Bill," *Newsweek*, November 21, 1955, 34; "Awakenings 1954–1956," *Eyes on the Prize*, episode 1, PBS Home Video (Los Angeles, 1986).

5. According to the American Commission on Civil Rights, by 1955 more than 2,500 black people had been murdered by white lynch mobs in the United States since the end of Reconstruction. In 1955, two NAACP leaders were lynched in Mississippi for their efforts to register blacks to vote. See "Fear Campaign," *Time*, October 4, 1968; "Bishop Cites States' Failure to Punish Perpetrators in Recent Murders of Negroes," *New York Times*, December 24, 1955.

6. Stephan J. Whitfield, *A Death in the Delta: The Story of Emmett Till* (New York, 1988), 96.

7. Elijah Muhammad, *Message to the Blackman in America.* (Newport News, Va., 1965), 42, 125.

8. Lerone Bennett Jr. *Confrontation: Black and White* (Baltimore, 1965), 174.

9. "Nation," *Time,* January 3, 1964, 26

10. Early census records on income and other statistics were often broken into two categories, white and nonwhite. Black people made up the overwhelming majority of people of color in the 1950s.

11. Nathan Wright Jr., *Black Power and Urban Unrest* (New York, 1967), 49, 54

12. In a UCLA study after the Watts rebellion of 1965, over 90 percent of blacks polled believed police beat those in custody. Nearly 50 percent personally knew someone who had been beaten by police. "The President's Commission on Law Enforcement and the Administration of Justice," in *Black Revolt: Strategies of Protest,* ed. Doris Y. Wilkinson (Berkeley, 1969), 84. See also John L. Cooper, *You Can Hear Them Knocking: A Study in the Policing of America* (Port Washington, N.Y., 1981), 34–35; W. Marvin Dulaney, *Black Police in America* (Bloomington, Ind., 1996), 13–26; Hugh Pearson, *The Shadow of the Panther: Huey Newton and the Price of Black Power in America* (New York, 1994), 49; August Meier and Elliot Rudwick, *CORE: A Study in the Civil Rights Movement, 1942–1968* (New York, 1973), 194.

13. There is evidence that African people have referred to whites as "devils" since the beginning of the Atlantic slave trade. An old term of derision for whites, "buckra," which is used in different parts of the African Diaspora, including the West Indies and North America, is traced to the Calabar Coast of West Africa and literally means "devil." See *Juba to Jive: A Dictionary of African-American Slang,* ed. Clarence Major (New York, 1994), 69. Africans in other parts of the continent have also referred to whites as devils or demons. *Likoundou* is a Sango term from Central Africa that means "devil." It is also used to describe whites. Several early black nationalists and militants referred to white racists at various times as "devils," including David Walker. See David Walker, *Appeal in Four Articles,* reprinted in *Classical Black Nationalism From the American Revolution to Marcus Garvey,* ed. Wilson J. Moses (New York, 1996), 70, 79, 86; so too have members of the UNIA. See Tony Martin, *Race First: the Ideological and Organizational Struggles of Marcus Garvey and the Universal Negro Improvement Association* (Dover, Mass., 1976), 187. Garveyite Archbishop George Alexander McGuire of the African Orthodox Christian Church implored his followers in the 1920s to view Satan anthropomorphically as white; see Ernle P. Gordon, "Garvey and Black Liberation Theology," in *Garvey: His Work and Impact,* ed. Patrick Bryan (Mona, Jamaica, 1988), 138. Though black people have intermittingly referred to whites as devils since the seventeenth century, no organization insisted on an innate and universal white deviltry.

14. Bennett, *Confrontation,* 232.

15. Cone, *Martin and Malcolm,* 174–74, 178.

16. Bayard Rustin's political career began with the Communist Party, and he later drifted into pacifist work with the Fellowship of Reconciliation (FOR), which was philosophically inspired by Gandhian nonviolent resistance. Some FOR-affiliated people founded the Congress of Racial Equality in 1942, further expanding these notions of nonviolence, which had not yet taken full root in the philosophy of most civil rights activists, North or South, by the late 1950s. Even after Rustin had been forced to leave Montgomery after his short time as an "adviser" to King and others, he complained that he needed a replacement to further instruct local activists on the principles of nonviolent action. Guns in leader's homes, including King's, were problematic, Rustin believed. For Rustin, nonviolence went beyond the peaceful actions of the Montgomery activists. Nonviolence, as Rustin envisioned it, dismissed the possibility of direct action self-defense, or what King would later call "retaliatory violence." It is this interpretation of nonviolence that has come to be the standard understanding of nonviolence in grassroots struggle since the late twentieth century. See Branch, *Parting the Waters,* 174, 178–80; Jervis Anderson, *Bayard Rustin: Troubles I've Seen, a Biography* (New York, 1998).

17. Martin L. King Jr., *Where Do We Go from Here: Chaos or Community?* (New York, 1967), 59.

18. Nationalists were not alone in criticizing King for his theories of love and nonviolence; mainstream supporters of the civil rights movement also expressed consternation with King's philosophies. Prominent black psychologist Kenneth B. Clark stated that it was "pathological" for a victim of violent oppression to be told to love his oppressor; see Kenneth Clark, *Dark Ghetto: Dilemmas of Social Power* (New York, 1965), 218. Also, as seen below, Roy Wilkins, executive secretary of the NAACP, was skeptical of King's hostility toward black self-defense.

19. I use the term *direct action self-defense* in place of simply *self-defense* to make a distinction between the larger exercise of self-defense and self-preservation inherent in the struggle for civil rights. All civil rights activists, I argue, are ultimately in favor of defending their humanity, lives, and livelihood, but in any immediate manner, many rejected the option to strike back physically when struck or shoot back when shot at.

20. Claude Andrew Clegg III, *An Original Man: The Life and Times of Elijah Muhammad* (New York, 1997), 130–31.

21. Ibid., 131.

22. In 1959 the Nation was excoriated in the white press with several negative media reports, such as the CBS report "The Hate that Hate Produced" and other hostile stories in *U.S. News and World Report, Newsweek,* and *Time* magazines. Despite the negative coverage, the Muslims had nearly doubled in membership by late 1960. See William Strickland, *Malcolm X: Make It Plain* (New York, 1994), 84–85.

23. Gordon Parks, "The Nation of Islam," *Life,* May 31, 1963, 32.

24. Clegg, *An Original Man,* 116; Cone, *Martin and Malcolm,* 193.

25. Clegg, *An Original Man,* 195.

26. Mattias Gardell, *In the Name of Elijah Muhammad: Louis Farrakhan and the Nation of Islam* (Durham, N.C., 1996), 234; Malu Halasa, *Elijah Muhammad* (New York, 1990), 81.

27. Halasa, *Elijah Muhammad,* 129–30.

28. King, *Where Do We Go,* 70; Cone, *Martin and Malcolm,* 75.

29. Quoted in Cone, *Martin and Malcolm,* 75–76.

30. Contrary to popular belief, the NOI did believe that some whites could be made into "Muslim Sons" after twenty to thirty years of study and discipline. While it was against the nature of whites to be morally sound, Elijah Muhammad taught, some whites can resist their genetic proclivities and seek salvation from the wrath of Allah when Armageddon comes. Through careful and tireless efforts, a white person could admit the truth of his "grafted" nature as well as submit to the will of God. Few whites, however, were willing to declare that they were devils, produced by the genetic manipulations of an evil scientist and by-products of bestiality with dogs. Moreover, the Nation was not willing to allow whites to enter its Mosques in order to study for the years necessary to seek salvation. In the final analysis, there was little hope for whites, since the earth was not expected to last too much longer. Elijah Muhammad, *Our Savior Has Arrived* (Hampton, Va., 1988), 11, and *The Fall of America* (Hampton, Va., 1988), 238–42.

31. Malcolm X, *Malcolm X Speaks,* ed. George Breitman (New York, 1965), 8, 12.

32. "Black Supremacy Cult in US—How Much of a Threat?" *U.S. News and World Report,* November 9, 1959, 112.

33. Martin Luther King Jr., *A Testament of Hope: The Essential Writings of Martin Luther King Jr.,* ed., James Kelvin Washington (San Francisco, 1986), 390.

34. King, *Where Do We Go,* 61.

35. "Black Supremacy Cult," 112–14.

36. Robert F. Williams, *Negroes with Guns* (New York, 1962), 67

37. Akinyele Umoja, "Eye for an Eye: The Role of Armed Resistance in the Mississippi Freedom Movement" (Ph.D. diss., Emory University, 1996), 170–78.

38. Ibid., 178.

39. Ibid., 179.

40. Ibid., 182.

41. Ibid., 180.

42. Though there has been some attention given to armed members of SNCC and the NAACP, there has been no substantive examination of armed agents of the SCLC. Because much of King's public image is predicated on his commitment to nonviolence, members of his organization have been particularly reticent on the degree to which members armed themselves. I was fortunate to interview a former armed agent of the SCLC who detailed how he and others selected .38 caliber handguns because they were easy to conceal in crowds. Other times they relied on rifles or shotguns. Anonymous informant, Anniston, Ala., May 26, 2002.

43. Blacks in Panola County reported on J. C. Saxon's brutality, which include stories of beatings, torture, rape and murder. The county, part of which is in the Delta, was not a hot point of civil rights activity, but did have its share of activism. Saxon's pathological and criminal behavior was tolerated by the white power structure, as he represented the first line of defense against challenges to white supremacy and injustice. Interviews with author, May 1999.

44. Branch, *Parting the Waters,* 615–17.

45. Ibid., 617.

46. Willie Mukasa Ricks, former member of SNCC, interview with author, February 23, 1997; for a more elaborate discussion of similar informal groups of militant poor black youth see Robin D. G. Kelley, *Race Rebels: Culture, Politics and the Black Working Class* (New York, 1994), 77–100.

47. Ricks, interview; Branch, *Parting the Waters,* 874.

48. Black militants, including the Black Panther Party, SNCC, the NOI, and RAM long admired the activities of the Deacons for Defense and Justice. Huey Newton and Bobby Seale pointed to them as inspiration, as well as to Robert F. Williams. See "Bullets in Bogalusa," *Newsweek,* July 19, 1965, 25; Ricks, interview.

49. Robert Carl Cohen, *Black Crusader: A Biography of Robert Franklin Williams* (New York, 1972), 176. Williams later became international chairman of the Revolutionary Action Movement, a revolutionary nationalist organization that was critical of the Nation of Islam's lack of activism. In fact, Malcolm X, before he departed the Nation, is reported to have discouraged one of RAM's founders from joining the Muslim organization on the grounds that he could be more viable in an activist-oriented nationalist organization. See Max Stanford, "The Revolutionary Action Movement (RAM): A Case Study of an Urban Revolutionary Movement in Western Capitalist Society" (M.A. thesis, Atlanta University, 1986), 78.

50. Cohen, *Black Crusader,* 132.

51. "The Awful Roar," *Time,* August 30, 1963, 49.

52. Cohen, *Black Crusader,* 127.

53. Roy Wilkins and Tom Matthews, *Standing Fast: An Autobiography of Roy Wilkins* (New York, 1977), 265.

54. Kenneth B. Clark, "Malcolm X Talks with Kenneth B. Clark," in *Malcolm X: The Man and His Times,* ed. John H. Clarke (New York, 1969), 168.

55. Cone, *Martin and Malcolm,* 102.

56. Ibid.

57. Wilkins and Matthews, *Standing Fast,* 317.

58. Cone, *Martin and Malcolm,* 101.

59. James Farmer, *Lay Bare the Heart: An Autobiography of the Civil Rights Movement* (New York, 1985), 222–24, 228.

60. Ibid., 225.

61. Ibid., 226–27.

62. Anderson, *Bayard Rustin,* 238.

63. Quoted in Meier and Rudwick, *CORE,* 206.

64. Farmer, *Laying Bare the Heart,* 224, 230.

65. "I Like the Word 'Black,'" *Newsweek,* May 6, 1963, 28.

66. Malcolm X, "Message to the Grassroots," in Clarke, *Malcolm X,* 279.

67. "I Like the Word 'Black,'" 27–28.

68. "The Awful Roar," 28; Wilkins and Matthews, *Standing Fast,* 293, "Birmingham's Choice," *Newsweek,* May 27, 1963, 27.

69. Richard Lentz, *Symbols, the News Magazines, and Martin Luther King* (Baton Rouge, 1990), 89–90.

70. "America's Most Influential Negro?" *Ebony,* February 1962, 31.

71. "Freedom—Now," *Time,* May 17, 1963, 25.

72. The range of misquotes was significant. Often, Malcolm X was depicted as an advocate of wanton violence against whites. Typically, his insistence that he was an advocate of peace was omitted from coverage. At his death, *Time* magazine and others noted that he suffered a fate not unlike what he advocated in life. See also Clegg, *An Original Man,* 127.

73. Ibid., 199–200.

74. Malcolm X, *Malcolm X Speaks,* 107; Cone, *Martin and Malcolm,* 267.

75. Quoted in Clayborn Carson, *In Struggle: The Student Nonviolent Coordinating Committee* (New York, 1981), 23.

76. Ibid., 93.

77. Quoted in David Garrow, *Bearing the Cross: Martin Luther King Jr. and the Southern Christian Leadership Conference* (New York, 1986), 296.

78. "I Like the Word 'Black,'" 28.

79. Willie Mukasa Ricks, interview with author, May 19, 1997.

80. Ibid.

81. Cleveland Sellers and Robert Terrell, *The River of No Return: The Autobiography of a Black Militant and the Life and Death of SNCC* (New York, 1973), 68.

82. Michael Flug, former member of CORE, interview with author, March 22, 1997.

83. Ricks, interview, May 19, 1997.

84. Quoted in Halasa, *Elijah Muhammad,* 98.

85. As noted above, James Farmer engaged Malcolm X in a series of debates while the latter was national spokesman for the Nation of Islam. Though he disagreed with Malcolm's politics, Farmer insisted that he was an affable friend. That he did not wish CORE members to attend OAAU meetings reflects his concern over Malcolm's skills at persuasion. He also must have realized the basic appeal that Malcolm's message had. Moreover, he likely understood the growing acceptance of the message within the movement. Flug, interview.

86. For further discussion of Malcolm X and his ideological evolution, see Clarke, *Malcolm X,* and *Ghosts in Our Blood: With Malcolm X in Africa, England and the Caribbean,* ed. Jan Carew (New York, 1994). Also see *The Autobiography of Malcolm X* for his own views on his evolution and decision to break from the NOI.

87. Garrow, *Bearing the Cross,* 476–77.

88. Wil Ussery, CORE national chairman, memo,1966, CORE papers, University Microfilms, Ann Arbor, Mich., reel 13, 76, p. 535.

89. Floyd McKissick, press release, n.d., CORE papers, Reel 13, 76, p. 535.

90. Floyd McKissick, *A Black Manifesto—CORE* (New York, 1966), 4.

91. Ibid., 5.

92. "CORE Hears Cries of 'Black Power,'" *New York Times,* 2 July 1966.

93. Dress number 19, a standard garment for Muslim women, was a long white dress with a head covering and long sleeves.

94. "CORE Adopts Policy Insisting on 'Black Power,'" *New York Times,* July 5, 1966.

95. McKissick, *A Black Manifesto,* 5.

96. Quoted in Anderson, *Bayard Rustin,* 314–15.

97. "Excerpts from the Speech by Wilkins," *New York Times,* July 6, 1966.

98. "Baptists to Shun Dr. King Rally," *New York Times,* July 7, 1966.

99. "President Points to Racial Actions," *New York Times,* July 6, 1966.

100. "Excerpts from the Talk by Humphrey," *New York Times,* July 7, 1966.

101. "CORE Chief Assails Humphrey for 'Racist' Views," *New York Times,* July 8, 1966.

102. King was still considered a "rabble rouser" by many whites because of his aggressive grassroots campaigns. In fact, King, according to many, was a radical among the civil rights establishment until the emergence of the NOI and Black Power. As noted, his 1966 criticism of U.S. military aggression in Vietnam caused considerable loss of support from whites and moderate blacks. See Herbert H. Haines, *Black Radicals and the Civil Rights Mainstream, 1954–1970* (Knoxville, 1988), 82–84, 96.

103. "Wilkins Assails CORE and SNCC" *New York Times,* July 8, 1966.

104. Harvard Sitkoff, *The Struggle for Black Equality* (New York, 1993), 135.

Chapter 3. A Party for the People

1. Though some former Panthers deny that the party was ever a black nationalist organization, Huey P. Newton details the party's political evolution from a "Black Nationalist Party" in 1966 to revolutionary nationalism to "Internationalists," or the system of beliefs known as "intercommunalism." Huey P. Newton, *To Die for the People: The Writings of Huey P. Newton* (New York, 1972), 31–32.

2. The official position of the Nation of Islam was to repudiate firearms. Members of the NOI, however, were rumored to have been armed since the early 1960s. In fact, several people were shot and killed by NOI members, most notably Malcolm X and the family of Hamaas Abdul Khaalis. While these killers may have been renegade members who did not follow NOI policy, FBI surveillance notes that in 1960 Elijah Muhammad suggested that his assistant buy a gun. Understanding the duplicity and illegality of FBI activities against

the NOI, however, one must question the veracity of the its claims. See Karl Evanzz, *The Messenger: The Rise and Fall of Elijah Muhammad* (New York, 2001), 222, 380–89.

3. Though there have been several examinations of armed resistance in the southern black freedom movement, examinations of armed agents of the SCLC have not been written. See chap. 2 for further discussion. Ramza Muhammad, Rudy Harlow, and an anonymous SCLC informant, interviews with author, December 20, 1995; July 14 and 16, 1996; May 2002.

4. Willie Mukasa Ricks, Julian Bond, James Foreman, and Askia Toure, interviews with author, February 22, 1997; July 20, 1990; July 27, 1999; April 21, 2000. Also see Charles Evers, *Have No Fear: The Charles Evers Story* (New York, 1996), Akinyele Umoja, "Eye for an Eye: The Role of Armed Resistance in the Mississippi Freedom Movement" (Ph.D. diss., Emory University, 1996), and Emile Cosby, "Common Courtesy: The Civil Rights Movement in Gibson County, Mississippi" (Ph.D. diss., Indiana University, 1996).

5. Taylor Branch, *Parting the Waters: America in the King Years, 1954–1963* (New York, 1988), 259–61.

6. Ricks, Bond, Foreman, and Toure, interviews.

7. Hugh Pearson, *The Shadow of the Panther: Huey Newton and the Price of Black Power in America* (New York, 1994), 25–28.

8. Huey P. Newton, *Revolutionary Suicide* (New York, 1995), 112.

9. Robert F. Williams, *Negroes with Guns* (New York, 1962), 95–100.

10. Quoted in Charlie Cobb, "Black Power," *Emerge,* June 1997, 41.

11. Bond, Ricks, interviews.

12. CAP eventually received federal funds, but due to hostility and anti-CAP activities from police organizations, the funding was significantly curtailed. CAP ceased to exist by late 1967. See "Riots," *Newsweek,* August 7, 1967, 33; Ron Wilkins, interview with author, June 30, 1996, and June 3, 1997.

13. Wilkins, interview.

14. *Revolutionary Nationalist* 1 (summer 1965): 2.

15. Bond, Ricks, and Forman, interviews; see also Clayborn Carson, *In Struggle: The Student Nonviolent Coordinating Committee* (New York, 1981), 192–95.

16. While Brown may be referring to the masses of black people, when he refers to them in less derisive terms, they are simply "Black." H. Rap Brown, *Die Nigger Die!* (New York, 1969), 62–63.

17. Carson, *In Struggle,* 195.

18. Ibid., 191–93. See Timothy B. Tyson, *Radio Free Dixie: Robert F. Williams and the Roots of Black Power* (Chapel Hill, N.C., 1999), and Umoja, "Eye for an Eye" for discussions of armed struggle and inchoate Black Power in the southern-based civil rights movement.

19. Martin Luther King Jr., *Where Do We Go from Here: Chaos or Community?* (New York, 1967), 58–59.

20. Ibid., 44.

21. Stokely Carmichael, "Power and Racism," in *The Black Power Revolt: A Collection of Essays,* ed. Floyd B. Barbour (Boston, 1968), 64.

22. Stokely Carmichael and Charles V. Hamilton, *Black Power: The Politics of Liberation in America* (New York, 1967), 41.

23. Clayborne Carson, *In Struggle: The Student Nonviolent Coordinating Committee* (New York, 1981), 153.

24. Andrew Young, *An Easy Burden: The Civil Rights Movement and the Transformation of America* (New York, 1996), 404.

25. Ricks, interview.

26. Quoted in Cobb, "Black Power," 43.

27. James Forman, interview with author, July 2000.

28. Carmichael and Hamilton, *Black Power,* 62.

29. Huey P. Newton, *Revolutionary Suicide* (New York, 1974), 113.

30. Ibid., 62

31. Ibid., 61.

32. Lawrence P. Crouchett, Lonnie G. Bunch III, and Martha Kendall Winacker, *The History of the East Bay Afro-American Community, 1852–1977* (Oakland, 1989), 53–55; Hugh Pearson, *Shadow of the Panther,* 50.

33. Akbar Muhammad (Max Stanford), "History of RAM—Revolutionary Action Movement," c. 1979, unpublished ms. in the author's possession, 28–29; Maxwell C. Stanford, "The Revolutionary Action Movement (RAM): A Case Study of an Urban Revolutionary Movement in Western Capitalist Society" (M.A. thesis, Atlanta University, 1986), 74–76.

34. Akbar Muhammad, 5–8; Akinyele Umoja and Ernest Allen, interviews with author, March 26, 2000; March 30, 2000.

35. Allen, interview.

36. Akbar Muhammad, 28–29. Beyond RAM documents, there is little evidence of RAM activities with the Five Percenters. Oral history among Five Percenters shows no evidence of RAM involvement. Since the organization was loosely organized, RAM activities were most likely confined to only a portion of the street group's membership; conversations with members of the Nation of Gods and Earths (Five Percenters), July 19, 2000. See also "Clarence Edward Smith," memo, SAC, New York, January 1, 1966, Bureau number 10 0444636, NY 10 0150520, FBI Archives.

37. Akbar Muhammad, 30.

38. Though RAM members have claimed that they formed Black Panther parties in other cities, including Detroit, Chicago, Los Angeles, Oakland, and Cleveland, evidence does not reveal that these groups were sizable or particularly active (ibid.). Henry English, Akua Njeri, Ron Wilkins, interviews with author. Ward Churchill and Jim Vander Wall, *Agents of Repression: The FBI's Secret War against the Black Panther Party and the American Indian Movement* (Boston, 1990), 45.

39. Askia M. Toure, interview with author, April 21, 2000.

40. Newton, *Revolutionary Suicide,* 63–65.

41. Ibid., 71.

42. Bobby G. Seale, *A Lonely Rage: The Autobiography of Bobby Seale* (New York, 1978), 129–30.

43. Bobby Seale, speech given at "It's About Time," Conference on the Thirtieth Anniversary of the Founding of the Black Panther Party, Oakland, Calif., October 13–15, 1996.

44. Bobby Seale, *Seize the Time: The Story of the Black Panther Party and Huey P. Newton* (Baltimore, 1991), 16–20.

45. Elaine Brown, interview with author, September 26, 2003.

46. Allen, interview.

47. Seale, *Seize the Time,* 109.

48. Harvard Sitkoff, *The Struggle for Black Equality* (New York, 1993), 185; see *U.S. News and World Report,* August 30, 1965, and *Newsweek,* August 7, 1967, on urban unrest and other disturbances and the role of the police, including interviews with police and community leaders.

49. Newton, *Revolutionary Suicide,* 110–13.

50. Ibid., 110.

51. Seale, *Seize the Time,* 4

52. Ron Wilkins, former CAP member and deputy chairman of the Western Division of SNCC, interview with author, June 30, 1996.

53. Seale, speech at "It's About Time."

54. "Montreal: Bobby Seale—Panthers Take Control," *The Black Panther,* December 21, 1968.

55. Frantz Fanon, *The Wretched of the Earth* (New York, 1963), 61.

56. There is a sizable body of literature on the pervasive nature of police brutality in black communities. See Lawrence M. Friedman, *Crime and Punishment in American History* (New York, 1993), 377, and *Black Revolt: Strategies of Protest,* ed. Doris Y. Wilkinson (Berkeley, 1969), 84. See also John L. Cooper, *You Can Hear Them Knocking: A Study in the Policing of America* (Port Washington, N.Y., 1981), 34–35, and W. Marvin Dulaney, *Black Police in America* (Bloomington, Ind., 1996), 13–26.

57. Newton, *Revolutionary Suicide,* 147–48; Seale, *Seize the Time,* 152–54

58. Akbar Muhammad, 28–30; Bobby Seale, *Seize the Time,* 125–32; Newton, *Revolutionary Suicide,* 130–32; Umoja, interview.

59. The Oakland-based Panther who threatened BPPP members in Los Angeles was later expelled for being an agent of the police. Whether he was an actual agent is unclear. Many people who were not agents were expelled for suspicion of being police agents. It is also unclear whether he acted on police orders to disrupt the expansion of the party. Legitimate Panthers such as Newton, Cleaver, and Seale were known to physically threaten people in other organizations. See "Tightening Up," *The Black Panther,* January 25, 1969, 17; Angela Y. Davis, *Angela Davis: An Autobiography* (New York, 1974), 163–65; Newton, *Revolutionary Suicide,* 131–32; Churchill and Vander Wall, *Agents of Repression,* 47–49.

60. James Forman, *The Making of Black Revolutionaries* (New York, 1981), 527; Ayuko Babu, James Forman, interviews with author.

61. Omar Barbour, interview with author, October 22, 1996.

Chapter 4. Swimming with the Masses

1. Maulana Karenga, "The Quotable Karenga," in *The Black Power Revolt,* ed. Floyd B. Barbour (Boston, 1968), 163.

2. Eldridge Cleaver, *On the Ideology of the Black Panther Party* (San Francisco, 1968), 2.

3. Ibid.

4. Ibid., 7.

5. Ibid.

6. Frederick Engels and Karl Marx, *The Communist Manifesto,* ed. Frederic L. Bender (New York, 1988), 65.

7. Frederick Engels and Karl Marx, *The Peasant War in Germany in Selected Works,* vol. 1 (New York, 1926), 84.

8. *A Dictionary of Marxist Thought,* ed. Tom Bottomore et al. (Cambridge, Mass., 1983), 292–93.

9. V. I. Lenin, "Marx on the Class Struggle and the Dictatorship of the Proletariat," in *Marx and Engels Marxism: A Collection of Articles* (London, 1936).

10. Cleaver, *Ideology,* 3.

11. Ibid., 1.

12. Bobby Seale, *Seize the Time: The Story of the Black Panther Party and Huey P. Newton* (Baltimore, 1991), 132.

13. Huey P. Newton, *Revolutionary Suicide* (New York, 1974), 46–53, 78–90

14. Ibid., 24

15. C. R. D. Halisi, interviews with author, May 17, 1996, and September 4, 1996.

16. Ayuko Babu, Daniel Johnson, interviews with author, June 6, 1997; May 30, 1997; Brown, *A Taste of Power,* 142–43.

17. Babu, Halisi, interviews. See also Davis, *An Autobiography,* for discussion of violent behavior of local Panthers. A very well done examination of the lumpen phenomenon is found in Chris Booker, "Lumpenization: A Critical Error of the Black Panther Party," in *The Black Panther Party Reconsidered,* ed. Charles E. Jones (Baltimore, 1998).

18. Elaine Brown, interview with author, September 26, 2003.

19. Akinyele Umoja, Ron Wilkins, interviews with author, March 26, 2000; June 30, 1996. See also Charles E. Jones and Judson L. Jeffries, " 'Don't Believe the Hype': Debunking the Panther Mythology," in Jones, *The Black Panther Party Reconsidered,* 45.

20. Quoted in Booker, "Lumpenization," 338.

21. RAM was also a revolutionary nationalist organization. It conforms to the definitions of revolutionary nationalism and generally identified with the label. The term *cultural nationalist* is perhaps a derisive label used by Newton in his context, as it is not a correct description of the ideology of the BPP of northern California, although its membership promoted "cultural renewal" among African Americans, African names, and African garb. Ernest Allen, Akinyele Umoja, interviews with author. See also Maxwell C. Stanford, "The Revolutionary Action Movement (RAM): A Case Study of an Urban Revolutionary Movement in Western Capitalist Society" (M.A. thesis, Atlanta University, 1986), 5–16; William L. Van Deburg, *A New Day in Babylon: The Black Power Movement and American Culture, 1965–1975* (Chicago, 1992), 152–54, 165.

22. Ibid., 130.

23. William Lee Brent, *Long Time Gone* (New York, 1996), 116.

24. Ibid., 116–20, 123.

25. Significantly influenced by the Nation of Islam, many black nationalist organizations rejected pork. Malcolm X was often known to deride the pig as a filthy animal fit only for consumption by whites. Arguing that, "you are what you eat," the Muslims joked that it was no mistake that the pinkish skin of whites resembled that of a pig. Pork was derived from the germ of a "cat, rat and dog," Elijah Muhammad said. Since so many black nationalists had their beginning in the Nation, many adopted its rebuke of swine. Us members, for example, avoided pork consumption and found it ironic that they were called "pork chop nationalists" by Panthers when Panthers often enjoyed pork ribs for dinner. See Elijah Muhammad, *How to Eat to Live* (Newport News, Va., 1988).

26. While Hampton avoided and discouraged the thuggish behavior found on the West Coast, he did herald his street appeal, as mentioned in this chapter. Profanity was important for Hampton to relate to the people most in need, he thought. He was also convicted in 1968 of stealing ice cream from a vendor and distributing it to children. It would be too simplistic to suggest that Hampton did not value the lumpenism celebrated by Newton, Cleaver, and Seale, but it is clear that lumpenism was not as virulent or destabilizing as it was on the West Coast. Local Panthers were not known to bully or engage in the confrontational politics of their California counterparts. The same can be said of chapters from Baltimore, New York, Indianapolis, and elsewhere. Fred Hampton, *Power Anywhere There's People* (Chicago, ca. 1970), Black Panther Party, political pamphlets, P201234, Northwestern University Special Collections, Evanston, Ill.; Henry English, Steve McCutchen, Akua Njeri, and Omar Barbour, former members of the Black Panther Party, interviews with author, July 23, 1995; October 27, 1996; August 14, 1995; October 22, 1996.

27. Newton, *Revolutionary Suicide,* 127; Wilkins, Allen, Babu, interviews.

28. "In Defense of Self-Defense," *The Black Panther,* June 20, 1967, 4.

29. FBI surveillance file, Black Panther Party, Charlotte, N.C., CE 157-6171; Newton, *Revolutionary Suicide,* 132; "In Defense of Self-Defense," 4.

30. "Elaine Brown's Poetry," *The Black Panther*, January 20, 1970, 20.

31. Quoted in Nefertiti Austin, "A Look at the Intersectional Experience of Black Women in the Black Panther Party" (M.A. thesis, University of California at Los Angeles, 1996).

32. Tracye Matthews, " 'No One Ever Asks, What a Man's Place in the Revolution Is': Gender and the Politics of the Black Panther Party, 1966–1971," in Jones, *The Black Panther Party Reconsidered*, 270.

33. Newton, *Revolutionary Suicide*, 30.

34. Ibid., 251.

35. Although Hampton implies that Karenga and Us members did not support armed struggle, the cultural nationalist organization was known to be armed. This speech even occurred after the shoot-out between Panther and Us members that left two Panthers dead. Hampton, *Power Anywhere There's People*, 32.

36. Ibid., 33.

37. There has been a very pervasive belief that the Panthers were particularly hostile to the women's liberation movement and feminism. In *Too Heavy a Load,* author Deborah Gray White discusses Elaine Brown's own frustrations with male chauvinism in the Black Panther Party. White quotes from a story in Brown's autobiography where she and other women are told to wait until men get their share of food before they eat, although women were responsible for cooking and cleaning after all people. The story is not about the Panthers but a visit Brown made to an Us organization function in San Diego, not Los Angeles, as White writes. White presents a problematic representation of the party, arguing that for her several years "[Elaine Brown] and other black women were regularly beaten by black men in the name of 'black manhood.' " Furthermore, a black feminist was "an enemy of black people." White gives no mention of the powerful rhetoric of Panthers (men and women) in support of feminism. She fails to mention that Brown became chair of the party and brought large numbers of women into major positions. Moreover, some men, such as her chief of staff, Larry Henson, demonstrated unwavering loyalty to her as well. While violence was a tragic and destabilizing part of Panther punishment, men were also beaten, sometimes by women or under the direction of women, including Brown. Still, violence against fellow members, men or women, was rare, and far from acceptable, as White implies. Similar misinterpretations and misinformation have cultivated an image of the party as virulently sexist. Closer examination of recollections by several Panther women reveals that while sexism existed in the ranks, it was no more virulent there than in society at large. Moreover, few organizations (black or otherwise) made attempts, as did the Black Panther Party, to explicitly challenge sexism. Matthews, "No One Ever Asks," offers the most well-balanced analysis of gender in the party. Also see Deborah Gray White, *Too Heavy a Load: Black Women in Defense of Themselves, 1894–1994* (New York, 1998), 219–20; Elaine Brown, *A Taste of Power: A Black Woman's Story* (New York, 1992), 108–9, 357–58, 369–71.

38. Brown, interview.

39. Huey P. Newton, *To Die for the People: The Writings of Huey P. Newton* (New York, 1972), 152.

40. Ibid.

41. Ibid., 154.

42. Eldridge Cleaver, quoted in *The Black Panthers Speak,* ed. Philip Foner (New York, 1995), 99.

43. "Roberta Alexander at Conference," *The Black Panther,* August 2, 1969, 7; "The Role of Revolutionary Women," *The Black Panther,* May 4, 1969, 9.

44. Hugh Pearson, in his book *In the Shadow of the Panther* (New York, 1994), provides a detailed discussion of Huey P. Newton's violence directed at women. Newton, as Pearson also details, was even more violent toward men. In fact, the Panther leader's rage was not discriminating. To call him a "misogynist" may be a simplistic take on Newton's violent character, which was not particularly directed at women.

45. Barbour, interview.

46. "Comrade Sister: Voices of Women in the Black Panther Party," unreleased documentary, 1995; Michael Zinzun, Bobby McCall, former members of the Black Panther Party, interviews with author.

47. Safiya Bukhari-Alston, "On the Question of Sexism within the Black Panther Party," 1992, available at: www.blackpanther.org (accessed December 28, 1996).

48. Brown, interview.

49. Njeri, interview.

50. Lee Lew-Lee, interview with author.

51. There were no official or precise records kept of national Panther membership. In my interviews, however, former Panthers have always given estimations of female membership at over 40 percent. Bobby Seale notes that by mid-1968 about two-thirds of Panther membership was female. Bobby Seale, Omar Barbour, Lee-Lew Lee, and Akua Njeri, interviews.

52. "Comrade Sister"; Giddings, *When and Where I Enter,* 317; Emory Douglass, former member of the Black Panther Party, interview with author, November 8, 1996.

53. Kathleen Cleaver and George Katsiaficas, eds., *Liberation, Imagination, and the Black Panther Party: A New Look at the Panthers and Their Legacy* (New York, 2001), 124.

54. Ibid., 126.

55. Brown interview.

56. "Reactionary Paper Tigers," *The Black Panther,* May 25, 1969, 4.

57. Hampton, *Power Anywhere There's People,* 36.

58. David Hilliard and Lewis Cole, *This Side of Glory: The Autobiography of David Hilliard and the Story of the Black Panther Party* (Boston, 1992), 262–65.

59. Ibid., 262.

60. Eldridge Cleaver, *Eldridge Cleaver: Post-Prison Writings and Speeches,* ed. Robert Scheer (New York, 1969), 132; Newton, *Revolutionary Suicide,* 39, 328–32; "Inside Report on Transformed Black Panthers," *Jet,* May 11, 1972, 29.

61. Newton, *Revolutionary Suicide,* 329.

62. Brown, interview.

63. Earl Anthony, *Spitting in the Wind: The True Story behind the Violent Legacy of the Black Panther Party* (Malibu, Calif., 1990), 21–24.

64. Earl Anthony, *Picking Up the Gun: A Report on the Black Panthers* (New York, 1970), 5.

65. Douglas, interview.

66. Ibid.

67. Barbour, interview.

68. Ibid.

69. McCall, interview.

70. Ibid.

71. McCutchen, interview.

72. Fame Studios in Alabama was a white-owned business with white musicians who performed for black artists like Wilson Pickett. White artists like David Hood, Jimmy Johnson, and Spooner Oldham admitted being inspired by black performers like Chuck Berry and Bo Diddly. See *The History of Rock N' Roll,* Warner Video (Los Angeles, 1995), and Arnold Shaw, *Black Popular Music in America: From the Spirituals, Minstrels, and Ragtime to Soul, Disco and Hip-Hop* (New York, 1986), 212–15.

73. It is important to note that black nationalists, taking their cue from the Nation of Islam, deconstructed the term *Negro* and used it derisively to describe politically backward, cowardly, Uncle Toms. A *nigger/nigga* was typically a more virulent pejorative for a Negro. Still, those who made copious attempts to affirm their street credibility and identification with the lumpen used the term as well, sometimes in reference to themselves. I have chosen to spell the word phonetically, using the "-a" instead of the "-er" ending. Umar Bin Hassan and Abiodun Oyewole, *On a Mission: Selected Poems and History of the Last Poets* (New York, 1996), 60–64.

74. Quoted in "The Last Poets," *Essence,* May 1972, 16.

75. Ibid.

76. Hassan and Oyewole, *On a Mission,* 5.

77. Ibid., 126–27.

78. Zinzun, interview.

79. Scot Brown, "In the Face of Funk: The Us Organization and the Arts of War," paper delivered at the Association for the Study of African American Life and History, Orlando, Fla., October 2002.

80. "Interview: The Impressions," *The Black Collegian,* November–December 1971, 15.

81. "On Cultural Nationalism," *The Black Panther,* February 2, 1969, 6.

82. "Music Legends: Curtis Mayfield," VH1, air date December 7, 1996.

83. "Revolutionary Culture," *The Black Panther*, February 2, 1969, 7.

84. Ibid.

85. Ibid.

86. Cleaver, *Ideology*, 8, 9.

87. Eldridge Cleaver, "Education and Revolution," *The Black Scholar* 1, no. 1 (November 1969): 49.

88. "On Cultural Nationalism," *The Black Panther*, February 2, 1969, 6.

89. "Panthers Assassinated by Us Organization," *The Black Panther*, January 25, 1969, 1, 3.

90. Hampton, *Power Anywhere There's People*, 20.

91. Sababa Akili and Kaimu Tukufu, Us statement, ca. 1970, Black Power, Political Pamphlets, P201234, Northwestern University Special Collections.

92. Hampton, *Power Anywhere There's People*, 21.

93. "African Splendor: Colorful Garb Reflects the Best of Two Worlds," *Ebony*, July 1973, 113.

94. For further discussion of fashions and the influence of "soul," see Van Deburg, *New Day in Babylon*, 192–204.

95. For a more elaborate discussion on Marcuse's position and the phenomenon generally, see Elinor Langer's "Notes for Next Time," *Working Papers for a New Society* 1, no. 3 (fall 1973).

96. "On Cultural Nationalism," *The Black Panther*, April 20, 1969, 8.

97. Barbour, interview; Hilliard and Cole, *This Side of Glory*, 236.

98. A survey of contemporary film and photos, too numerous to name here, from black demonstrations reveals the influence of the Panther beret on the movement; *College Chips* (Decorah, Iowa), February 28, 1969, 2; Sandy Miller, interviews with author, September 12, 2000.

99. *Time*, October 25, 1968, 62; *Newsweek*, October 25, 1968, 63–65; *New York Times*, October 19, 1968, 1; see also *Fists of Freedom: The Story of the '68 Summer Games*, HBO, Inc. (Los Angeles, 1998).

100. U.S. Olympic organizers viewed Carlos and Smith's action as a violation of the policy to abstain from politics during the games and banned the two men from Olympic participation for life and sent them back home. Harry Edwards, leader of the Olympic Project for Human Rights, also changed his dress as the campaign gained momentum. He replaced his suits and ties with dark glasses and an ever-present black beret. Ultimately, he argued, his militant image kept him in the press: "The white media fed on that [militant image]." *Time*, October 25, 1968, 62; *New York Times*, October 17, 1968, 1; October 18, 1968, 1; and October 19, 1, 45; *Fists of Freedom*.

101. Regina Jennings, "Why I Joined the Party: An Africana Womanist Reflection," in Jones, *The Black Panther Party Reconsidered*, 260–61; Barbour, interview.

102. The Black Power movement gave rise to an explosion of artistic expression, known as the Black Arts movement. Often called a celebration of the "black

aesthetic," young playwrights and poets such as Larry Neal, Askia Toure, Amiri Baraka, Sonia Sanchez, and Nikki Giovanni emerged as representatives of a new, dynamic and highly politicized vanguard of black literati. The young militant artists even affected older poets like Gwendolyn Brooks. Typically, these artists embraced cultural nationalism and had more favorable relations with the Us organization than the Panthers, who often derided them as "pork chop nationalists." While there has been no substantive book-length study on the Black Arts movement, Komozi Woodard's *A Nation within a Nation: Amiri Baraka (LeRoi Jones) and Black Power Politics* (Chapel Hill, 1999) and Van Deburg's *New Day in Babylon* are very good studies on significant elements of the movement. There are several articles worth reading by artists and scholars on the subject. See Larry Neal, "The Social Background of the Black Arts Movement," *Black Scholar* 18, no. 1 (January–February 1987); Imamu Amiri Baraka, "Why I Changed My Ideology: Black Nationalism and Socialist Revolution," *Black World,* July 1975; Robert Blauner, "The Question of Black Culture," in *Black America,* ed. John F. Szwed (New York, 1970).

103. In fact, there were rumors in Chicago that initiates were required to kill a white person in order to join the party. Njeri, interview.

104. English, interview; Ward Churchill and Jim Vander Wall, *Agents of Repression: The FBI's Secret War against the Black Panther Party and the American Indian Movement* (Boston, 1990), 57–58.

105. Brown, *A Taste of Power,* 205.

106. Marlon Brando attended the funeral of Lil Bobby Hutton in 1968 and remained one of several celebrities, including actress Jean Seberg, who publicly demonstrated support for the party. Some supported secretly. English, interview.

107. Foner, *Black Panthers Speak* (New York, 1995), xxiv.

108. Jonina M. Abron. " 'Raising the Consciousness of the People': The Black Panther Intercommunal News Service, 1967–1980," in *Insider Histories of the Vietnam Era Underground Press: Voices of the Underground, Volume 1,* ed. Ken Wachsbergen (Tempe, Ariz., 1993), 352; Malu Halasa, *Elijah Muhammad* (New York, 1990), 81.

Chapter 5. "Move Over or We'll Move Over on You"

1. William Van Deburg, *New Day in Babylon: The Black Power Movement and American Culture, 1965–1975* (Chicago, 1992), 12–13.

2. Stokely Carmichael, "SNCC-1966," Social Protest, Northwestern University Special Collections, Evanston, Ill., 1.

3. I have chosen to use the term *rebellion* in place of *riot* in reference to the civil unrest that hit Los Angeles in August 1965 because of the politically charged nature of the disturbance. The incident was a direct reaction to oppressive conditions against which the poor rebelled. Riot suggests chaotic, unorganized, destructive and lawless behavior, as opposed to rebellion, which carries a more accurate connotation of resistance—violent or not. Studies have shown that wanton

destruction of property was not the aim of the Watts rebellion. White stores were targeted for destruction, while black stores, public schools, libraries, homes, and churches were spared. See Gerald Horne, *The Fire This Time: The Watts Uprising and the 1980s* (Charlottesville, Va., 1995).

4. For a discussion of how people gravitated to various black nationalist organizations, see Van Deburg, *New Day in Babylon*, 112–19.

5. Ernest Allen, Donald Warden, and Ayuko Babu, former Black Panther Party members, interviews with author.

6. Although some local Muslims and others claim that Ron Everett (Maulana Karenga) was a member of the NOI, Karenga insists that he attended the Temple, especially when Malcolm was speaking, but was not a registered member. Maulana Karenga, conversation with the author, March 21, 2003.

7. "Violence in the City—An End or a Beginning? A Report by the Governor's Commission on the Los Angeles Riots," Los Angeles, 1965, 75, 78.

8. "The Explosion in L.A.," *The National Guardian*, 25 August 1965.

9. "Law Enforcement and Criminal Law Aspects of the Los Angeles Riots," published by the California Assembly Interim Committee on Criminal Procedure, Los Angeles, November 18–19, 1966, 65–68.

10. "Violence in the City," 1–2.

11. Ibid., 3.

12. While the official policy of the NOI was a disavowal of firearm use and armed struggle in general, pockets of FOI were involved with firearm training. On several occasions, members of the Nation were arrested on charges of shooting black people. The most popular case, of course, is the assassination of Malcolm X. Other major cases include the killing of Hanafi Muslims in Washington, D.C., in 1973. For a more detailed discussion of the Us Organization and its founder, see Scott Brown, *Fighting for Us* (New York, 2003). C. R. D. Halisi, Ernest Allen, and Ron Wilkins, interviews.

13. Maulana Ron Karenga, *The Roots of the US-Panther Conflict: The Perverse and Deadly Games Police Play* (San Diego, 1976), 1–3; Maulana Ron Karenga, "Overturning Ourselves: From Mystification to Meaningful Struggle," *The Black Scholar* 3, no. 3 (October 1972): 6–7, Ron Crook Wilkins, Clyde Halisi, Daniel Johnson, interviews with author.

14. In Los Angeles, a Chicano gang system largely operated separately from black gangs. It was not significantly influenced by the Watts rebellion's overt black-centered discourse. Chicano youth would, however, be significantly influenced by the Black Power movement and, in turn, influence Chicano gangs. Varying levels of Chicano nationalism have been found in Chicano gang culture since the early 1970s, as discussed later in the book.

15. Yusuf Jah and Shah'Keyah Jah, *Uprising: Crips and Bloods Tell the Story of America's Youth in the Crossfire* (New York, 1995), 122–23.

16. Hakim Jamal, *From the Dead Level* (New York, 1972), 219; Frederick Knight, "Justifiable Homicide, Police Brutality, or Governmental Repression? The

1962 Los Angeles Police Shooting of Seven Members of the Nation of Islam,"
Journal of Negro History 79 (spring 1994): 187.

17. Ibid., 219.

18. Ibid., 221.

19. Ibid., 222–23; Knight, "Justifiable Homicide," 190; Wilkins, interview.

20. Karl Evanzz, *The Judas Factor: The Plot to Kill Malcolm X* (New York, 1992), 123.

21. Ron Wilkins, interview with author. In must be noted that despite the reluctance to physically attack whites, there are a handful of cases of physical confrontations between Muslims and police. On April 14, 1972, two NYPD officers were beaten and stomped by Fruit of Islam after barging into Harlem's Mosque no. 7. One officer was killed, most likely hit by another officer who was firing into the building. A mini-riot occurred, forcing police to retreat. See "5 Policemen Hurt in Harlem Melee," *New York Times,* April 15, 1972; "Incident in Mosque Leads Police to List Sensitive Locations," *New York Times,* Mary 14, 1972.

22. *Chicago Defender,* September 1, 1964, 2; September 2, 1964, 2; September 3, 1964, 4.

23. "AD NIP" folder, including posters, flyers; *African Descendents Manifesto,* 1967, pamphlet, iv, 1, 8, 18, 30, 34–37, Social Protest Collection, CU-309, the Bancroft Library, University of California, Berkeley (UCBSPC), 18:20.

24. The Black Congress was co-founded by Walter Bremond and Ernest Priestly in the fall of 1967. The Congress consisted of various black organizations that would lobby for viable programs for the black community and act as an organizing force to mobilize blacks and minimize factionalism among African Americans. Wilkins, Johnson, Halisi, interviews with author.

25. Elaine Brown, *A Taste of Power: A Black Woman's Story* (New York, 1992), 115–16; Wilkins, interview.

26. Huey Newton and Bobby Seale valorized lumpen behavior of Panthers in their writings. Both proudly recount their physical conquests over the "Paper Panthers" in San Francisco. For more discussion of Panther intimidation, see Brown, *A Taste of Power,* 124; also see *The Black Panthers Speak,* ed. Philip Foner (New York, 1995), xx–xxi, and Hugh Pearson, *The Shadow of the Panther: Huey Newton and the Price of Black Power in America* (New York, 1994), 230–34, 260–68, on reputations of Panthers acting as thugs.

27. Johnson, interview.

28. Halisi, interview.

29. Johnson, interview.

30. Lee Lew-Lee, former member of the Black Panther Party, interview with author.

31. Some members of the Nation of Islam claim that Elijah Muhammad directed ministers to model themselves after the very successful Malcolm X. Others insist that Malcolm X modeled himself after John Shabazz. Regardless of the origins of his style, many in the Los Angeles community viewed Minister

Shabazz as a "Malcolm clone"; Ramza Muhammad, Rudy Harlow, and Ron Wilkins, interviews with author, December 20, 1995; July 14 and July 21, 1996; June 30, 1996, and June 3, 1997.

32. Arthur Miller, interview with author, September 12, 2000; for further information on the experiences of African American students on white college campuses, see *Black Power and the Student Rebellion*, ed. James McEvoy and Abraham Miller (Belmont, Calif., 1969), and Harry Edwards, *Black Students* (New York, 1970).

33. "National Association of Black Students Formed," *New York Times*, August 29, 1969.

34. Floyd Hayes III, interview with author; Alphonso Pinkney, *Red, Black, and Green: Black Nationalism in the United States* (New York, 1976), 187; "The Plight of Black Studies," *Ebony*, December 1973.

35. "The Most Integrated School in America," *Express* (San Francisco), June 9, 1999, 9.

36. "The Negro," *Newsweek*, October 21, 1963.

37. Across the country, particularly the Northeast and major cities in the Midwest, white ethnic identity gave way to a primary racial "white" identity, as contests over housing and race ensued. The Chicago phenomenon was not unique, although it was particularly virulent. See Robert Slayton, *Back of the Yards: The Making of a Democracy* (Chicago, 1988); Ronald P. Formisano, *Boston against Busing: Race, Class, and Ethnicity in the 1960s and 1970s* (Chapel Hill, 1991); and Jonathan Rieder, *Canarsie: The Jews and Italians of Brooklyn against Liberalism* (Cambridge, 1985).

38. Diane Heller, Deborah Reynolds, and Karen Triche, interviews with author, August 29, 2001. Reynolds and Triche were members of the school's Black Student Union, Nommo. "Public School Survey Shows 52% of Students Are Negro," *Chicago Tribune*, October 25, 1967, 10; Chicago Board of Education, "Student Racial Survey," September 1968, Bureau of Research Development Special Projects, Chicago.

39. The chant had another variation: "A fight! A fight! A black and a white! The white can't fight, but the brother's alright!" The author attended a Los Angeles racially mixed magnet school in the late 1970s and remembers these very well. Amy Albert attended racially mixed schools in Oakland, California, in the late 1970s and recalls identical chants. The chants, I assume, had survived from a few years earlier. Amy Albert, interview with author, March 13, 2002. For additional discussions of black students in majority white schools, see Rovell P. Solomon, *Black Resistance in High School: Forging a Separatist Culture* (Binghamton, N.Y., 1992).

40. Miller, interview.

41. David Dawley, *A Nation of Lords: The Autobiography of the Vice Lords* (New York, 1973), 113–15; Reynolds, Triche, and Heller, interviews.

42. Dawley, *Nation of Lords*, 113.

43. The term *chucks* is used in reference to whites in a letter addressed to a black student organization from a black student in 1970. Barney C. Young, "Letter Addressed to Black United Front Representatives Council, MSU," in "Black United Front Newsletter," June 4, 1970, 7, Black United Front Newsletter folder, Archives and Special Collections, Thomas J. Dodd Research Center, University of Connecticut Libraries. There are many personal stories of friends and family who were engaged in this informal renegotiation process. It is a fascinating phenomenon that deserves additional scholarly attention. Several books give peripheral comment, including Wallace Terry, *Bloods: An Oral History of the Vietnam War by Black Veterans* (New York, 1984); Clayborne Carson, *In Struggle: The Student Nonviolent Coordinating Committee* (New York, 1981), on students and SNCC; and Alphonso Pinkney, *Red, Black, and Green: Black Nationalism in the United States* (New York, 1976), for general references.

44. Untitled Flyers, UCBSPC 18:1; *New York Times,* February 9, 1968. There were scores of uprisings of black students on college campuses—white and black schools—between 1968 and 1975. Recent scholarship on the subject is rare. See *Black Studies: Myths and Realities,* ed. Martin Kilson et al. (New York, 1969), and *Black Studies in the University,* ed. Armstead Robinson et al. (New York, 1969). William Van Deburg offers a good cursory look at the subject in *New Day in Babylon.*

45. *Newsreel* (San Francisco), flyer, UCBSPC18:4; "To All Black People" and "Black Student Union," UCBSPC 18:9.

46. James Turner, "The Sociology of Black Nationalism," *The Black Scholar* 2, no. 4 (December 1969): 19; Angela Y. Davis, *Angela Davis: An Autobiography* (New York, 1974), 191–94

47. "The Plight of Black Studies," *Ebony,* December 1973.

48. Reprinted from the *Peninsula Observer,* distributed by the Free University (Menlo Park, Calif.), 7, UCBSPC 18:1.

49. Available at: www.abpsi.org/history.html (accessed August 27, 2001).

50. Available at: http://ssw.unc.edu/professional/NABSW.html (accessed August 27, 2001).

51. C. V. Roman, M.D., founding member of the National Medical Association and author of the historic 1908 manifesto, www.nmanet.org/nonflash.htm (accessed August 17, 2001).

52. The Black United Front (BUF) of Michigan State University valued its place at the mostly white university but also emphasized the utility and importance of black control of black organizations and programs. For the student members of BUF, this control was a prerequisite for black power. Therefore, an Office of Black Affairs was important for them. Moreover, the director should not be appointed by white administrators, which would undermine black autonomy. Only black students had the right to appoint a director, they argued. Reflecting the popular sentiment of the era one student asked, "How the hell can the white man *give* Black people Black Power?" (emphasis in original). The larger concern for African American professional organizations similarly reflected this notion.

"Black United Front Newsletter," June 4, 1970, 4, Black United Front Newsletter folder, Archives and Special Collections, Thomas J. Dodd Research Center, University of Connecticut Libraries.

53. Muhammad, *Message,* 31–32; Claude A. Clegg III, *An Original Man: The Life and Times of Elijah Muhammad* (New York, 1997), 47.

54. Clegg, *An Original Man,* 240; Elijah Muhammad, *Message to the Blackman in America* (Newport News, Va., 1965), 57.

55. The differentiation between classical and modern forms of black nationalism derives from the work of Wilson J. Moses, as mentioned in the introduction. Other scholars, however, have also pointed out the civilizing mission as a trope of nineteenth-century black nationalists. For a thorough examination of this theme, see Yekutiel Gershoni, *Africans on African-Americans: The Creation and Uses of an African-American Myth* (New York, 1997), and Tunde Adeleke, *Unafrican Americans: Nineteenth-Century Black Nationalists and the Civilizing Mission* (Louisville, Ky., 1998).

56. Since 1938 the NOI had had no major theological shift and only minor ideological adaptation to resistance to white supremacy. Claude Clegg argues that the NOI was more radical before Elijah Muhammad's imprisonment for sedition during World War II. This radicalism was circumscribed by his confrontation with the state and the success of his conservative political and economic programs, according to Clegg. Though Muhammad did not advocate any confrontations with the state, the cosmology and its classical black nationalist agenda remained largely unchanged. For a more detailed discussion of the ideological stasis of the Nation of Islam, see Clegg, *An Original Man,* esp. 238–39.

57. Martin Luther King Jr., *Where Do We Go from Here: Chaos or Community?* (New York, 1967), 3–4.

58. "The Cities," *Time,* August 11, 1967, 11.

59. "Gamble in the Ghetto," *Newsweek,* January 31, 1966, 24–25; King, *Where Do We Go,* 45–46.

60. Quoted in David Garrow, *Bearing the Cross: Martin Luther King Jr. and the Southern Christian Leadership Conference* (New York, 1986), 443.

61. Ibid, 443–44.

62. Nicholas Lehman, *The Promised Land: America's Great Migration* (New York, 1989), 64.

63. Clegg, *An Original Man,* 237–38.

64. Willie Mukasa Ricks, interview with author, February 22, 1997.

65. Quoted in Garrow, *Bearing the Cross,* 488.

66. Ibid., 489–500; "The Touchiest Target," *Newsweek,* August 15, 1966, 29.

67. *The Promised Land,* episode 3, Discovery Channel, 1995; "The Touchiest Target," *Newsweek,* August 15, 1966, 29.

68. Quoted in James H. Cone, *Martin and Malcolm and America: A Dream or a Nightmare* (New York, 1991), 226.

69. Ibid., 230, 229.

70. Martin Luther King Jr., "The Role of the Behavioral Scientist in the Civil Rights Movement," address to the meeting of the Society for the Psychological Study of Social Issues, American Psychological Association, Washington, D.C., September 1967, UCBSPC 18:15, pp. 1–7.

71. Nancy Weiss, *Whitney Young Jr. and the Struggle for Civil Rights* (Princeton, N.J., 1989), 223.

72. Roy Wilkins and Tom Matthews, *Standing Fast: An Autobiography of Roy Wilkins* (New York, 1977), 329–32.

73. "Uncle Roy Stoops Again," *The Black Panther,* January 25, 1969, 5.

74. "A Frank Interview with Roy Wilkins," *Ebony,* April 1974, 35; "Races," *Time,* August 11, 1967, 13; Van Deburg, *New Day in Babylon,* 45, 12.

75. "Races," 21; Weiss, *Whitney Young,* 184.

76. Van Deburg, *New Day in Babylon,* 119.

77. "Black Parleys in Capital Hail Nixon and Thurmond," *New York Times,* December 6, 1972.

78. "Races," 13.

79. Weiss, *Whitney Young,* 184.

80. Mark Chapman, *Christianity on Trial: African American Religious Thought before and after Black Power* (New York, 1996), 76; *Time,* November 17, 1967, 87.

81. Black Methodists for Church Renewal, "Black Power Paper, 1968," quoted in *Black Theology: A Documentary History,* vol. 1: *1966–1979,* 2d rev. ed., ed. James Cone and Gayraud S. Wilmore (New York, 1993), 224; Vincent Harding, "The Religion of Black Power," quoted in ibid., 49.

82. Joseph R. Washington Jr., "Are American Negro Churches Christian?" in Cone and Wilmore, *Black Theology,* 1:104–5.

83. Joseph A. Johnson Jr., "Jesus the Liberator," in ibid., 1:204–5; quoted in Chapman, *Christianity on Trail,* 42, 70.

84. "Black Power Moves on Churches," *U.S. News and World Report,* August 26, 1968, 46.

85. Lee Lew-Lee, *All Power to the People! The Black Panther Party and Beyond,* video documentary, Electronic News Agency (Los Angeles, 1996); "This Will Tide Us Over to Liberation," *The Black Panther Intercommunal News Service,* April 8, 1972.

86. Quoted in Huey P. Newton, *To Die for the People* (New York, 1972), 72

87. Ibid., 64–65, 74.

88. Doug McAdam, *Political Process and the Development of Black Insurgency, 1950–1970* (Chicago, 1982), 151–53

89. Many states maintained unenforceable laws that sanctioned oppression and / or racial segregation. Several southern states, for example, kept antimiscegenation laws on the books, despite the *Loving v. Virginia Supreme Court* ruling of 1967 that outlawed antimiscegenation laws. Mississippi even maintained laws that regulated the trade in enslaved people until 1995, despite the Thirteenth Amendment, which outlawed slavery.

90. Clegg, *An Original Man,* 252.

Chapter 6. Rainbow Radicalism

1. Rodolfo Acuna, *Occupied American: A History of Chicanos,* 3d ed. (New York, 1988), 180, 254–55.

2. "Border Crossings," *L.A. Weekly,* June 24–30, 1988, 22; "The Los Angeles Chicano Area—Cultural Enclave," *San Francisco Chronicle,* October 10, 1970, 12.

3. "Hail 'La Raza' and Scorn the Establishment," from www.brownberet.org/bbraza.html (accessed July 16, 1999).

4. "Border Crossings," 22; "Cultural Enclave," 12; Marguerte Viramontes Marin, "Protest in an Urban Barrio: A Study of the Chicano Movement" (Ph.D. diss., University of California, Santa Barbara, 1980), 123–24.

5. Ibid., 124–25.

6. Bobby Seale, *Seize the Time: The Story of the Black Panther Party and Huey P. Newton* (Baltimore, 1991), 115.

7. "Hail 'La Raza.' "

8. Some have argued that the word Chicano evolved from sixteenth-century Castilian pronunciation of Mexico, where the "x" had a "sh" sound: Meh-shee-ko. For the people, Meh-shee-kanos, "Chicanos" emerged among isolated rural peasants whose pronunciation was unmodified into the nineteenth century. Conservative and moderate Mexican-Americans, hostile to the new word for identity, however, insisted that the word is a Castilian word, meaning "one who practices fraud." Still, others said that it was a blend of two words, reflecting the demographic makeup of the new militants: Mexicano and Chico, literally meaning "Young Mexican." Yet others argued that it had historically been a pejorative term for poor Mexicans. See Tony Castro, *Chicano Power: The Emergence of Mexican America* (New York, 1974), 131; "Cultural Enclave," 12; Acuna, *Occupied American,* 338.

9. Elio Carranza, *Pensamientos on Los Chicanos: A Cultural Revolution* (Berkeley, 1969), 4–5; Castro, *Chicano Power,* 13.

10. Boyd C. Schafer, *Nationalism and Internationalism: Belonging in Human Experience* (Malabar, Fla., 1982), 41–47.

11. Marin, "Protest in an Urban Barrio," 128.

12. *La Causa,* December 1970.

13. Marin, "Protest in an Urban Barrio," 131.

14. Ibid., 135.

15. Ibid., 55.

16. Ibid., 143; Castro, *Chicano Power,* 12–14.

17. Acuna, *Occupied American,* 337–38.

18. Castro, *Chicano Power,* 13–17; "In Memory of 1970 Protest," *Los Angeles Times,* August 31, 1980.

19. "Police Spying on L.A. Activist Groups," *Los Angeles Times,* July 19, 1978, B2. There is a growing body of literature on the illegal activities of the FBI and its program, COITELPRO. See especially Ward Churchill and Jim Vander Wall, *Agents*

of Repression: The FBI's Secret Wars against the Black Panther Party and the American Indian Movement (Boston, 1988), and Brian Glick, *War at Home: Covert Action against U.S. Activists and What We Can Do about It* (Boston, 1989).

20. Castro, *Chicano Power,* 133.

21. Acuna, *Occupied American,* 348.

22. *The Asian Student* (Berkeley) 3, no. 1 (November 1974): 3; 2, no. 1 (March 1974): 3, 9–10.

23. *The Asian Student* 2, no. 1 (March 1974): 9–10.

24. Ibid.

25. *La Causa* 1, no. 1 (November 1, 1993): [4]. Note that this is a different newspaper created under the same name as the original Brown Beret organ of 1969–73.

26. *Chicanismo* 1, no. 6 (1970): [1].

27. Ibid., 2.

28. *The Asian Student* 1, no. 1 (November 1973): 13.

29. Ronald Takaki, *Strangers from a Different Shore: A History of Asian Americans* (New York, 1989), 13–15.

30. Some have argued that Richard Aoki is a co-founder of the Black Panther Party with Newton and Seale. Such a position conflicts, however, with official party history. Bobby Seale states that Aoki was a "consultant" and comrade to him and Newton but not a founder. Bobby Seale, conversation with author, April 18, 2002; "Yellow Power," *Giant Robot* no. 10 (spring 1998): 71; Seale, *Seize the Time,* 72–73, 79.

31. "Yellow Power," 71.

32. *Hokubei Manichi,* December 9, 1968, [2].

33. Asian American Political Alliance, flyer, ca. 1969, Social Protest Collection, CU-309, the Bancroft Library, University of California, Berkeley (UCB-SPC), 18:25.

34. Asian Student Union, flyer, n.d., UCBSPC 18:27.

35. Ibid.

36. "Yellow Power," 79–80.

37. Ibid.

38. Ibid.

39. Ibid.

40. Ibid., 76.

41. Ibid., 79–80; Robin Kelley and Betsy Esch, "Black Like Mao: Red China and Black Revolution," *Souls* 1, no. 4 (fall 1999): 26.

42. "Yellow Power," 76.

43. Ibid., 74.

44. Ibid., 75.

45. Alvin M. Josephy Jr., *Red Power: The American Indians' Fight for Freedom* (New York, 1971), 3.

46. Churchill and Vander Wall, *Agents of Repression,* 118.

47. Ibid., 119.

48. Russell Means with Marvin J. Wolf, *Where White Men Fear to Tread: The Autobiography of Russell Means* (New York, 1995), 228–30.

49. Churchill and Wall, *Agents of Repression,* 119.

50. Native American Solidarity Committee, flyer, UCBSPC 18:37c.

51. Native American Solidarity Committee, flyer, UCBSPC 18:37b.

52. *Minneapolis Star,* June 28, 1975, 5; Native American Solidarity Committee, flyer, UCBSPC 18:37c.

53. Young Lord Organization, flyer, n.d., UCBSPC 18:33.

54. Huey P. Newton, *Essays from the Minister of Defense,* pamphlet, 1967, Black Panther Party, political pamphlets, P201234, Northwestern University Special Collections, Evanston, Ill., 11.

55. "From Rumble to Revolution: The Young Lords," *Ramparts,* October 1970; Young Lord Organization, flyer, n.d., UCBSPC 18:33; see also David Hilliard and Lewis Cole, *This Side of Glory: The Autobiography of David Hilliard and the Story of the Black Panther Party* (Boston, 1993), 229.

56. Ibid.

57. Ibid.

58. There was a strained relationship between the Chicago Panthers and the primarily white Weather Underground, an offshoot of the Students for Democratic Society. In 1968 Minister of Information Eldridge Cleaver directed Fred Hampton to apologize to the SDS and other local white radicals for comments considered offensive to Panther allies. Hampton refused. The friction developed after Hampton rejected a request that the local Panthers support tactics to protest the 1968 Democratic National Convention in Chicago. One of the tactics rejected was to throw urine-filled balloons on police. The Panthers were also unwilling to dissuade youths from breaking into an SDS office in a poor black Southside neighborhood. The SDS, Chicago Panthers argued, should have an office in a white community. In the white community they could work to eradicate racism from among their white brothers and sisters. Some Weather Underground members, including Bernardine Dohrn, were physically intimidated and berated as "bourgeois mother country radicals," while the largely working-class Young Patriots were "respected" by Panthers. Interview with Akua Injeri, July 1996. See also Elaine Brown, *A Taste of Power,* 198.

59. Some of the white radical organizations that modeled themselves after the Panthers are the White Panther Party of Michigan, the John Brown Party of California, and Rising Up Angry in Chicago. Steve Tappis, a founder of Rising Up Angry, explains that "It seemed like the only ones around that did what we wanted to do, and did it well, were the Panthers." Rising Up Angry used the Panther paper as a model for its own, as had the John Brown Party, which also adopted a 10–point program modeled after the Panthers' program. Dozens of white organizations created alliances with the Panthers. Many adopted the rhetoric of the Panthers, as had the young radical left in general. Slogans and terms such as "All power to the people" and "pigs" came into common use in

radical circles. Hilliard and Cole, *This Side of Glory*, 230–33; misc. flyers, UCBSPC 18:1.

60. "Palante Siempre Palante! A Look Back at the Young Lords," at http://netdial.caribe.net/~dfreedma/beginnin.htm (accessed July 30, 1999).

61. Felipe Luciano, speech, St. Lawrence University, April 1997.

62. "Palante Siempre Palante!"

63. Komozi Woodard, *A Nation within a Nation: Amiri Baraka (LeRoi Jones) and Black Power Politics* (Chapel Hill, 1999), 138–40.

64. See David R. Roediger, *Wages of Whiteness: Race and the Making of the American Working Class* (New York, 1991).

65. *La Causa* 1, no. 1 (May 23, 1969): 2.

66. Adelante Tigeres Angelines, flyer, March 1968, UCBSPC 18:30.

67. *La Causa* 1, no. 2 (July 10, 1969): 3.

68. Marin, "Protest in an Urban Barrio," 144.

69. Ibid., 144–45.

70. *Palante Siempre Palante: The Young Lords,* documentary written, produced, and directed by Iris Morales, Latino Education Network (New York, 1996); *Young Lords Party, Palante, Young Lords Party* (New York, 1971), 117.

71. *The Asian Student* 1, no. 1 (November 1973): 13.

72. Los Siete, flyer, ca. 1970, UCBSPCC 18:32.

73. Richard Newman, interview with author, August 4, 1999.

74. Seale, *Seize the Time,* 210–11.

Conclusion

1. Harvard Sitkoff, *The Struggle for Black Equality* (New York, 1993), 124.

2. *Malcolm X: The Man and His Times,* ed. John Henrik Clarke (New York, 1969), 10; Maulana Karenga, *Introduction to Black Studies* (Los Angeles, 1992), 175.

3. "The Panthers," *ABC News,* April 13, 1970.

Epilogue

1. Bobby Seale, statement made in *All Power to the People! The Black Panther Party and Beyond,* documentary by Lee Lew-Lee, Electronic News Agency (Los Angeles, 1996); Seale, interview with author, October 1998.

2. "Bobby Seale's Evangelical Fire Turns to Warmth of Barbecue," *The Sunday Oregonian,* July 11, 1982.

3. Committee for Justice, "The State vs. Huey P. Newton" (Oakland, 1979), Black Panther Party, political pamphlets, P201234, Northwestern University Special Collections, Evanston, Ill.

4. Jonina Abron, "Final Report," Jonina Abron box 7/19/90, Black Panther Party collections, Moorland-Spingarn Research Center, Howard University, Washington, D.C.

5. "Armed and Intellectually Dangerous," *Village Voice,* 5 September 1989, 24; Hugh Pearson, *The Shadow of the Panther: Huey Newton and the Price of Black Power in America* (New York, 1994), 315.

6. Claude A. Clegg III, *An Original Man: The Life and Times of Elijah Muhammad* (New York, 1997), 205.

7. Karl Evanzz, *The Messenger: The Rise and Fall of Elijah Muhammad* (New York, 2001), 419–20.

8. Ibid., 279–80.

9. Clifton E. Marsh, *From Black Muslims to Muslims* (Metuchen, N.J., 1995), 106–9.

10. "Muslims Keep Lid on Drugs in Capital," *Washington Post,* April 26, 1988; "Gang Youth Get Farrakhan Peace Message," *Los Angeles Times,* October 9, 1989.

11. "The Right Man for the Job," *U.S. News and World Report,* October 15, 1995.

12. "New Black Panthers Emerge in Texas," *Chicago Tribune,* September 15, 1996.

Essay on Sources

Histories of Black Power

For a movement of its magnitude and significance, the literature on the Black Power era is conspicuously thin. The earliest writings on the movement came from participant-observers. The first book to engage the new slogan was *Black Power: The Politics of Liberation in America* (1967), written by Stokely Carmichael and Charles Hamilton. The book cogently describes the fundamental ideals and aspirations of Black Power. It does not, however, substantively engage the cultural facets of Black Power, as later books would. A series of anthologies on black protest was published between 1968 and 1976; many of them provided voice to the leading advocates of black radicalism. *The Rhetoric of Black Power* (1969), edited by Robert Scott, features writings from several who were engaged in the Black Power debates, from Martin Luther King Jr. to Stokely Carmichael.

A few books place the Black Power movement in a historical context of black resistance, viewing it as an intensification of the black freedom movement that is as old as the laws and practices that circumscribed black freedom in America. The following books give the reader a broad look at black resistance to racial subjugation from as early as the colonial era through to the urban unrest of the 1960s: *The Black Power Revolt* (1968), edited by Floyd B. Barbour; *Chronicles of Black Protest* (1968), edited by Bradford Chambers; Robert Goldston, *The Negro Revolution* (1968); and *Black Brotherhood* (1971), edited by Okon Edet Uya. Another collection that provides the voice of the movement leaders and participants is *The Black Revolution* (1970), published by *Ebony* magazine. Though much of the earliest work on Black Power came from participants, scholars and others also examined the movement and ideas surrounding the nebulous slogan. In one instance, the worlds of the academy and activist politics joined forces. Academic proponents of black studies programs began publishing the *Black Scholar* in 1969. In virtually every issue of the journal between 1969 and 1976, there were articles (too many to list here) written by or pertaining to major figures of the Black Power era.

Robert H. Brisbane, *Black Activism: Racial Revolution in the United States, 1954–1970* (1974); Nathan Wright Jr., *Black Power and Urban Unrest;* and Edward

Peeks, *The Long Struggle for Black Power* (1971), as well as Benjamin Muse, *The American Negro Revolution: From Nonviolence to Black Power, 1963–1967* (1968); Theodore Draper, *The Rediscovery of Black Nationalism* (1970); and Alphonso Pinkey, *Red, Black and Green* (1976), are good overviews of the era, though they all lack the privilege of chronological distance. Of these books, Draper offers the most cynical examination of black nationalism, which, he argues, is a problematic reaction to racism, offering no substantive overhaul of the system, instead promoting "fantasy nationalism."

Some very good studies have been produced since 1990. No book offers a more comprehensive examination of the cultural contours of the era than William Van Deburg, *New Day in Babylon* (1992). Komozi Woodard's impressive biography of Amiri Baraka, *A Nation within a Nation* (1999), also provides a good overview of the role of culture in the Black Power movement. Though not entirely focused on Black Power, Dean E. Robinson's *Black Nationalism in American Politics and Thought* (2001) builds on the work of Wilson J. Moses and his categorization of black nationalism into "classical" and "modern" types. Other books that include substantive discussion of the Black Power era but are much broader in scope are Rod Bush, *We Are Not What We Seem* (1999); John T. McCartney, *Black Power Ideologies* (1992); and Kinfe Abraham, *Politics of Black Nationalism* (1991). Recent edited volumes include *Is It Nation Time?* (2002), edited by Eddie S. Glaude Jr., which provides scholarly essays on black nationalism and Black Power. *Modern Black Nationalism* (1997), edited by William Van Deburg, includes a number of primary documents and essays from the Black Power era.

The Nation of Islam

The publications on the Nation of Islam (NOI) are numerous. Scholarship on the organization extends as far back as 1938, when Erdmann D. Beynon published in the *American Journal Sociology* the first scholarly article on the NOI. Scholarly examinations of the Nation of Islam tend to be highly polemical. Two of the most balanced examinations are the terribly overlooked Mattias Gardell, *In the Name of Elijah Muhammad: Louis Farrakhan and the Nation of Islam* (1996), and the very impressive biography of Elijah Muhammad by Claude A. Clegg III, *An Original Man* (1997), which provides substantive information on the development of the organization Muhammad led for forty years. The most celebrated monograph about the Nation, C. Eric Lincoln, *Black Muslims in America* (1961), introduced the specifics of the organization to a much wider audience, evoking criticism from the ranks of the NOI. E. U. Essien-Udom, *Black Nationalism: A Search for an Identity in America* (1962), did not receive the attention that it deserved, perhaps due to an issue of timing. Essien-Udom, in fact, offers a more comprehensive and balanced study of the Nation than Lincoln does. Other books on the Nation include Martha E. Lee, *The Nation of Islam* (1988); Louis E. Lomax, *When the Word Is Given* (1962); and Clifton E. Marsh, *From Black Muslims to Muslims* (1996).

Elijah Muhammad and other members have written a number of books on the core beliefs and values of the Nation: *Theology of Time* (1992), *The Fall of America* (1973), *Message to the Blackman in America* (1965), *Our Savior Has Arrived* (1974), and *The Supreme Wisdom* (1957) are all written by Elijah Muhammad. A number of books transcribe speeches by Malcolm X, the former national spokesman for the NOI, from his time in the Nation and after his departure: *Malcolm X Speaks* (1965), *The End of White World Supremacy* (1971), *Malcolm X: By Any Means Necessary* (1989), *Malcolm X: February 1965, the Last Speeches* (1992), *Malcolm X on Afro-American History* (1970), and *Malcolm X Talks to Young People* (1991). Louis Farrakhan, current leader of the Nation, has published *A Torchlight for America* (1993), which promotes the NOI as a viable alternative to the confusion and "moral crisis" in America. Other books include Prince-A-Cuba, *Before Adam, the Original Man* (1992) and *The Teachings of Both* (1994) edited by Atiyah Majied. These works generally provide a mix of vituperative and more moderate language of the NOI, where the organization is, of course, lauded as a model of black uplift and enterprise.

The Black Panther Party

It is unusual that, for an organization of its historical significance and popular familiarity, there is no monograph on the history and development of the Black Panther Party. The two best sources are edited volumes: *The Black Panther Party Reconsidered* (1998), edited by Charles E. Jones, and *Liberation, Imagination and the Black Panther Party* (2001), edited by Kathleen Cleaver and George Katsiaficas. Both volumes provide very lucid, scholarly essays on various facets of the party, from lumpenism to gender politics. A number of dissertations focus on various facets of the party, as do several books: Jennifer Smith, *An International History of the Black Panther Party* (1999), concentrates on the international politics of the Party; Gilbert Moore, *A Special Rage* (1971), looks at the trial of Huey Newton; and Gail Sheehy, *Panthermania* (1971) examines the struggles of the New Haven chapter. Michael Newton, *Bitter Grain* (1991), and Gene Marine, *The Black Panthers* (1969), both provided generally good pedestrian narratives of the Panthers. For party politics, see Huey P. Newton, *To Die for the People*, (1995), and Eldridge Cleaver, *Eldridge Cleaver: Post-Prison Writings and Speeches* (1969), edited by Robert Scheer. See also *The Black Panthers Speak*, (1995), edited by Philip S. Foner.

Participant Narratives

There are numerous books from Nation of Islam and Black Power movement participants, which include a degree of intimate knowledge but lack critical distance. The most popular is the *Autobiography of Malcolm X* (1965), written with Alex Haley. The classic African American narrative is a powerful look at the life of Malcolm and the black freedom movement. Bobby Seale's *Seize the Time* (1970) is typical in its insider's praise of the organization's worth; although Seale does confront issues such as rogue behavior or jackanapes. His autobiography, *A Lonely Rage* (1978), provides a greater degree of criticism and analysis of the party, as well as his own political evolution. Huey Newton's *Revolutionary Suicide* (1973) provides a limited look into the author's life and development. George Jackson, inmate and prominent Panther, received notoriety as a revolutionary behind bars. His *Blood in My Eye* (1972) and *Soledad Brother* (1970) discuss the urgent need for critical resistance and revolutionary change in America. Eldridge Cleaver's classic *Soul on Ice* (1968) is one of the most controversial books from the period. Though mistaken as party politics at times, it was written before he joined the party, as a collection of his prison essays and intellectual explorations.

Several biographies represent a microcosm of the black freedom movement in that they provide a first person narrative of political awakening and the attraction to radical politics. Typically, these are stories of young people who are confronted with racism and oppression and make a conscious break with older generations to challenge white supremacy more forcefully, meeting intense resistance, particularly from the state. Similar themes occur in the following autobiographies: Angela Y. Davis, *An Autobiography* (1988); Elaine Brown, *Taste of Power* (1992); William Lee Brent, *Long Time Gone* (1996); Assata Shakur, *Assata, an Autobiography* (1987); David Hilliard, *This Side of Glory* (1992); Ann Moody, *Coming of Age in Mississippi* (1968); Johnny Spain, *Black Power, White Blood* (1996); and Cleveland Sellers, *River of No Return* (1973). See also James Farmer, *Lay Bare the Heart* (1985). Martin Luther King Jr.'s books, *Stride toward Freedom* (1958), *Strength to Love* (1963), *Why We Can't Wait* (1964), *Where Do We Go from Here?* (1968), all provide insight into important elements of overarching ideas and philosophies, as well as tactics in the movement. Several autobiographies are important additions to the body of work on the black freedom movement, including Charles Evers, *Have No Fear: The Charles Evers Story* (1997); James Farmer, *Freedom—When?* (1965); James Peck, *Freedom Ride* (1962); Roy Wilkins, with Tom Matthews, *Standing Fast* (1982); and James Meredith, *Three Years in Mississippi* (1966). In his autobiography, *Spitting in the Wind* (1990), Earl Anthony admits to being an informant to authorities while in the Black Panther Party. James Foreman, *The Making of Black Revolutionaries* (1985), is a great insight into SNCC and Black Power. The following books give personal insight into the tumultuous Freedom Summer of 1964: Sally Belfrage, *Freedom Summer* (1965); Len Holt, *The Summer That Didn't End* (1968); and Tracy Sugarman, *Stranger at the Gates* (1966). Also see Nicholas Von Hoffman, *Mississippi Notebook* (1964), and *Letters from Mississippi* (1965), edited by Elizabeth Sutherland.

Biographies

There have been several very informative biographies and autobiographies about and by personalities from the Nation of Islam and the Black Power movement. (Also see "participant narratives" above.) For black nationalism, no figure is as studied as

Malcolm X. Some biographies and edited volumes include Bruce Perry's *Malcolm: The Life of a Man Who Changed Black America* (1991), one of the most ambitious undertakings in biographical research on the subject; *Ghosts in Our Blood: With Malcolm X in Africa, England, and the Caribbean* (1994), edited by Jan Carew; *Malcolm X: The Man and His Times* (1969), edited by John H. Clarke; and Michael Eric Dyson, *Making Malcolm: The Myth and Meaning of Malcolm X* (1995). See also George Breitman, *The Last Year of Malcolm X* (1967); William Strickland, *Malcolm X: Make It Plain* (1994); and Joe Wood, *Malcolm X: In Our Own Image.* The following are personal testimonies to Malcolm's life: *Malcolm X: As They Knew Him* (1992), edited by David Gallen; *Malcolm X: The Man and His Times* (1969), edited by John H. Clarke; and Benjamin Karim, *Remembering Malcolm* (1992). James Cone does a great job in contrasting the lives of Malcolm X and Martin Luther King Jr. in *Martin and Malcolm and America: A Dream or a Nightmare* (1991), which demonstrates the profound similarities the men shared, as well as their strengths, foibles and ideological shifts.

Martin Luther King Jr., though not a nationalist, is an important figure to the modern black freedom movement and is the most examined civil rights figure. The most celebrated and thorough works are Taylor Branch's two-volume *Parting the Waters* (1988) and *Pillar of Fire* (1998), and David J. Garrow's *Bearing the Cross: Martin Luther King Jr. and the Southern Christian Leadership Conference* (1986). Clayborne Carson's *The Autobiography of Martin Luther King Jr.* (2001) utilizes King's own writing in this work published over thirty years after his death. See also David Lewis, *King: A Biography* (1978); Lawrence D. Reddick Jr., *Crusader without Violence* (1959); William Robert Miller, *Martin Luther King Jr.* (1968); Lerone Bennett Jr., *What Manner of Man* (1968); and John J. Ansbro, *Martin Luther King Jr.: The Making of a Mind* (1982). See also August Meier's "On the Role of Martin Luther King," *New Politics* 4 (winter 1965). Ralph D. Abernathy's *And the Walls Came Tumbling Down: An Autobiography* (1989), evoked uproar when Abernathy chose to discuss some of the more intimate details of movement leaders' lives. Timothy Tyson's *Radio Free Dixie: Robert F. Williams and the Roots of Black Power* (1999) is a very good examination of an icon of black radicals whose political beginnings were with the NAACP. An earlier biography on Williams is Robert Carl Cohen's *Black Crusader: A Biography of Robert Franklin Williams* (1972).

The rise of Louis Farrakhan as a major figure in national discussions of race in the 1980s and 1990s generated a flurry of activity from white and black writers who generally dismissed the NOI leader as a xenophobic charlatan. Karl Evanzz, *The Judas Factor: The Plot to Kill Malcolm X* (1992), argues that the NOI leadership, including Farrakhan and Elijah Muhammad, were behind the assassination of Malcolm X, as well as other criminal behavior. The following books are highly critical of the chief organizer of the Million Man March and the organization he leads: Florence H. Levinsohn, *Looking for Farrakhan* (1997); *The Farrakhan Factor* (1999), edited by Amy Alexander; Elreta Dodds, *The Trouble with Farrakhan and the Nation of Islam* (1997); Robert Singh, *The Farrakhan Phenomenon* (1997); and Arthur Magida, *Prophet of Rage* (1996).

Despite his historical importance, there are only a handful of biographies on Elijah Muhammad, including the aforementioned *An Original Man* (1997), by Claude A. Cleage III, and Karl Evanzz, *The Messenger: The Rise and Fall of Elijah Muhammad* (1999). See also the hagiographic *Elijah Muhammad* (1990), by Malu Halasa.

Hugh Pearson's *The Shadow of the Panther* (1994) is the only real biography of Huey P. Newton. Pearson provides considerable detail of Newton's activism and demons, erroneously extending Newton's pathology to the party as a whole. Though not a biography, Judson L. Jeffries, *Huey P. Newton: The Radical Theorist* (2002), is a useful study of Newton in the context of his politics.

Organizations

Good examinations of the major organizations include Clayborne Carson's formidable study, *In Struggle: SNCC and the Black Awakening of the 1960s* (1981), as well as August Meier and Elliot Rudwick, *CORE: A Study in the Civil Rights Movement, 1942–1968* (1973); Cleveland Sellers and Robert Terrell, *The River of No Return: The Autobiography of a Black Militant and the Life and Death of SNCC* (1973); Howard Zinn, *SNCC: The New Abolitionists* (1965); and Inge Powell Bell, *CORE and the Strategy of Nonviolence* (1968). Scot Brown, *Fighting for US* (2003) is an important study of the leading exponent of cultural nationalism from the period.

Histories of the Civil Rights Movement

The most significant overviews of the movement are Manning Marable, *Race, Reform, and Rebellion: The Second Reconstruction in Black America, 1945–1990* (1991); Kevin Gaines, *Uplifting the Race: Black Leadership, Politics, and Culture in the Twentieth Century* (1996); Rhoda Lois Blumberg, *Civil Rights: The 1960s Freedom Struggle* (1984); Adam Faircloth, *Better Day Coming: Blacks and Equality, 1890–2000* (2001); Richard King, *Civil Rights and the Idea of Freedom* (1992); Doug McAdam, *Political Process and the Development of Black Insurgency, 1930–1970* (1999); Harvard Sitkoff, *The Struggle for Black Equality, 1954–1992* (1993); Robert Weisbrot, *Freedom Bound: A History of America's Civil Rights Movement* (1990); *The American Negro Revolution: From Nonviolence to Black Power, 1963–1967* (1968); Jack Bloom, *Class, Race, and the Civil Rights Movement* (1987); Alton Morris, *The Origins of the Civil Rights Movement* (1984); Steven F. Lawson, *Running for Freedom: Civil Rights Movement, 1940–1970* (1974); Herbert H. Haines, *Black Radicals and the Civil Rights Movement, 1954–1970* (1988); Pat Watters, *Down to Now: Reflections on the Southern Civil Rights Movement* (1993); Hugh Davis Graham, *The Civil Rights Era* (1990); and Benjamin Muse, *The American Negro Revolution* (1969).

For more a limited scope of time but important books, see Taylor Branch, *Parting the Waters: America in the King Years, 1954–1963* (1988), and its equally brilliant follow-up, *Pillar of Fire: America in the King Years, 1963–1965* (1998);

Benjamin Muse, *Ten Years of Prelude: The Story of Integration since the Supreme Court's 1954 Decision* (1964); and Numan V. Bartley, *The Rise of Massive Resistance: Race and Politics in the South During the 1950s* (1969). See also Anthony Lewis, *Portrait of a Decade: The Second American Revolution* (1964); and Howell Raines, *My Soul Is Rested: Movement Days in the Deep South Remembered* (1977), and Clayborne Carson et al., *The Eyes on the Prize Civil Rights Reader* (1991). Henry Hampton and Steve Fayer, *Voices of Freedom: An Oral History of the Civil Rights Movement from the 1950s through the 1980s* (1990), collect personal testimonies. There are some very informative anthologies on the movement, including *New Directions in Civil Rights Studies* (1991), edited by Armstead L. Robinson and Patricia Sullivan; *Conflict and Competition: Studies in the Recent Black Protest Movement* (1971), edited by John H. Bracey Jr., August Meier, and Elliott Rudwick; *The Negro Protest* (1963), edited by Kenneth B. Clark; *The Negro in Twentieth-Century America: A Reader on the Struggle for Civil Rights* (1967), edited by John Hope Franklin and Iosidore Starr; *The Civil Rights Movement in America* (1986), edited by Charles W. Eagles; and *Have We Overcome?* (1979), edited by Michael V. Namorato.

Race and Society

Good theoretical discussions of the movement, race and society include James Baldwin, *The Fire Next Time* (1963); Lerone Bennett Jr., *The Negro Mood* (1965); Debbie Lewis, *And We Are Not Saved: A History of the Movement as People* (1970); and Lewis Lomax, *To Kill a Black Man* (1968). Black opinions were never static or monolithic. For perspectives in the opinions of white and black Americans, see Louis E. Lomax, *The Negro Revolt* (1962), as well as Edward Peeks, *The Long Struggle for Black Power* (1971); Samuel Lubell, *White and Black: Test of a Nation* (1964); and Richard Lemon, *The Troubled Americans* (1970).

Women

There is no scholarly monograph on women in the modern civil rights or Black Power movements; however, there are a growing number of essays and articles on the topic. There are also several very strong biographies on movement women, described in the biographies and autobiographies section above. A number of recent books give considerable attention to the role of gender in the black freedom struggle. Lynne Olson's *Freedom's Daughters: The Unsung Heroines of the Civil Rights Movement from 1830 to 1970* (2001) is the first major monograph on women in civil rights activity, although Olson's focus extends over a hundred years before the modern civil rights movement. There are also good edited volumes, including *Women in the Civil Rights Movement: Trailblazers and Torchbearers, 1941–1965* (1990), edited by Vikki Crawford, Jacqueline Anne Rouse, and Barbara Woods; and *Sisters in the Struggle: African-American Women in the Civil Rights–Black Power Movement* (2001), edited by Bettye Collier-Thomas and V. P. Franklin.

For general histories that include substantive discussion of women's activities and roles, see Paula Giddings, *When and Where I Enter: The Impact of Black Women on Race and Sex in America* (1984), and Deborah Gray White, *Too Heavy a Load: Black Women in Defense of Themselves, 1894–1994* (1999). *Black Women in White America* (1992), edited by Gerda Lerner, is a superb anthology on black women from slavery through the civil rights movement. See also Michele Wallace, *Black Macho and the Myth of the Superwoman* (1990), which discusses black male sexism and its role in muting black feminism; Willi Coleman, "Black Women and Segregated Public Transportation: Ninety Years of Resistance," in *Black Women in United States History*, vol. 5 (1989), edited by Darlene Clark Hine; and Dolores Janiewski, *Sisterhood Denied: Race, Gender, and Class in a New South Community* (1985).

Federal Government and Black Power

There is a relatively sizable body of scholarship on the role of the federal government in the civil rights movement and a growing corpus on the federal government's relationship to Black Power. Several books engage the role of the president in civil rights issues, including Mark Stern, *Calculating Visions: Kennedy, Johnson, and Civil Rights* (1992); James Duram, *Moderate among Extremists: Dwight D. Eisenhower and the School Desegregation Crisis* (1981); and Ruth P. Morgan, *The President and Civil Rights–Policy Making by Executive Order* (1970). For two of the most critical examinations of the shortcomings of the presidency, see Allan Wolk, *The Presidency and Black Civil Rights: Eisenhower to Nixon* (1971), and Hugh Davis Graham, *Civil Rights and the Presidency: Race and Gender in American Politics, 1960–1972* (1992). See also Leon E. Panetta and Peter Gall, *Bring Us Together— The Nixon Team and Civil Rights Retreat* (1971). For a look at the role that recalcitrant congressmen played in stifling civil rights laws, see the somewhat dated J. Anderson, *Eisenhower, Brownell, and the Congress: The Tangled Origins of the Civil Rights Bill of 1956–1957* (1964).

Many of the above books provide context to the ideological underpinnings of black rage and the rise of Black Power, born of racial oppression. Though the government denied that it was involved in a conspiracy to disrupt the black freedom movement, Congressional hearings in 1975 confirm the charges. Many books have detailed the aggressive campaigns to destroy the Black Power movement. Dhoruba Bin Wahad, *Still Black Still Strong* (1993), provides a first-person narrative of repression. Huey P. Newton, *War against the Panthers* (1996), was Newton's posthumously published doctoral dissertation. Like the following books, Newton's study explores many sources made public by the Freedom of Information Act. Ward Churchill and Jim Vander Wall, *Agents of Repression* (1990), looks at the FBI's infamous Counter Intelligence Program (COINTELPRO) and its campaign again the Panthers and the American Indian Movement. Brian Glick, *War at Home* (1990), examines COINTELPRO as a tool of repression for dissent in general. John Copper, *You Can Hear Them Knocking* (1981), looks at police aggression across the country. Michael

Friendly and David Gallen, *Martin Luther King Jr.: The FBI File* (1993), and David J. Garrow, *The FBI and Martin Luther King Jr.* (1981), both expose the efforts of the FBI to sabotage King. Kenneth O'Reilly, *Black Americans: The FBI File* (1994) and *"Racial Matters": The FBI's Secret File on Black America, 1960–1972,* demonstrates the degree of intrusion into citizen's lives and evasion of legal process common among federal agencies to disrupt activist groups.

Index

Books in the Series